CAUGHT IN A TRAP
KIDNAPPING ELVIS

Chris Charlesworth

Published 2017 by Red Planet Publishing Limited
Text © Chris Charlesworth 2017

This edition © Red Planet Publishing Limited 2017
Paperback ISBN: 978 1 9113 4658 6
First Edition

Printed in the UK by CPI

'Suspicious Minds'. Words & Music by Francis Zambon ©1968,
reproduced by permission of Sony/ATV Music Publishing Ltd.

'Peace In The Valley'. Words & Music by Thomas A. Dorsey
©1937, reproduced by permission of Carlin Music Corporation.

Cover design: Lisa Pettibon

For more information on Red Planet books visit:
www.redplanetzone.com

CAUGHT IN A TRAP
KIDNAPPING ELVIS

PROLOGUE

On Monday, August 18, 1975, Elvis Presley opened a two-week engagement at his regular Las Vegas showroom, the Hilton Hotel. Midway through the 8.00 pm performance he appeared to tire, and thereafter frequently sat down to rest while his backing vocalists entertained the capacity audience.

The American show business magazine Variety was critical of the show, stating: *'Presley may be suffering from a continual disability. His overweight condition and lack of stamina, and poor vocal projection, may spring from such a malady. It is difficult for him to maintain any credible vocal lines or lyric commitments. He spends more time playing with his ringside romps with femmes, but tosses nearly every member of his backup quintet a lengthy solo. In addition he lumbers around in travesties of his earlier karate moves or trademark pelvic gyrations... his [\$2,500] jumpsuit costume [is] an obviously poor design that stresses his ballooning midriff.'*

Three days later the engagement was cancelled. On the orders of his manager, Colonel Tom Parker, all traces of Presley's presence were abruptly removed from the hotel, apart from a notice in the foyer that stated, 'The remainder of the Elvis Presley engagement has been cancelled due to illness.'

That same day Elvis was flown to Memphis where he was admitted to the Baptist Memorial Hospital on Walnut Grove Road to be treated for 'fatigue'. He remained in hospital until September 5, although during the final two weeks of his stay he returned to his home, the mansion called Graceland he'd bought in 1957, for a few hours each day.

On Saturday, September 10, while out riding around Memphis on one of his many motorcycles, Elvis was given a speeding ticket by Patrolman Robert T. Logan.

Elvis Presley was not seen in public again until December 2 when he opened a further season at the Las Vegas Hilton to make up for the cancelled shows in August. He arrived in Las Vegas on November 27.

The story that follows is the first detailed account of the events that occurred in the life of Elvis Presley during the period between September 10 and November 27. In Presley biographies and chronologies published since the singer's death in 1977 it is suggested that he remained ensconced at Graceland convalescing for several weeks, an unusually uneventful period in Elvis' life.

In fact, it was just the opposite...

Chapter One

(August 18 – 21)

Elvis felt awful. His head ached and his stomach churned.
His eyes, protected from the glare of bright helium stage
lights by thick reflective wrap-around sunglasses, refused
to focus properly. His eyelids were yellow and puffy.
The gelatinous glob of grease that kept his mop of dyed
black hair in place had melted under the intense heat of
the lights and oozed down over his forehead and bloated
cheeks until it settled beneath the neck of his white silk
shirt where it mingled with his sweat. There was a damp,
shaded area beneath both of his armpits that grew larger
by the minute. The lumbering pain in Elvis' intestines,
the result of a grossly enlarged colon, just wouldn't go
away. He was chronically constipated. Though he'd eaten
prodigiously, Elvis hadn't enjoyed a satisfactory bowel
movement for three straight days.

At nearly 300 pounds, Elvis was at least 100 pounds
overweight and there were times when it seemed to him
that his legs were unable to carry the enormous load. He
wore a tight corset around his stomach to rein in the fat
but he still moved like a hippo, swaying unsteadily across
the stage, leaning against the grand piano for support. He
was in a foul temper.

It was the middle of the afternoon, quite early in the
day by Elvis' usual crepuscular standards, and he was
attempting to rehearse a couple of sentimental ballads
before the night's opening show. The musicians started
and stopped both songs several times, and with each
interruption it seemed less likely that they'd ever reach

the end of either. The whole rehearsal was a shambles and everyone present knew it. They also knew that it was Elvis' fault that the rehearsal was a shambles, that he was unable to concentrate because he didn't really care one way or another about the songs, the show or anything else for that matter.

Unable to continue, Elvis again signalled for the band to stop playing and spoke briefly with two of his bodyguards. They laughed self-consciously; the kind of laugh that men use when they know something isn't particularly funny but when it is prudent to laugh all the same. Then Elvis turned his attention back to the band.

'You know what?' he sneered, looking directly at his old friend, guitarist Charlie Hodge. 'I hate this fucking place Charlie, I hate it!'

Hodge, who had known Elvis since 1958 when they met as fellow GIs on a transport ship to Germany, unstrapped the acoustic guitar that he played on stage and grinned. 'Me too, boss,' he muttered, almost inaudibly.

His thoughts on Las Vegas evidently concluded, Elvis turned abruptly on his heel and left the stage area. Five minutes later came an announcement from his dressing room that the rehearsal was over. The musicians, by now used to Elvis' tantrums, were surprised the rehearsal had lasted as long as it had, or even that it had taken place at all.

That was the way it was with Elvis these days.

Upstairs in his suite of rooms, 66-year-old Colonel Thomas Andrew Parker, Elvis Presley's rotund, bombastic, cigar-smoking manager, surveyed the mess of clutter spread out before him on the king-sized bed. Chief amongst the piles were several heaps of eight-by-ten black and white glossy photographs of Elvis, and in all of them Elvis was sleek and handsome, quite unlike the man who had just brought his rehearsal to an abrupt halt.

There was Elvis in the shiny black leather outfit that he wore for the 1968 'Singer Special', the famous Christmas TV show that had played such an important part in his popular and artistic renaissance during the late Sixties; there was Elvis in a dramatic karate pose, wearing one of the brilliant white jump-suits that had been designed for his first Las Vegas season a year later; there were stills from his movies, from Love Me Tender in 1955 to Change Of Habit in 1969; and there was even Elvis as he was in 1961, straight out of the army, his hair newly styled, his sexuality neutered, his wide face beaming like a fat Tom cat. This was one of Colonel Tom's favourites. Every one of the pictures was captioned 'Elvis Presley, RCA Records & Tapes' and every one was taken long before Elvis' physique entered its sad decline.

As well as the pictures there were other items, leaflets, stickers, badges, handouts, flyers, posters and more, all of them drawing attention to Elvis' forthcoming stint at the Hilton. Brightly coloured, cheap and clearly designed by someone for whom good taste was not a priority, they were all part of Colonel Parker's lifelong mission to raise Elvis consciousness and make plenty of money as a consequence. Other managers of entertainers gave away these tawdry promotional items. The Colonel sold them.

His reverie was interrupted by the phone. It was Joe Esposito, commanding officer of the Memphis Mafia, Elvis' private but by no means élite security force.

'Colonel... Elvis just broke off the rehearsal. I don't think he's feeling too good right now. He might pull out of the show. What do we do?'

'Where is he?'

'Up in his room.'

'Leave Elvis to me.'

'He's in a foul temper right now Colonel. I dunno whether it's a good idea to call him...'

'I said leave him to me, Joe,' Parker interrupted.

'If you say so Colonel.'

Colonel Parker replaced the receiver, sat back in his gilded armchair and took another puff from his long cigar. Once again it seemed he needed to have words with his boy.

Over the years the Colonel had grown accustomed to Elvis' complaints but lately they'd grown louder and more frequent, and Elvis himself had become more and more difficult to control. Aside from when he'd orchestrated the marriage to Priscilla Beaulieu in 1967, he'd always made a point of staying out of Elvis' private life but he'd heard a thing or two about the recent goings-on at Graceland and knew full well that not only was Elvis behaving like a spoilt child most of the time but there was no one in Memphis capable of restraining him. Vernon Presley, Elvis' father, was a spineless old man who had never been able to stand up to anybody, least of all his headstrong, breadwinning son; the Memphis Mafia, the guys who looked after Elvis' needs in the guise of 'good buddies', were largely a bunch of sycophantic yes-men too afraid of losing their undemanding jobs to ever enter into a dispute with Elvis; and the women around Elvis, including Priscilla, simply and sensibly walked out when the going got too rough.

Since the death of Elvis' mother in 1958, Colonel Parker was the only person in the world to whom Elvis would submit, but as Elvis grew older the submissions had become harder and harder to enforce. At one time the partnership was based on trust but now it was based purely on hard cash; each needed the other to generate the income they required to maintain their lifestyles, but the Colonel had always managed to hoodwink Elvis into believing he needed his manager more than his manager needed him.

If for no other reason, Elvis needed the Colonel because he knew of no one else who could coordinate his career. It had been the Colonel's deliberate long-term strategy to ensure that Elvis was entirely bereft of alternative managerial, legal or financial advice. In his 20-year career Elvis had known no other adviser; indeed, the Colonel had summarily eliminated all other potential professional advisers who had come within his orbit. The Memphis Mafia, the only men with regular access to Elvis, were carefully vetted for lack of imagination or ambition.

Without the Colonel, Elvis would be lost. For a start a new manager would not know how to get his hands on Elvis' money because all of Elvis' funds were channelled through the Colonel's companies. Were Elvis to try to leave the Colonel, the newcomer would have enormous difficulty in unravelling the financial strands that the Colonel had knitted over the years. To maintain his lifestyle, Elvis would require constant injections of cash, which the new manager would have to provide himself since the actual sources of funds – RCA Records, the William Morris booking agency, the Hill & Range music publishing company and various film companies – were all in Parker's pocket. Once the new manager realised the professional, financial and personal complications surrounding Elvis, he might question the sense in trying to manage the King of Rock'n'Roll.

Weighed against the fiscal side of the Elvis equation
were the Colonel's personal needs. Sure, he needed
Elvis to maintain his own income, much of which he
squandered on Las Vegas gaming tables, and at his time
of life he wouldn't welcome having to start over with a
new client, but there was another, less tangible, aspect
to Parker's need. For the Colonel, Elvis fulfilled a hidden
craving to fleece anyone and everyone he met, to always
come out on top of a business deal, to always have the
last laugh. In their 20-year relationship, Colonel Parker
had never truly come to terms with Elvis' music, his art,
or even begun to appreciate it. From the very beginning,
when the teenage girls screamed their silly heads off, he'd
always thought deep down that Elvis was a novelty act,
certainly an original, but a novelty act all the same. And
all showmen know that it takes a great showman to sell
a novelty act and an even greater showman to sell that
act over and over again for 20 years. The Colonel wanted
to be remembered as the greatest showman of them all,
bigger than Zeigfeld, bigger than Ringling Brothers, bigger
even than PT Barnum, and because of this he always
regarded Elvis' success as largely due to his own talents as
a manager and promoter. In short, he needed Elvis Presley
to satisfy his vanity as well as to fill his purse.

So the Colonel picked up the telephone and dialled
Elvis' suite. It rang several times before Linda Thompson,
the former Miss Tennessee and Elvis' on-off, 25-year-old
girlfriend for the past two and a half years, answered.

'This is Colonel Parker. I need to speak to Elvis.'

'He's in the bathroom.'

'Just put me through.'

Linda called out to Elvis who was at that moment

astride the toilet. He picked up the extension in the bathroom. 'Yeah,' he grunted.

'You okay, Elvis?'

'No, Colonel. I'm sick.'

'Can you go on with the show tonight?'

There was a pause. Elvis wanted to say 'No' but it wouldn't come out. Instead he said, 'I guess so, if I have to. I don't know. I don't want to.'

'Stay there. We need to talk. I'm coming up.'

Elvis replaced the receiver, pulled up his pants and walked into the bedroom. Linda looked at him expectantly. 'Sorry, you gotta' beat it sugar. Colonel Parker's on his way up. We got business to take care of.'

Linda knew better than to argue. 'Will I see you later, honey?'

'Sure. Just go down and hang out with some of the guys for a while. I'm sorry.' Elvis walked towards the door of the suite and opened it so she could leave. Linda gathered up her purse and some clothes, ambled towards Elvis with the intention of kissing him then thought better of it. Elvis playfully spanked her behind as she walked through the door, then closed it behind her. He was alone. He went back into the bathroom and swallowed a red pill from a bottle on the shelf by the washbasin. It was the third painkiller he'd taken since quitting the rehearsal less than an hour earlier; sooner or later they'd start to work. In the meantime he had to deal with the Colonel.

Elvis dreaded showdowns with Colonel Parker because he'd never been able to stand up to the man who controlled his career. The first time he'd ever met Parker, back in 1955 when he was a struggling rockabilly singer, he'd called him 'Sir' because Parker was older and a respected country music agent but even now, 20 years and millions of dollars later, the relationship between them had never really changed. Elvis no longer called the Colonel 'Sir' but he didn't call him Tom either. Just like everybody else, he called him 'Colonel' which always came out sounding like a term of deference even though Parker was no more a military Colonel than the old guy with a white suit and beard who sold Kentucky Fried Chicken. Indeed, the Colonel – a Dutchman whose real name was Andreas Cornelis Van Kujik – had successfully hidden his real identity from the world since he arrived in America by jumping ship in 1929.

The occasions when Elvis and Colonel Parker were alone together had become fewer and farther between as the years passed and these days they were almost always unpleasant encounters. When others were present there were appearances to maintain but when they were alone the Colonel always spoke his mind while Elvis, eternally inarticulate in such situations, tended to snarl and sulk like a cornered dog.

Elvis went back into the bathroom and stashed his pill bottles into a leather case. He didn't want the Colonel to see them. He was lying on his bed, staring vacantly at the ceiling of his suite when there was a knock at the door. The Colonel had his own key and could let himself in at any time. His knock implied a feigned respect.

'That you Colonel?'

'Yeah, son.' Parker often called Elvis 'son' when they were alone together. It irritated Elvis, and Parker knew it.

'Come on in.'

Colonel Parker opened the door and walked inside. Elvis didn't move. Parker drew up a chair by his bedside and the two men who between them had generated what some estimated to be a billion dollars of income stared hard into each other's eyes.

'We gotta talk, son,' said the Colonel. 'I'm worried about you. You're sick and if you can't perform we're in trouble.'

Elvis looked away. He didn't speak.

'I only want what's best for you son but...' The Colonel hesitated. '... but it seems to me that sometimes you're... you're throwing it all away.'

Elvis fixed the Colonel with a steady glare and spoke for the first time. 'I don't wanna do the show tonight... I...'

The Colonel stared right back and spoke before Elvis could continue. 'You gotta do tonight's show. I ain't going into that showroom tonight to tell the audience you ain't going to sing for them. You know how much money we'll lose if you cancel again? Almost a million dollars. Think... a million dollars thrown away, and you can't afford that.'

'Whaddaya mean I can't afford it. I can afford what I like.'

'You can't afford what you like unless you work. You spend too much money anyways. This is something else I wanna talk about... you got too many guys on the payroll, you spend too much money on girls and Graceland and cars and planes and everything. You give stuff away to total strangers. Your pappy told me how you spend all the time. It's gotta stop.'

'Don't you talk to me like that. I can spend what I like. It's my money, ain't it?'

'Not if you don't have it, it ain't.'

The Colonel saw this was getting nowhere and that the longer they bickered the worse the atmosphere would become. If things got too out of hand there was always the danger that Elvis really would walk out of the hotel and all the way to the airport and then the run of shows would have to be cancelled, and that had to be avoided at all costs, if for no other reason than the Colonel owed the Hilton Hotel over half a million dollars in gambling debts. Though he didn't know it, Elvis was the collateral that enabled Parker to buy credit. He decided to play soft.

'OK Elvis. Why don't you just rest up awhile? Maybe you'll feel better and we'll talk later. I gotta go see about some things.'

Elvis didn't look at the Colonel. He'd always found it difficult to stare the Colonel in the eye when he was arguing with him and now he just stared at the wall, not speaking.

'We'll talk later, OK?' said Parker, rising from his chair and walking towards the door. Elvis didn't respond until the door closed behind his manager and when he did he made sure the Colonel was out of earshot. 'Fuck you, asshole,' he said, wishing for the thousandth time that he had dared say it to the Colonel's face.

Elvis leaned over, picked up the telephone by his bed and dialled. 'That you Marty? Is Linda there? Good. Get Doctor Nick on the line for me. I need some more medication.'

The main showroom at the Las Vegas Hilton hotel holds 1,000 diners seated at large white tables on tiered levels in a 60-degree arc facing the 100 foot stage. The decor is blue and white, the roof is sprinkled with tiny white lights like stars in the sky and huge glass chandeliers hang low from the ceiling. With two shows a night over a two week run, 28,000 fans get to see Elvis for 90 minutes in this room during his twice yearly stints at the hotel. The cost of the tickets for an Elvis show is $20 each, which includes two drinks or half a bottle of cheap champagne, but many of the fans spend at least $200 during their stay. Most of this is lost on the gambling tables.

The hotels in Las Vegas might have been designed with Elvis in mind. Primarily residential casinos that never close, a night-time atmosphere is maintained by the total lack of daylight anywhere on the ground floors, while the absence of clocks discourages gamblers from heeding the passage of time. Night and day thus merge into one long, eternal spell. The gaming rooms in each are located in vast lobbies and are situated so that every journey, from the check-in desks to the elevators, from the elevators to the dining room, from the dining room to the bar, from the bar to the front doors and round again, involves passing through the casino. When Elvis plays Vegas, there isn't an empty hotel room in town.

Elvis Presley fans are a curious breed whose loyalty often strains the credulity of non-believers. For many there is no limit to the lengths they will go to support their idol, and no limit to the expense this might incur. Many of these fans look upon Elvis as a deity, the God of Music, the King of Rock'n'Roll, blessed with a Golden Voice whose every utterance is flawless. These fans will brook no criticism of their idol under any circumstances. They are the lifeblood of Colonel Parker, the oxygen that keeps Elvis Inc's heart beating.

Many such fans came from all over the world to see The Elvis '75 Summer Festival. As always, there was a large contingent of wealthy fans from Japan and a small delegation from the Brazilian Fan Club who had flown up from Rio de Janeiro especially for the opening night. None of these fans had ever seen Elvis before but like dedicated Elvis fans all over the world they'd collected all his records, seen all his films and read the books. They were now on the edge of Elvis nirvana – seeing him in person.

Some of the European fans that flew into Vegas
had seen Elvis before, especially those from England
who came on the bi-annual trip organised through the
remarkably efficient Official Elvis Presley Fan Club of
Great Britain whose secretary, Todd Slaughter, was a by-
word for devotion amongst true Elvis believers. Elvis had
never once visited the United Kingdom to perform, nor
even performed outside of the United States apart from
a handful of shows in Canada early in his career, but this
mattered not one iota. It was as if his absence created
a vacuum that could be filled only with a trip to Vegas.
Many of Elvis' British fans would already have visited
Memphis and Elvis' birthplace in Tupelo on their way out
to Nevada: theirs was the ultimate Elvis experience that
climaxed with the live show.

Most visitors to Vegas, of course, were American fans
and many of these, too, had seen Elvis numerous times.
For some, though, it was the first time they were seeing
Elvis on stage and in many cases they'd waited years for
the chance.

Among the latter, preparing breakfast at her home in
Memphis, was Sandra Pandel, who'd admired Elvis since
she was a teenager. Her husband Delmore had bought a
pair of tickets six weeks before as a surprise present for
Sandra for their second wedding anniversary on August
21, four days into the Elvis summer season. Although only
23 and too young to remember Elvis in his Fifties pomp,
Sandra was a true believer, the kind of fan for whom he
was as sacred as Jesus. Delmore gave her an envelope
containing the tickets over the breakfast table and when
she opened it she squealed with delight.

'Elvis tickets! Oh my, oh my, honey. Are they real? Can

we afford it? Oh, honey. I can't believe it. I just cannot believe it's true,' she shrieked.

'It's true,' said Delmore. 'You're going to see Elvis at last, you and me.'

'It's a dream come true,' gushed his wife. 'It truly is. Oh Del baby, I do love you.'

Delmore didn't share his wife's unrestrained enthusiasm for Elvis but knew that the tickets would make her happy and that was all he really cared about for he loved her deeply. Sure, he'd probably enjoy seeing Elvis himself. He quite liked his records; hell, they were a darn sight better than some of the records made by these longhaired drug-taking groups that were everywhere you looked these days. He was a country music fan himself; he liked Johnny Cash and Merle Haggard, singers who showed some respect for the American values he'd respected himself since his daddy taught him the right way to live all those years ago. He believed at all times in looking and acting like a man.

Delmore grinned at his pretty young wife. Her outsize yellow t-shirt stopped half way up her thighs, and when she turned to face him Del could see that it was all she wore. 'C'mon over here honey,' he drawled. 'Thank me properly.' Sandra glanced at her husband. He was sitting at the kitchen table wearing only the loose cotton shorts he slept in. He hadn't shaved and his hair was uncombed, but she liked what she saw.

'I'm supposed to go to work in half an hour,' she said unconvincingly. There was a gimlet sparkle in Del's eye that he knew she couldn't resist, so she smiled back at him teasingly. 'Just for a moment, then.'

Del pushed back his chair, stood up and leant against the kitchen wall, admiring his wife as she crossed the room towards him. She stood on tiptoe to put her arms around his neck and pressed herself seductively against his chest, kissing him full on the lips. His rough chin and firm stomach excited her. 'Yes,' she whispered into his ear. 'I guess I do need to thank you properly.' Sandra stepped back from his embrace and pulled the t-shirt over her head, then fell back naked into his arms and kissed him again, urgently, hard on his lips. Del held her tight, her small breasts pressed against his bare chest, and began to stroke her back, moving his hands down her spine to caress the curves below. Sandra felt Del's hardness rising inside his shorts and slid her hand inside to fondle him, then moaned softly as his fingers probed between her legs. 'Quickly,' she gasped, as he swept her up in his arms and carried her to their bedroom.

Delmore Pandel came from a family of old fashioned grafters, poor but honest believers in the American Dream much like the small Presley family that raised the surviving twin they named Elvis Aron. His father had never held down a steady job but managed somehow while his mother stayed home to bring up a family of seven. Del was born in 1948, the last of the brood, but he was no mama's boy. Schooling was never his style and he quit without graduating in 1965 to join the US marines, which made both his parents real proud. Seven years later, after a tour of duty that included three years in Vietnam, he'd been invalided out with a broken ankle that wouldn't set properly and a sergeant's disability pension to fall back on if things got tough.

Army life, with its harsh discipline and allegiance to God and country, had suited Delmore and he often missed the camaraderie of the barracks. But a year later, his ankle

just about healed, he'd settled down and married Sandra
Mason, a one time runner-up in the annual Miss Jackson
Pageant, and he'd driven a massive 18-wheel truck
for a living ever since. He was an expert truck driver,
able to handle the biggest of rigs and take them across
the highways of America as fast as any other driver he
knew. He brought home around $200 most weeks which
was enough for him and Sandra to pay the rent on their
apartment and live comfortably if they didn't try to get
above themselves.

Delmore had always liked the outdoors. He took a
pride in his physical appearance, exercised regularly with
his own weights and was the kind of man who would
never back down in a fight. He wouldn't go looking for
one, mind, but woebetide the man who crossed him. He
loved to hunt and fish, and after a long haul across the
country in his truck there was nothing he liked better than
to head off into the Kentucky Hills with a couple of guns,
some rods and lines, and his wild buddy Roy whom he'd
known since his days in the army.

Delmore also liked to make Sandra happy. With leaving
school early and going straight into the army, he hadn't
known many women apart from the whores who hung
around camp but when he saw her working as a waitress
in a diner down in Germantown just two months after
he'd quit the army, he asked her for a date and after their
first night out together knew instinctively that she was the
girl for him. Sandra was younger than him by five years
but she too quickly realised he was the man for her. Del's
steady hand and genuine sincerity swept her off her feet
and they were married within three months of that first
visit to the diner.

Sandra was happy with her husband; he was big and

strong and good-looking, working steady and a good provider. He didn't drink overmuch, which was rare in a Memphis workingman of his background, and didn't seem to mind too much about her infatuation with Elvis Presley. Previous boyfriends had grown tired of this but Del just shrugged it off. 'Honey,' he'd say. 'I don't mind you liking Elvis. Shit. I like plenty of girl singers myself but I won't ever get to meet them. Just you go right ahead.'

Sometimes Sandra thought that maybe Del thought she just wasn't good enough to attract a man like Elvis. Maybe he was right. Sandra, too, had quit school early but being as pretty as she was with her long and curly blonde hair, turned up nose and wide smile, she'd had plenty of boyfriends until Del came along. She thought that when the light caught him right he looked a bit like Elvis with his dark quiffed hair and tough, slim physique. He was certainly the best looking and strongest man she'd ever met, and he was a pretty smooth operator in bed. The only trouble spot in their marriage was that after two years of regular sex without any form of birth control she hadn't fallen pregnant. They'd been to the doctor who pronounced them both capable of having children, so what was the matter?

'I just don't know what to do,' Sandra told her ever-inquisitive parents whenever she visited them at their home in Jackson. 'I guess we'll just have to keep trying and it'll happen someday.'

On the morning that Del left the Elvis Presley tickets on the breakfast table, after he'd left the house to see about another trucking contract, becoming pregnant was again on Sandra's mind. A couple of nights in a Las Vegas hotel offered an opportunity for plenty of loving, she thought, before heading off into town with plans to stop off at that

new lingerie shop she'd noticed at the corner of Union
and Main.

On the evening of August 18, after the aborted
afternoon rehearsal and the sharp encounter with Colonel
Parker, Elvis Presley twice dragged his weary body on
to the stage of the Hilton International and did his best
to please the audience of first night fans. He was tired,
often out of breath, and he sat down several times to rest
between songs. The instrumentalists in his backing band,
notably lead guitarist James Burton, all took lengthy solos,
as did the individual members of his quintet of black
backing singers.

Elvis slurred his way through a dozen hits, forgot
some of the words and actually poked fun at his own
shortcomings. As always, he toyed with the women in the
front rows, allowing them to shake his hand and handing
out the white scarves that were systematically passed
to him by Charlie Hodge, his rhythm guitarist and old
Army buddy. In return he listlessly accepted items of frilly
underwear with which he wiped his brow before passing
them back to Hodge with the best leer he could muster up.
Watching from the side-lines backstage, Colonel Parker
seemed unconcerned, though it often occurred to him
that giving away all those white silk scarves was unduly
generous.

After little more than 60 minutes the show climaxed
with a rendering of 'American Trilogy', the dramatic
segued arrangement of 'All My Trials', 'Dixie' and 'The
Battle Hymn Of The Republic' that was usually a show
stopper, followed by 'Can't Help Falling In Love', the big
hit ballad from the movie Blue Hawaii that Elvis habitually
used to close his shows. In the event it was an anti-

climactic finalé brought about by Elvis' apparent rush to leave the stage. Sometimes, but not often, Elvis came back for an encore but not tonight. When Elvis quit the stage nowadays, he quit for good.

Afterwards Elvis retired to his room with Linda Thompson, took a handful of the painkillers that had been delivered by his personal doctor earlier in the evening and lay on his enormous bed holding Linda's hand while they watched television together. Unable to relax, he decided to throw a party at 2.00 am, inviting those members of the Memphis Mafia who had flown with him to Vegas, the wives and girlfriends who accompanied them, some members of the band and certain privileged members of the Hilton staff. All had to be summoned from wherever they were by Joe Esposito and not all were eager to attend though they did so anyway. It didn't pay to snub Elvis. Colonel Parker, downstairs playing the gaming tables, was not present.

The party broke up at six and Elvis went to bed with a book on religion and half a dozen powerful sleeping pills to knock him out. He didn't awaken the next day until after four, and immediately cancelled plans for another rehearsal. He was due on stage again at eight and until then he sat in his suite guzzling banana sandwiches that were passed to him slice by slice by Linda. Colonel Parker didn't call.

As Elvis scoffed his banana sandwiches in Las Vegas, Delmore Pandel stopped by the travel agency in downtown Memphis to pick up his plane tickets and motel reservation voucher for the two nights he and Sandra were to spend in the American gambling capital. They planned to arrive a day early, rest up on their first night, see Elvis the following evening and fly back to Memphis the next day. They couldn't afford to stay at the Hilton, of course, and had instead taken a room at a motel on the outskirts of town. Nevertheless, this was costing $60 a night and what with the plane tickets and their meals and drinks, together with the Elvis tickets, Del didn't expect much change from $500.

Elvis had better be worth it, he though to himself as he handed over a wad of cash to the travel agent. He'd been saving up for this for several months and had foregone many a night's beer drinking with his pal Roy over the past few weeks. Roy, single, unsympathetic and given to playfully goading Del about his marriage, couldn't understand it at all.

'Elvis is fat and forty,' Roy had laughed when Del told him about his Vegas plans. 'He's over the hill. You're goddamned crazy man, fuckin' crazy as shit.'

They were in their favourite bar, the JayKay Saloon, and Roy was sounding off loudly as usual. 'Elvis goddamned Presley. Jesus man. I'd sure like to have a talk with that guy someday. There was a girl I once screwed a time or two who liked to jack off listening to him singing. Couldn't help herself. Caught her doing it once on her living room floor in the middle of the night. Hell, was she mad at me. Kicked me out of her apartment there and then. Threw my clothes out after me. Never saw her again after that night.'

Royston Kruger had been Del's best buddy for nigh on seven years. They'd met in the Army, and were shipped out to Vietnam together in 1968. Serving in the same platoon out there, they'd seen some dirty action that they didn't often speak about but which bound them together in ways that few would understand.

They'd quit the army round about the same time,
Del because of his ankle and Roy because he was fed
up with the discipline, and returned to their homes in
Memphis looking for work. Del, who'd driven trucks
in the army, soon found a job behind the wheel again,
but Roy hadn't enjoyed the same luck. Eventually he'd
become a cop, but he quit after a year because he didn't
like the responsibility and was now working for a private
security set-up that patrolled banks, office buildings and
warehouses. Like Del, his army experiences had made
him tough, handy with a gun and his fists, and together
they made a formidable team. Luckily for the Memphis
Police Department they were both honest. It never
occurred to them, as it might have done to other men, to
utilise the skills they'd learned in the army for dishonest
ends.

Roy was single and seemed to run through girlfriends
at a rate that made Delmore blink. Del was the steadier
of the pair, content with Sandra; Roy, wilder and invested
with a mad streak that had always endeared him to Del,
wanted everything and never wanted to wait for it. If
Sandra had been another kind of girl, she might have
disliked Roy but instead she found him fun. He wasn't as
good looking as Del, so there was never any competition
and the three of them often went out together, sometimes
with Roy's latest date, to drink beers at the JayKay when
Sandra wasn't waitressing down at the diner or Roy on the
night patrol at some riverside warehouse on the banks of
the Mississippi.

Delmore picked up his plane tickets to Vegas and
headed for home. Across town Sandra was choosing a
new nightdress from a rack of lacy see-through items
in the lingerie store. Subconsciously she found herself

fantasising about what Elvis would prefer and basing her selection on what she would wear for him in the unlikely event that such an occasion might arise. It made the shopping expedition all the more enjoyable, and in the end she picked out a very short pure white number with thin shoulder straps, a low neckline and matching see-through panties with ribbons that tied in bows on either side. It was perfect for a bride to wear on her wedding night, and just the sort of thing that Sandra thought would turn Delmore – and Elvis – on.

Sandra Mason never forgot the first time she fell in love with Elvis Presley. She was just 15 and it was nearly Christmas and there was an Elvis Presley special being aired on TV, his first TV appearance since just after he left the army in 1960. At the time she'd finally decided that she preferred Paul McCartney to Ringo Starr because Paul had lovely eyes and sang so beautifully, but The Beatles were getting a bit weird anyway what with John leaving his wife for that funny-looking Japanese woman, and her churchgoing parents hated all the English groups, especially The Rolling Stones.

She remembered reading somewhere that John had once been a fan of Elvis Presley and though most of her friends, especially the boys, thought Elvis was old hat, if John Lennon liked him then there might be something good about Elvis. So that night, three weeks before Christmas, when most of her friends were swooning to Paul McCartney singing 'Hey Jude' at her friend Jeannie-Rae's party, she opted to stay home and watch Elvis on television.

The Singer Special, which Sandra and millions of others saw on the night of December 2, 1968, turned out to be a major triumph for Elvis, and she was entranced, especially

when, guitar in hand, the leather-clad King of Rock'n'Roll
raucously led his band through a slew of hits from the
Fifties, 'Heartbreak Hotel', 'Hound Dog' and 'All Shook Up'
among them. But it was when Elvis sang 'One Night' that
Sandra became a true convert. Somehow, in this one song,
Elvis communicated to her the power and possibilities of
passionate sex and she had never forgotten the effect it
had on her.

Since that night Sandra had managed to collect
virtually every Elvis Presley recording that had ever
been released. She'd seen all his films at least twice and,
even though she thought some of the movies he made
in the Sixties were a bit lacklustre, she stoutly defended
Elvis against anyone who dared speak ill of him. She had
collected photographs for seven years and now had 23
scrapbooks of Elvis pictures at home. She'd joined the fans
hanging around Graceland on many occasions and had
even caught sight of what looked remarkably like Elvis in
the back of a long black Cadillac one evening. The figure
with the black hair and quiff was wearing sunglasses and
she'd taken a hurried picture of the car that came out
blurred but was still the pride of her collection. The one
thing she'd never managed to do, however, was to see
Elvis on stage.

Remembering all this in a flash, she paid $22.50 for
the skimpy nightdress and hurried home to make Del's
dinner. That night they planned to go out for a few beers
with Del's friend Roy, and the night after that they'd be in
Vegas.

Once again, on the evening of August 19, Elvis Presley
managed to deliver the goods to the audience of second
nighters at Vegas. The shows were no more inspired than

the opening night but the crowd didn't seem to care. Elvis often wondered to himself just how little he could get away with as far as these shows were concerned. It was the same dilemma that had confused The Beatles during the heady days of Beatlemania, when they toured the world regularly and never heard a note they played or a word they sang.

Elvis had long ago reached the conclusion that his audience had really come simply to look at him and that his singing was an added extra. Could he just stand there and smile for 60 minutes, talking occasionally or even sit down while the band played on? Would the audience be satisfied if he just wandered on and took a few bows while the musicians played his hits in the background?

So Elvis went through the motions again, mumbling inelegant renderings of 'Hound Dog', 'All Shook Up' and 'Blue Suede Shoes', laughing his way through 'Are You Lonesome Tonight' and murdering 'Love Me Tender'. His karate moves were a travesty of the way he performed them three years ago and again he seemed to draw more pleasure from fooling around with women in the front than actually performing.

There were no encores and Elvis retired early with Linda. This time there was no party and only Doctor Nichopoulos, Elvis' personal physician, visited his suite during the night. Again Elvis slept well into the following day, waking just before 3pm on August 20 with another dreadful pain in his lower intestine.

'Well, all I can say is that I hope he's damn well worth it. All that money. Jesus Christ.' Roy slapped his hand down hard on the bar top. It was not the first time he'd used that phrase during the evening and it wouldn't be the last. Del and Sandra just laughed.

'Roy,' said Sandra. 'I have never ever seen Elvis and I love him. So just stop being such a killjoy. It's the nicest thing Del has done for me and I love him for it.'

'Aw shucks... you don't say,' said Roy.

'Yes, I do say,' said Sandra. 'Now get me another beer. No, on second thoughts get me a vodka and lime. We're celebrating.'

'Now, honey, don't overdo it here.' Delmore pretended to look concerned. 'We don't want you waking up with no bad head in the morning when we gotta' fly out to Vegas in the afternoon, remember.'

'As if she could forget partner,' laughed Roy. 'Let her be. She's enjoying herself.'

Sandra, Del and Roy all enjoyed themselves at the JayKay bar that night. They didn't leave until after 2am by which time all three were pleasantly tipsy. As they parted company at the corner of Dogwood and Eighth Street, Roy finally dropped his cynical mask.

'Listen you guys, have a great time in Vegas,' he called out, walking unsteadily towards his apartment. 'Give my best regards to Elvis. Right now I wish I was coming with you. I really do.'

The pain in Elvis' abdomen grew steadily worse during the late afternoon of August 20 and Dr Nichopoulos was called to prescribe further medication. Again Elvis threatened to call off the evening's show, and this time his complaints were louder and longer than ever before. Eventually, two hours before Elvis was due on stage, Colonel Parker was called to his suite.

Elvis, with Linda Thompson and Dr Nichopoulos by his side, summoned up all his will power for the confrontation. 'Colonel,' he said. 'I really am sick. I can't go on with the shows. I really can't.'

'It's true Colonel,' confirmed Dr Nichopoulos. 'Elvis really ought to be in the hospital, not on stage. He shouldn't have to perform tonight.'

This time the Colonel, with as much bad grace as he could summon up, finally relented. 'OK, do what you want. It's your career, your fans, your goddam money. But I ain't going out there tonight and telling that full house you ain't gonna' sing for them, son. Tell your pappy to make the announcement.'

Elvis was backed into a corner. He couldn't force his father Vernon to go through the embarrassment of standing on the Hilton stage and telling his fans the show was off. That would be too humiliating for him and too much to ask. He would do tonight's show but the remainder of the engagement would be cancelled.

Del and Sandra arrived at Memphis International Airport with an hour to spare before their five o'clock plane to Vegas, and, still slightly hung over, killed time sipping black coffee in the bar. The flight took four hours and with the time difference they landed at Las Vegas McCarran International shortly before seven. They took a cab to their motel, unpacked and went to a nearby diner to eat. Both were tired after the previous night's partying and they decided to have an early night so as to be in the best of spirits for the following evening.

Sandra had packed her new nightdress but she left it in the suitcase for the time being. She would wear it after the Elvis show, she decided. She and Del were fast asleep before midnight.

Elvis' final midnight performance at the Hilton in August 1975 was noted more for its slapstick humour than musical quality. He took more pleasure from playing with two water pistols handed to him by some playful girls in the front row than he did from singing another litany of all too familiar hits. Relieved that the decision to close the current run had been taken, Elvis seemed to relax on stage and giggled childishly as he sprayed the band several times with jets of water that they took in good humour. He took his final bow shortly after one o'clock and went hurriedly to his suite via the private elevator that serviced his dressing room.

At 6am the following morning, while Delmore and Sandra were still asleep, Elvis left his suite in the Hilton hotel and took the elevator to the basement. Surrounded by bodyguards and accompanied by Linda and Dr Nichopoulos, he made his way unsteadily to a limousine in the underground car park that drove at speed to McCarran airport where his private plane was waiting. It was shortly after 7.30 am when the plane took off for Memphis.

When he landed at Memphis International three and a half hours later Elvis was taken directly to a private ward on the 18th floor of the Madison Wing of the Memphis Baptist Memorial Hospital where he would remain for almost three weeks.

As Elvis' plane flew eastwards through the morning sky, Colonel Parker and his staff bustled around the public areas of the Hilton, removing all evidence of Elvis' presence with an efficiency only the Colonel, in his best bullying mood, could inspire. All external billboards and neon signs were removed, all posters in the hotel's foyer and elsewhere were pulled down and all the leaflets, stickers, pennants and flyers that the Colonel had distributed so liberally were packed away for future use.

Peggy Lee was hastily contracted to take over Elvis' outstanding nights and by mid-morning, every trace of Elvis Presley's presence in the hotel had been removed. All that remained was a solitary sign in the hotel lobby: 'The remainder of the Elvis Presley engagement has been cancelled due to illness.'

Exhausted by the previous day's travel, Del and Sandra slept until late. They awoke refreshed, made themselves coffee and Del took a shower while Sandra flicked through the channels on TV. She found the mid-morning local news and weather on Channel 7.

'The weather is sunny and dry, top temperature in the high eighties with low humidity,' announced the weatherman.

Always the same out here I guess, thought Sandra, glancing out of the motel room window at the clear blue sky above. She was just about to turn off the television when the newscaster returned. As he spoke, a recent picture of Elvis flashed on to the screen.

'Finally... Rock'n'Roll King Elvis Presley has cancelled his current two-week engagement at the Hilton Hotel showroom with eleven more nights still to run. A spokesman for the hotel said that Presley had been taken ill and had to return to Memphis for immediate hospital treatment. The exact nature of his illness has yet to be confirmed but it is understood to be fatigue coupled with a severe stomach complaint. The hotel very much regrets the inconvenience to fans of the singer and has guaranteed that all tickets for his upcoming shows will be honoured at a future Presley engagement.

'News of Presley's illness will come as no surprise to fans who have already seen the shows during the current Presley season. Reports indicate that Presley was having difficulty breathing on stage and appeared listless and overweight. Is this the end for the King? We'll have more on Presley's sudden cancellation later in the day.'

When Delmore came out of the bathroom Sandra was sobbing quietly on the bed. Between sobs, she explained to her husband what she'd heard on the TV.

Del had always prided himself on being able to control his temper but this time he let fly, picking up an ash tray and hurling it at the television set. With a mighty crash, the screen exploded into a thousand tiny diamonds.

'The son of a bitch,' spat Del with a fury that Sandra barely recognised from her normally even-tempered husband. 'The fuckin' son of a goddamned bitch. Never mind honey, I'll make it up to you somehow. I promise I will. Just you wait.'

Chapter Two

(August 22 – September 30)

Frankie Wilson sat at his desk in the reporters' room at the *Memphis Press-Scimitar* and typed out his latest story on Elvis' illness.

'The 40-year-old singer has had a history of stomach and bowel complaints in recent years but his personal doctors at the Memphis Baptist Memorial Hospital are confident that Elvis will soon recover.

'He's sitting up in bed and joking with his nurses,' Doctor Sam Anschuler told me this morning from Elvis' bedside. 'He's even asked two of them to move into Graceland with him during his convalescence'.'

Wilson pulled the sheet of paper from his elderly manual typewriter and read through what he'd just written. It was, as always, slanted positively. Elvis was a local hero; the readers of his paper did not want to hear bad news or read negative things about Elvis, so Frankie dutifully handed in his optimistic account of Elvis' latest hospitalisation to an appreciative copy editor.

'How is Elvis?' asked the editor, knowing that Frankie's own words carried more weight than the story in his hand.

'He'll pull through, but I sometimes wonder whether he'll see 50,' replied Frankie.

'Really?'

'Yeah, really.'

'Why?' asked the curious editor.

Frankie put a finger to his lips but didn't elaborate. He knew better than to reveal all he knew about Elvis, even to his colleagues on the paper. The more he created the impression that he was privy to inside information on Elvis, the likelier it was that he'd retain their respect and hang on to his very comfortable job.

Frankie Wilson had covered the Elvis beat for the *Memphis Press-Scimitar* for 19 years. He was the paper's Entertainment Correspondent in 1956 when Elvis, then 21, broke through on to the national charts with 'Heartbreak Hotel' and he'd already interviewed the Hillbilly Cat – as the *Press-Scimitar* had called him – a couple of times that year when he was stirring things up with his wild style of singing and guitar playing. At first Frankie shared the general opinion that Elvis was a flash in the pan and that the novelty of rock'n'roll, and Elvis with it, would quickly fade. He was wrong, of course, as were millions of others of his generation. But Frankie wasn't too set in the conservatism of the American Fifties, the Dwight D. Eisenhower years, to be unable to do a swift about-turn on Elvis, and he'd hung on to his coat tails ever since.

Whenever there was a story about Elvis in the *Press-Scimitar*, it almost always carried Frankie's by-line. Over the years he'd met Elvis and his manager Colonel Parker many times, and he was pretty friendly with some of the guys in the Memphis Mafia. He'd heard a few distasteful things about Elvis, of course, things he could never report in the paper, but he kept his mouth shut which meant they trusted him as much, if not more, than any other newspaper reporter in the country. It was a privileged position, of course, and one that he valued highly, not least because most newspaper reporters were *persona non grata* as far as Colonel Parker was concerned. Frankie didn't believe he'd ever compromised himself with the *Press-Scimitar*, even though Elvis had once paid for a pair of plane tickets to Hawaii so he and his wife Grace could take a holiday to celebrate their 20th wedding anniversary. He still had the note that accompanied the tickets, written in Elvis' own handwriting. 'To my good friend Frankie,' he'd written. 'Thanks for all your help. Sincerely, Elvis.'

Sometimes Frankie pondered over where his loyalties really lay, with the *Press-Scimitar* or with Elvis. He knew how difficult it would be if a really big Elvis story came along that showed him in a bad light, meaning he had to make a choice between the two, but it had never happened yet. Sometimes he felt like he was sitting on a rickety barbed wire fence that pricked his backside whenever he moved one way or the other.

He decided to call Charlie West, one of the Elvis' guys, to see if he knew when Elvis was really going to be released from the hospital. He went back to his desk and dialled the number.

'Charlie? Frankie here, Frankie Wilson at the *Press-Scimitar*. How are things?'

'Real quiet with the boss in the hospital. Real quiet Frankie.'

'Any idea when he's coming out?'

'Can't say for sure Frankie, but I think he's gonna' spend some time of the day at Graceland and maybe sleep nights in the hospital, y'know. He's definitely looking a whole lot better than he was in Vegas.'

'Yeah.' Like all good reporters, Frankie was an adept at not interrupting the flow of a conversation that might lead to a possible confidence. The well-aimed 'Yeah' would hopefully encourage Charlie West to continue.

'Yeah. I think Elvis just got wound up about the shows. He knew he couldn't cut it properly on stage and that worried him, so he couldn't sleep, so he just got more and more wound up and felt worse and worse. Now he doesn't have to do any shows he can relax and he'll get better.'

'That's good,' said Frankie. 'He'll be back at Graceland soon then?'

'Yeah, I think so. All being well, anyway.'

'Great. Well I gotta run. Let's meet for a beer sometime Charlie.'

'Yeah, let's do that real soon. OK Frankie. Bye.'

Frankie hung up. At least his story about Elvis getting better seemed to be true. That was a relief.

Elvis Presley bored easily. Like many others upon whom Dame Fortune had showered fame and riches, the mundane was anathema to contentment and Elvis needed a constant charge to keep him amused. It could be any of many things: music, movies, pretty girls, fast cars, motor bikes, funfairs, travel, practical jokes, vandalism, food, sport, drugs or – his current favourite – impulsive gestures of unexpected random generosity, latterly the gift of expensive cars to total strangers. Hospital was boring and as soon as he was feeling better than he did in Vegas, Elvis wanted out.

When he was first admitted to the hospital, immediately after his return from Vegas, huge sheets of aluminium foil were affixed to the windows of his room to keep out the sunlight. This enabled Elvis to maintain his Dracula-like routine of sleeping during daylight hours and coming alive at night, and the hospital was quite willing to bend their rules for such a famous patient.

The official word was that Elvis was under treatment for 'exhaustion', but the truth was far more serious. Elvis' liver was malfunctioning due to a grossly enlarged colon and he was suffering regular and painful intestinal spasms. His constant use of 'medication' – powerful, numbing pain killers during periods when he was awake and sleeping pills when he chose to sleep – and a junk food diet had upset his metabolic system, causing his weight to fluctuate wildly and putting additional pressure on his heart.

Elvis briefly considered an intestinal by-pass operation but ruled that out when it was explained to him that henceforth he would have to adhere to a strict, frugal diet. Linda Thompson visited his private ward regularly and the pair would watch afternoon game shows on television together, and tune in to the hospital's internal TV system, so they could check out the action in the public wards. Ever a snoop, this eased Elvis' boredom for a while. So, after he'd been bedridden for two days, did a surprise phone call from the man who was once the highest in the land.

'Yeah,' said Elvis when his bedside phone rang unexpectedly. The line was silent for a few seconds. Then a voice he didn't recognise came on the line.

'Is that Mr Elvis Presley?'

'Yeah,' said Elvis curiously. All calls to his bedside were supposed to have been screened by the hospital switchboard. 'Who's that?'

'This is Ron Zeigler, the secretary to Richard Nixon, the former President of the United States. One moment please.'

The one and only time Elvis had met Nixon was at the White House in 1970. Earlier this year he had phoned him when Nixon was himself hospitalised. Now, it seemed, the ex-President was returning the courtesy. The hot line crackled.

'Hello Elvis, it's Richard Nixon here. I'm speaking from

my home in California. I just wanted to call to say how sorry I was to hear that you were unwell, and that I hope most sincerely that you'll be feeling much better soon.'

Caught off his guard, Elvis was momentarily speechless. 'Thank you sir... er, Mr President, sir,' was all he could mumble in reply.

From the library of his San Clemente home, Richard Nixon tried to sound chatty. 'What's the problem, Elvis?' he asked.

'Er, just fatigue sir,' replied Elvis. 'I just been working too hard I guess. A bit of a stomach problem too, so the doctors tell me. But I'm feeling better every day sir. I should be outta' here real soon.'

'That's good,' said Nixon. 'Well just you look after yourself now. You're an important man in this country, our country.'

'Thank you sir.' Elvis felt deeply flattered. He admired the former President, any President, very much. Emboldened by Nixon's bonhomie, he decided to share some thoughts on current affairs. 'I think you did a fine job up there in the Capitol, Mr President, sir, and I want to say that you had my full support in that Watergate business I kept seeing on television. I know you're an honest man, Mr President, sir, and you had our country's best interests at heart. I think that those people who were trying to harm you were, er, unpatriotic citizens who didn't deserve a President like you, sir, er Mr President.'

Nixon coughed discretely. Elvis' grasp of the Watergate situation was evidently untainted by political reality. He decided to bring the conversation to an end.

'Thank you very much, Elvis. I am confident that my position in history is secure,' he said, sounding far more confident than he really felt. 'I gotta go now... State business, you know. Bye and best wishes Elvis.'

'Of course. Thank you for calling, sir.' Elvis hung up and a swell of pride surged through his huge body. Goddam it, the former President himself calling to wish him well. Wait till he told the boys about that.

Later the same day Elvis took a similar call from Frank Sinatra who also wished him well but his buoyant mood didn't last. After a few days in the hospital he was itching to get back to his toys at Graceland, so much so that the hospital staff had little choice but to discharge him earlier than they planned.

Linda visited Elvis every day and there was a sack of get well cards waiting to be opened at the foot of his bed. But Elvis was still bored.

So was Sandra Pandel.

Ever since the disappointment of Elvis' Vegas cancellation, she'd been listless, forgetful and just plain bad tempered. It was unbecoming and quite inappropriate for a waitress, and the manager at the Germantown Diner where she worked five days a week, a fussy, balding, middle-aged Italian who liked his staff to call him Mr Armando, was becoming increasingly intolerant of her attitude.

'Sandra, this is not good enough, not at all good enough,' he scolded her when she arrived 30 minutes late for the second morning in succession. 'It's 8.30 already and you're supposed to be here by eight, as you well know. There's been complaints from customers and the kitchen staff. Yesterday you served wrong dishes to the wrong customers, got the orders mixed up and you look a mess too.'

Sandra bit back an angry riposte. 'I'm sorry Mr

Armando. I really am. I'll work later tonight to make up for it.'

Mr Armando shrugged. 'OK,' he said. 'OK. But watch it. OK.'

Sandra took off her coat and headed for the bathroom to fix her make-up. Locking the door behind her, she pushed her hair back from her face and stared into the mirror. Mr Armando was right. She certainly wouldn't win any beauty competitions these days, she thought, staring at the rings around her eyes, her pale features and unwashed hair. Del was away on a road trip, hauling machine tool parts to Cleveland and then on to Chicago, and when she didn't have anyone around to look pretty for, she often let things slide.

Sandra was reasonably confident that Mr Armando wouldn't fire her, if for no other reason than he liked to flirt with her after a glass of lambrusco in the evening. She had never responded, of course, and nor would she. Hurriedly Sandra applied lip-gloss and mascara and brushed her hair as best she could. Reasonably satisfied with her appearance, she went out to the kitchen, put on her waitresses' overall, pulled it up above her knees and walked out behind the counter, putting on her best smile.

Mr Armando looked at her admiringly. It always amazed Sandra that she could change his mood by altering her appearance to suit his lechery, just as it always amazed Mr Armando that certain women could change their appearance for the better so dramatically in a matter of minutes with the aid of make-up and a hairbrush. 'You look very nice now Sandra,' he said, winking. 'No mistakes today, hey?'

Sandra clenched her teeth and smiled sweetly one more time. 'Can I help you, sir,' she asked a customer sat at the counter. 'Double bacon and fries, eggs over easy, coffee,' he said, not even bothering to look up from his copy of the *Memphis Press-Scimitar*.

Sandra was clearing away the plates when she came across the same copy of the *Press-Scimitar*, now discarded, and during her break she took it with her to the back of the kitchen to read with her cup of coffee. The headline on an inside page caught her eye. 'Elvis Out Of Hospital Soon' it read and the story below carried the by-line of Frankie Wilson. Sandra read the story twice and might have cut it out to save if her enthusiasm for Elvis hadn't been at an all time low. She'd read Frankie Wilson's stories about Elvis in the *Press-Scimitar* many times and she'd wondered what sort of a man he was.

For the rest of the day, Sandra kept thinking about Frankie Wilson at the *Press-Scimitar* and it made her mix up at least three orders, causing the increasingly angry Mr Armando to threaten her with the sack unless there was a marked change in attitude. By the time Sandra left the diner at six she was pretty angry herself and she'd found it hard not to answer back the beleaguered manager. She resolved to call Wilson at his office just to tell him how Elvis had disappointed her and other fans by cancelling. Maybe it would get back to Elvis and he'd do a special show in Memphis.

She made the call when she arrived home, but Wilson was out so she left a message with a night duty man who promised he'd ask Wilson to call her back the following day. Sandra left the number of the diner as well as her own. Then she began to tidy the apartment, starting with the bedroom where, in the drawer of her dressing table, the new negligee she'd bought for the Vegas trip lay unworn and undisturbed.

That morning Delmore Pandel had woken up in the back of his cab. He'd spent the night parked in a service area off Route I-90 West, and he was as stiff as a board. He made himself a coffee using the small kerosene stove he always carried with him, and munched on a day-old ham sandwich from an airtight plastic container.

He was due in Chicago later that day with the remainder of his cargo of machine parts but he'd made a couple of calls from the road yesterday and picked up another job, delivering a load of beer crates and empty kegs to Milwaukee, just north of the Windy City. With a bit of luck, he'd pick up another load of full beer kegs to take down to Nashville from a contractor he knew in Milwaukee who'd given him similar contracts on a couple of occasions before. That meant a nice round trip, earning all the way, and a decent cheque at the end of the week.

He finished his breakfast, got behind the wheel and started up the big motor. Easing the truck into first gear, he moved slowly forward, turning the giant wheel and heading back out towards the freeway. When he was up to speed, he switched on the radio. Elvis Presley was singing 'Suspicious Minds'.

'We can't go on together...,' Elvis' voice crackled from the speaker above his head, *'with suspicious minds... We can't build a dream...'*

'Fucking Elvis,' Del spat out of the cab window. Of all the songs in the Elvis Presley catalogue, 'Suspicious Minds' was probably his all time favourite, but he switched channels anyway, settling eventually on a country station that was playing 'Jolene' by Dolly Parton.

The wasted trip to Las Vegas had cost Del almost $600, and the lingering resentment towards Elvis wouldn't go away. There'd been the plane fares, $120 each, the motel, another $120, and incidentals along the way, not least the TV set he'd smashed for which the motel demanded $200. His tickets to see Elvis, at $20 each, were re-usable the next time that Elvis played the Hilton in Las Vegas but no one seemed to know when that was going to be and Del doubted whether he'd be able to afford the plane tickets or overnight stay again.

But Del's misgivings were inconsequential compared to the way Sandra had reacted. From the day she first saw Elvis on that TV special in 1968 she'd desperately wanted to see him in person and the disappointment had affected her very badly, almost as if someone close to her had died. When they returned home, Sandra had pulled out the 23 Elvis scrapbooks she kept in her closet and carried them down into the garage where Del parked his pick-up truck and motor bike. 'I don't think I'll be looking at them much now, and I need some extra space in here anyway,' she said.

Their life had returned to normal but it wasn't the same as before and Del was baffled as to why Sandra should react so strangely. It seemed irrational on her part and he couldn't figure it out. He'd rashly promised to take her back to Vegas to use the tickets again whenever Elvis re-appeared, but she didn't appear keen. Whatever was the matter, Del blamed Elvis personally for what had happened and the way it seemed to be affecting their relationship, or at least the way Sandra's mind had snapped. Even when they made love she seemed to be going through the motions.

'Fuckin' fat son of a bitch, treating his fans like shit,' he muttered to himself as he drove along. The more he muttered to himself, the more he thought about the issue, the madder he became.

A couple of nights earlier, a week after returning from Vegas, he'd met up with Roy in the JayKay, and Roy had shared his disappointment remarkably sincerely considering his cynical attitude towards Elvis. Roy seemed to enjoy badmouthing Elvis.

'The fat motherfucker,' Roy had spat. 'He should be made to pay back the money you lost, and everybody else's. He's goddamned rich enough. Fatigue, you say... more like plain simple laziness if you ask me. He's over the hill and always has been, ever since he came out of the army at any rate.'

Del could only agree. 'I'd really like to do something to get back at him,' he told Roy. 'I really would.'

'Yeah, well. Maybe someone ought to teach Elvis goddamned Presley a lesson in manners. It ain't right that he let folk down like he done to you and Sandy,' said Roy. Then they turned their attention back to the baseball on TV but Roy couldn't seem to concentrate. Whenever Del looked towards his friend, Roy's eyes didn't seem to be focusing on TV set. When he commented on the play Roy seemed to be a million miles away, and when they left the bar later the evening Roy turned to Del with a strange look on his face. 'Y'know, maybe there is something we can do about Elvis Presley,' he said.

'What's that?' asked Del. 'Rob Graceland?'

'No. That'd be stupid. But there is something. I gotta think about it first.'

The conversation went no further and the following day Del set off for Cleveland. He wasn't due back in Memphis for another three days.

Royston Kruger always knew there was more to life

than the cards he'd been dealt. He was the kind of man who jumped at opportunities without giving too much thought to the consequences, and he figured that sooner or later one of those opportunities would turn up trumps. But he wasn't one to brood, nor to bear grudges against those who might have failed him in the past. 'Tomorrow is another day', Scarlet O'Hara's famous line from Gone With The Wind, might have been written especially for Roy.

Apart from Delmore and Sandra, he had no close friends. The other security officers where he worked were all older than him and married with families, and he hadn't made any friends during his short spell in the Memphis Police. He'd had more than his fair share of girlfriends but he'd never managed to sustain a relationship with a girl who hadn't at one time shared his bed, and he would never have been able to establish a friendship with a single or, apart from Sandra, a married woman with whom he did not wish to share a bed.

Roy had no family either. He was an only child, born in Memphis just after the Second World War to third generation German immigrants who'd married in 1941, three months before Japan attacked Pearl Harbour. His father, Marcus Kruger, was anxious to fight against the Nazis in order to prove his loyalty to America, and had wasted no time in volunteering for the forces. Separated by the war, his bride Helen spent three anxious years waiting for her husband to return from his posting in Europe. It was a cruel irony that after surviving three years of vicious fighting in France and Germany, he would arrive home in time to conceive Roy but die in a car wreck six months before his son was born.

Helen Kruger, already 36, never really recovered from

the loss of her husband. Asthmatic and painfully thin, she died from pneumonia in 1950 and Roy was raised by an uncle and aunt who lived in Knoxville in Kentucky. Never one for a great deal of what he termed 'book learnin'', Roy returned to Memphis to look for work at 16, and after a year of casual labouring jobs ended up joining the army where he met Del, who was the same age as himself.

Like Del, Roy had become an excellent soldier. He liked the macho atmosphere of boot camp and if he hadn't felt that life owed him something better he'd have stayed in the army for the remainder of his days. But deep down he was restless. A rebel by nature, the rules and regulations of army life, the constant deference he was obliged to show to officers, the dull routine of guard duty, bored him to death. Twice he was disciplined for being out of line and threatened with discharge but each time he'd somehow talked his way out of trouble, promising to be a good soldier. Eventually, after a third disciplinary charge over a bar fight, he left the army and found what he hoped was a more rewarding job with the police but, again, the need to conform was alien to him and he quit after six months. Now, guarding a warehouse of produce in the early hours, he wondered whether he'd made the right choice.

Roy wanted to make his mark, and he wanted to be rich without having to work too hard. But at the same time he didn't want to risk breaking the law and ending up in jail where he knew he'd go stir crazy. Something had to turn up sooner or later, he thought as he smoked another cigarette and drank coffee to head off the 5am tiredness that came over him when he worked nights. He was thinking about Del and Sandra's ill-fated trip to Las Vegas when, as if by serendipity, Elvis Presley came on the radio singing 'All Shook Up'. Two nights ago in the JayKay, when Del told him about Elvis cancelling the show, a crazy idea had flashed through his head, and now, alone and at a loose end, he began to contemplate it again.

It was such a crazy idea that for once he hadn't blurted it out loud to Del, but now that he thought about it in a sober frame of mind, maybe it wasn't quite so crazy after all.

'Hell, it could be done. If Elvis was careless enough, it could be done,' he thought to himself. They'd have to plan it very carefully, choose their moment and not falter under any circumstances. 'God, what a thing to do,' Roy whistled to himself. Then he settled back against the cushions of the armchair provided for his late night comfort, closed his eyes and tried to sleep. What prevented him from dropping off was this crazy idea that occupied his mind.

Mr Armando picked up the telephone in the Germantown diner and was annoyed to discover that the caller was asking for Sandra Pandel. He'd told his staff they couldn't accept personal calls at work, and what with Sandra's other misdemeanours of late, this was too much.

'Who is this?' he demanded. 'What? The *Press-Scimitar*. OK. OK. OK. Wait a minute.'

'Sandra,' he shouted across the diner to where she was serving behind the counter. 'There's some reporter guy from the *Memphis Press-Scimitar* on the line for you. You famous now, or something? I've told you before about no calls at work.'

Sandra ignored Mr Armando and rushed to the phone. 'Hello,' she said.

'This is Frankie Wilson at the *Press-Scimitar*. I have a message to call you... something about Elvis Presley.'

Sandra gulped. She hadn't really expected Wilson to return her call and neither had she worked out exactly what she was going to say, other than to complain about Elvis' cancellation. 'Well,' she began, 'me and my husband went out to Las Vegas to see Elvis at the Hilton Hotel two weeks ago and he cancelled the show and we lost a lot of money because of it, and I don't know whether we can afford to go to Las Vegas again to see him with the same tickets and... and I don't know what to do. I think that was real bad of Elvis to cancel.'

'But Elvis was sick,' said Wilson, as reasonably as he could. 'He couldn't perform. In any case, what's this got to do with me?'

'Well, they shouldn't have sold us the tickets in the first place then,' said Sandra, unreasonably.

'What do you expect me to do about it?' asked Wilson.

'Well, maybe you could have a word with Elvis or someone close to him. Maybe persuade him to do a show here in Memphis. I bet the fans would love that.'

'A show just for you?' Wilson was becoming irritated, regretting now that he'd bothered to call back this stupid woman, but he never knew for sure whether a call would waste his time or lead to a valuable tip-off. 'I couldn't do anything of the kind, Mrs er... Pandel. You can get a refund on your tickets if you can't use them next time, you know.'

'What about our plane fare... and the motel. My husband saved up and we wasted our money.'

Wilson was on the verge of hanging up. 'I'm sorry, there's nothing I can do. Good morning.'

Sandra, left listening to the dial tone, slammed the phone down. Mr Armando came over. 'What was all that about? I told you no personal calls at work.'

'Oh, fuck off,' she spat, loudly enough for every

customer in the diner to hear.

'Right, that's it Sandra. You're fired. Get out... now!'

Sandra Pandel had no wish to argue. She threw off her apron, grabbed her purse and marched straight out of the door.

Five days after being admitted to the hospital, on August 26, Elvis was allowed to visit Graceland for four hours. He wasn't discharged finally until September 5, but on each intervening day he'd been allowed home for a few hours. Two nurses, Marion Cocke and Kathy Seaman, whose names were the cause of much ribald humour among the guys, were assigned shift duties at Graceland, Seaman from 9 am to 2 pm, Cocke from 11 pm to 7 am.

Elvis charmed the two nurses, just as he'd charmed most of the women he'd ever met. 'Yes, ma'am,' he would say whenever they required him to submit to tests. His courteous manners captivated them both into a campaign designed to restore him to full health as speedily as possible. There were times when Elvis seemed to them to be more like a small boy who needed mothering than a millionaire entertainer, the most celebrated singer in the whole of the United States. It was part of Elvis' all-round appeal to women of all ages; he could, when he wanted, be everything every woman had always desired, Gable's Rhett or Valentino's Sheik, Olivier's Heathcliffe or Brando's Kowalski.

Dr Nichopoulos assured everyone at Graceland and elsewhere that Elvis was not suffering from any serious medical problems and that he would be restored to full health in two to three months. The period in hospital enabled Elvis to detoxify and he was feeling as well as he'd done in ages. With no work on his immediate

schedule and no pressure from the Colonel, he was able
to relax with Linda, his family and his entourage of male
friends. After two weeks Elvis solemnly promised the
nurses that he would undergo their recommended weight-
loss regime, an unlikely undertaking, and they went back
to their normal duties at the hospital.

Despite the precarious position of his finances – and
knowing it would anger the Colonel – Elvis bought
expensive cars as farewell presents for both nurses
and four brand new Harley Davidson motor cycles on
which he hoped soon to go for night time runs with his
bodyguards. He also flew off to Fort Worth to personally
supervise the work on his latest toy, an 880 Convair jet
he'd christened *Lisa Marie* after his daughter, that was
being refitted and readied for his personal use.

In a frivolous moment, Elvis bought three 'super-
cycles', small three-wheeled vehicles similar to golf carts,
and in the twilight of the late summer evenings he and
Linda would ride around the neighbourhood surrounding
Graceland. He killed time supervising the building of an
additional trophy room on the ground floor of his house as
more space was needed to house the growing collection of
gold albums and other awards, and he busied himself with
plans for the construction of a building to house a sauna
bath elsewhere on the estate.

Life at Graceland settled into an easy routine. Colonel
Parker never called and, as ever, all activity centred
around Elvis' needs. Vernon Presley occasionally
admonished his son for overspending, but Elvis took little
notice. Linda was in sporadic attendance, excusing herself
whenever Elvis took a call from his ex-wife Priscilla, now
ensconced in Los Angeles with seven-year-old Lisa-Marie
and her lover Mike Stone, Elvis' former karate instructor.

Linda flew to and from Los Angeles, where she hoped to establish an acting career, and when she was away Elvis dated other girls.

Priscilla rarely visited but told Elvis she was delighted he'd chosen to take a long rest. 'Colonel Parker works you too hard,' she told her ex-husband on the phone, not for the first time. 'You know my feelings about Parker... I've never trusted that man Elvis, and I think you ought to...'

'Now, don't you worry about my business Cilla,' Elvis interrupted. He was well aware that Priscilla did not share his loyalty towards the Colonel, or any of the guys he employed for that matter; in fact, the constant presence of Parker and the Memphis Mafia had been one of the many factors that led to their eventual divorce. 'Let me worry about the Colonel.'

Since separating from Elvis three years ago, Priscilla had become far more independent and while she would never have dared to question Elvis in years gone by, she nowadays demonstrated a level of assertiveness that Elvis, eternally the male chauvinist, found plain irritating.

'But you never do worry about him...'

Elvis had no wish to get into another bickering session with Priscilla over the Colonel, so he abruptly changed the subject to Lisa-Marie, and they talked vaguely about the next time his daughter would visit Memphis. Elvis doted on his daughter and like all rich part-time fathers demonstrated his love largely by spoiling her with expensive presents and pandering to her capriciousness. In reality, he had about as much in common with a seven-year-old girl as he had with Richard Nixon.

There was a very definite hierarchy system at work amongst the residents of Graceland. Everybody was frightened of Elvis, and of how his moods might change, and everyone apart from Elvis deferred to Vernon Presley who was family. Elvis gave ground only to the Colonel who never visited, so he always got his own way, either by charm or bullying. Everyone apart from Elvis and Vernon deferred to Linda Thompson when she visited, but only when Elvis was around. When he wasn't the Memphis Mafia guys who came and went talked about her behind her back, often lasciviously, as they did about any woman below the age of 30. Some of them even thought that Vernon Presley was becoming a senile old fool, which wasn't far from the truth.

Two other elderly relatives of Elvis, his uncle Vester Presley, Vernon's elder brother who had married Clettes, the sister of Elvis' mother Gladys, and grandmother Minnie-Mae, Vernon's mother, known to one and all as Dodger, also lived at Graceland but kept themselves largely to themselves in their own quarters at the rear of the house. Minnie-Mae's sanctum was the kitchen, where she prepared Elvis' sumptuous fried meals, while Vester spent his days doing odd jobs or on duty at the front gate, amiably talking to the fans who gathered and vetting those who went in or out.

There was a regular compliment of bodyguards and good buddies – the Memphis Mafia – who came and went as and when they were summoned. Their leader was the long serving and uniquely discrete Joe Esposito, unquestionably the most trusted and capable of Elvis' retainers, who acted as tour manager, handling all arrangements for Elvis' concert tours, and liaised regularly with Colonel Parker over arrangements. Joe was based in Los Angeles but checked in at Graceland most days to see whether he was needed, but with Elvis' professional engagements temporarily on hold his services weren't required at present. Others who danced attendance on the King included Elvis' cousin, Billy Smith, the rotund Lamar Fike, guitarist and Army buddy Charlie Hodge, Jerry Schilling, who flew in from his home in Los Angeles whenever he was needed, and old timers Marty Lacker and Sonny and Red West and their cousin Charlie. George Klein, the Memphis disc jockey who was in the same class as Elvis at Humes High School back in 1953, was an honorary member of this troupe who never missed an opportunity to party with Elvis.

Settled into Graceland for a long spell, it was the new Harley-Davidson bikes that gave Elvis most pleasure, and by the middle of September he was regularly riding out at night with a posse from the Memphis Mafia for company.

'I've been fired.'

Sandra had waited for an hour after Delmore arrived home to give him the news, and it couldn't have come at a worse moment. The hoped-for run from Milwaukee carrying beer kegs to Nashville hadn't come through so he'd returned with an empty rig and it looked like September was going to be a slim month for both of them unless they dipped into the savings account that had already been eroded by the trip to Las Vegas.

'What happened?'

Sandra explained matter of factly that Mr Armando had never liked her and that he was a lecherous womaniser, and by the time she'd finished Del couldn't have cared less about his wife's job. She said she would go out looking for something similar the next day and the matter was dropped.

Over the next couple of days Del was booked for some short rides, to Lexington and back, down to Birmingham

in Alabama, and across to Jacksonville on the coast of
northern Florida. He would be home most nights and
Sandra was glad of it. They never mentioned Elvis, but
they never forget their Vegas disappointment either.
Sure enough, Sandra found another job within 48 hours,
this time working in the restaurant of a nearby Howard
Johnson motel for which she was required to wear a
green hat and matching nylon waitress' dress with short
sleeves and buttons down the front that Del took delight
in undoing whenever the opportunity arose.

Del met Roy in the JayKay three nights later, and when
they'd ordered their drinks and settled down, Roy was
uncharacteristically subdued.

'What's up buddy?' he asked.

'I got something on my mind, but I don't wanna talk
about it here. What say we grab a six pack and head on
over to my place?'

'What's this about?'

Roy turned to Del and put his fingers to his lips. 'Just
finish up. I'll tell you when we get to my place.'

The two men finished their beers and bought six cans
to go, then headed off to Roy's apartment. Not until they
went inside and settled in Roy's untidy living room did
Roy speak.

'I've been thinking,' he began. 'This business about
Elvis. Now I don't want you to laugh when I say this or
even to say anything at all to me until I'm finished. OK?'

'OK.' Del was curious. He'd never seen Roy behave so
mysteriously.

'Right,' said Roy, lowering his voice. 'Here's what I've
been thinking. We oughta kidnap Elvis Presley, talk to him,
teach him a lesson, ransom him, whatever... but I think we
could snatch the motherfucker. I really do.'

Del stared at Roy with a mixture of disbelief and amazement. 'Kidnap Elvis,' he repeated. 'Kidnap goddamned Elvis fucking Presley. You gotta be out of your crazy fucking mind, Roy.'

'Shhhhh.' Roy put his fingers to his lips. 'Not so loud Del. I knew you'd say that, exactly that, but it ain't so stupid as you think. I heard Elvis goes out riding his bike at night. I heard his bodyguards are a soft bunch. I heard all sorts, and I think two well organised guys could do it.'

'What about Sandra?'

'Well, she'd have to be a part of it too, sooner or later. I think maybe we could get him to sing for her.'

'Sing for her? Are you out of your mind?' Del opened another can of beer and took a deep swig.

'Just hear me out, man. Just hear me out. First of all we gotta do some reccies, just like we used to in 'Nam on those villages, you know. Keep our heads down and watch, except we'll keep watching Elvis' house, Graceland... we'll do it in shifts, so we can build up a pattern of Elvis' movements. Where he goes and with whom. Whether he's in a car or on a bike, and how many people are with him. We'll have to do it at night, so we watch the house at night, discretely. Maybe pretend we're fans or something.'

'Even if we do manage to get him, what do we do with him?' asked Del.

'Take him to the Kentucky Hills to the mountain cabin near Lake Cumberland that we use for hunting. We'll rent it for a week, like we usually do. Get him outta state, away from Memphis. We can hide him there for a while.'

Del was far from convinced. 'Are you trying to tell me that you and me can just go out there one night and snatch Elvis Presley... just like that?'

'Yeah, I am,' said Roy. He chuckled mischievously. 'And even if we failed, we'd probably be famous for trying.'

'And end up in jail.'

'Come on, we're too clever for that. Remember our army training. We're bound to have surprise on our side. Nobody has ever attempted to kidnap Elvis, so nobody will be expecting it. It's the last thing anybody will expect. Surprise is our best weapon. Also, we'll plan it down to the last detail, and we'll have fall back positions if things go wrong. I've heard that those guys that surround Elvis aren't as tough as they think they are. In any case they're not always there and we can probably take three of them anyway. Elvis won't fight... he's sick, too fat as well. He won't be a problem. We can use your flat bed to take him to the cabin.'

Del continued to stare at his friend in amazement. Roy really was serious about this, he thought.

'We'll have to get into shape ourselves,' Roy continued. 'We're probably already in better shape than Elvis' bodyguards but we should go down a gym for a couple of weeks. Take some time off work.'

'I can't afford to do that. I'm short this month as it is.'

'Never mind, I'll fund you. I've got some money put away.'

As Roy continued to talk, Del's objections seemed to be more and more futile. It was Roy's enthusiasm as much as anything that gripped Del but he was still far from convinced when he left Roy's place some time after midnight. Sandra was still awake when he arrived home.

'You're kinda late honey,' she said as he came through the door of their apartment. It wasn't an admonishment, just a statement of fact.

'Yeah.. I er, went back to Roy's for a couple of beers.

There was something he wanted to show me.'
'What was that?'

'Oh, nothing... just a letter and some pictures from an old Army buddy. No one you'd know.'

Lying in bed later next to Sandra, Del thought more and more about Roy's plan to kidnap Elvis Presley. 'Crazy bastard,' he kept murmuring as he drifted off to sleep.

During the second week of September Roy handed in his notice at the security firm where he worked, collected some back pay and sold an old Chevvy and a couple of shotguns he'd been meaning to unload for months. His savings amounted to just over $4,000, enough to stake Del and himself during the weeks when they would be busy stalking Elvis and holding him captive. He was determined to go ahead with his idea and he knew that Del would come round to his thinking soon. In the meantime he put together plans and a timetable.

Roy wasn't to know that Elvis had no plans of his own right now, but he guessed correctly that the singer had set aside some time for recuperation after his much-publicised illness. Roy had decided to spend three weeks watching Graceland, to carefully note the comings and goings of the Presley entourage in order to establish if there was any pattern to his movements. Once they knew of a pattern they would be half way to their goal. They could then decide how to actually go about snatching Elvis and when was the best moment. He inquired about renting the cabin the hills during the second week of October and was pleased to learn it was available for the entire month.

Roy started his reconnaissance campaign on the evening of September 10, a Saturday, unbeknownst to him the same day that Elvis was given a speeding ticket by Patrolman Robert T. Hogan. On an old pedal cycle he'd had for years, Roy cycled down Elvis Presley Boulevard until he reached the singer's famous home. It was set back from the road, almost hidden by oak trees at the end of a drive that wound uphill towards the mock Gothic porch with its four imposing Corinthian pillars on either side of the front door. There were about half a dozen fans hanging around the tall wrought iron 'music' gates that were famously decorated with musical notes and two outlines of the house's celebrated occupant. The slate walls on either side of the gates were low enough for a man to climb quite easily, but Roy was sure that there'd be two or three men patrolling the grounds, watching out for intruders.

Roy parked his bicycle across the street from Graceland and went into a restaurant on the opposite side of the road. The place sold Elvisburgers, but Roy settled for a coffee and watched the comings and goings across the street through the window. It had already occurred to him that he would have to vary his own comings and goings so as not to attract attention, and that Del would have to do his share of surveillance too.

Roy lingered for an hour, ordering a second coffee and reading a copy of the Memphis Scimitar. No one arrived or left Graceland. Some fans came and went, and several of them had their photographs taken with the famous gates in the background. So Roy left the burger bar and sauntered across the street to mingle with them.

'Is Elvis home?' he asked two girls in halter-tops and blue jeans.

'Yeah, he's home right now,' one of them replied. 'Vester Presley, that's Elvis' uncle... he was here earlier and he told us that Elvis is here in Memphis right now, somewhere up in the house. We're waiting around 'cos he's bound to come out sooner or later.'

Thus enlightened, Roy decided to linger.

'You a big fan, mister?' asked the other girl, the prettier of the two.

'Sure am,' said Roy. For once in his life he had no wish to get into conversation with a pretty girl, so he lit a cigarette, walked away and leaned against the wall twenty feet away.

Roy waited another hour, watching the house and the fans as the sun set and dusk approached. Still, no one had entered or left the house by the front gate, but as darkness fell he could see lights twinkling in the Graceland windows. Most of the fans had left now, including the two girls he'd spoken to earlier. The presence of other fans made him seem less conspicuous and he decided to wait. At 11pm he ran out of cigarettes and went back to the burger bar to buy more. He was pleased to note that different staff were on duty.

By midnight there were only three fans plus himself left, and he was just about to call it a night when he heard what sounded like motor cycles kick-starting somewhere in the grounds of Graceland. Moments later, three bike riders, all dressed in black leather and wearing helmets, swooped down the drive towards the gate. The noise from their exhausts was deafening after the silence of the last two hours. One of the riders dismounted and opened the gate, using a key to unlock a large padlock. He held the gate open for the other two riders who sped through, out into Elvis Presley Boulevard, then locked the gate behind him. One of the riders, the heaviest, glanced backwards at Roy and the fans and waved before accelerating away. The fans shrieked.

Roy had just set eyes on his prey for the first time.

It was the freedom of the night, as much as the speed
that Elvis craved; the fleeting chance to cast off the
downside of his monumental fame and behave like a
normal human being. He'd long ago become accustomed
to being unable to do such everyday things as drive into
town and buy a shirt, or go to a restaurant with a date, or
even stroll down a street, without being accosted by fans
or stared at like a monument. He'd even inured himself to
the eternally unreal situation at Graceland, where even
in the privacy of his own palatial home he was forever
on show, constantly the star, and expected to look and
behave like Elvis, the King of Rock'n'Roll, presiding over
his courtiers.

At night on the road astride his bike, cocooned in his
sleek black leathers, his face hidden behind the shaded
visor of an oversized crash helmet, Elvis could at least
taste something akin to freedom, if only temporarily.
Cruising along the wide street that the city of Memphis
had chosen to name after him, he deliberately avoided
looking up at the green street signs with their legend
'Elvis Presley Boulevard' for they were yet another of the
constant reminders that his life was not his own. Riding
his bike at night, even along the street that bore his own
name, was probably as close to normality as Elvis Presley
was ever likely to know.

It was as if in his black leather outfit and impenetrable
helmet he'd become an invisible man, a recurring fancy of
his imagination that he'd entertained since having once
seen a film based on a book by HG Wells. The thought of
entering a crowded room in which no one was able to see
him, or to walk the streets unobserved, was a fantasy that

thrilled him as much as the speeds he could attain astride his bike.

Waving to the half dozen or so fans by the gate was a symbolic gesture for him, like waving goodbye to that aspect of his life. For the next hour he would be free, and he doubted whether there would be any fans left when he returned in an hour's time after his burn up along Route 55, down into Mississippi and back.

In the event there was one fan waiting for him when he returned, a solitary man smoking a cigarette and leaning against the wall with a pedal cycle. Elvis couldn't remember whether he'd been there when he left, but as he was entering the Graceland gate at the end of his ride he turned and waved all the same.

The man waved back, got onto his bicycle and pedalled away into the night.

When Roy arrived back home he pulled out a notebook and wrote down his observations:

September 10: Kept watch from 2100 hours until 0130. E and 3 others left G on motorbikes at 0012 hrs. Turned left heading south at speed. Returned 0115 hours. No other persons left or entered G. 5 or so fans in locality.

When he'd finished Roy hid the notebook in the cupboard beneath his kitchen sink. On the front, as an afterthought, he wrote 'Plumbing Notes' in capital letters. It was too late to call Del, so he waited until the morning, waiting until Sandra would have left for work.

'Elvis goes out riding his bike at night. I saw him,' he told his friend. 'I don't know where he goes or how often, but I'm sure we can find out. He takes some men with him. There were three last night but it might not always be three.'

'You mean you were there all night?' Del sounded sceptical, but Roy carried on regardless.

'No, not all night, only until he came home. He even waved at me, not that he'd have been able to recognise me in the dark. We could take him on one of these night rides. I'm sure of it. I'm keeping a log of his movements in a notebook. I think we should keep the log going for at least three weeks, then see if there's a pattern so we can anticipate his moves.'

'Where's the notebook?' asked Del.

'It's hidden. Don't worry. No one will find it. I'll try again tomorrow night, then maybe you can have a go.'

'OK,' replied Del, then hung up. The following morning he arranged to store his big truck at a lorry park on the edge of town, handing over a $20 fee and telling the owner he wouldn't need it for at least a month, maybe longer.

Roy's notebook, September 11
Arrived at G at 2000. 4 fans. 7 fans arrived 2100 am. Gates locked, no action at house. Upper lights on. One car carrying 2 men (not E) left G at 2145. Car returned with driver only at 2212. All fans but 3 left at 2230. E and 2 others left G on motor bikes at 0015, headed south. All 3 returned 0133. Lights at G remained on until at least 0330, probably later.

On September 12 Del took over the watch duties and, following Roy's style, made an entry in Roy's notebook. *D arrived at G at 2100. 11 fans outside. One car carrying 2 men and girl arrived at 2215. Same car + passengers + one other carrying E, 2 men and 1 girl left at 2345. Car carrying E, 2 men and girl returned 0030. E and 2 men left G on motor bikes at 0115, headed south. All 3 returned 0245. Lights at G remained on until 0430, probably later.*

Thereafter Roy and Del worked alternate nights, systematically making entries into the notebook.

Roy's notebook, September 13
Arrived at G at 2100. 3 fans outside who left at 2215. No traffic in or out of G all night up to 0200.

Roy's notebook, September 14
Arrived at G at 2045. 8 fans outside who left at 2300. E and 1 man left G on motor bikes at 0010, headed south. Both returned at 0125.

It was this last entry that most excited Roy Kruger.

'Del, if he occasionally goes out with just one other rider it'll be as easy as shooting fish in a barrel to grab him,' he told his partner on the phone the next day.

'Really, he went out with just one other guy?'

'Sure did.'

'Maybe we should try to follow him on our bikes to see where he goes.'

'Yeah. I gotta feeling he heads for a freeway someplace so he can open up that big bike of his.'

'He always heads south, so that means he's probably making for Route 55,' said Del. 'What do you say we try to intercept them on that.'

'No. We gotta make the hit before he reaches the freeway.'

Early the following evening Del and Roy met at Roy's apartment and studied a large-scale street map of Memphis. After some discussion they decided to reccie together for the first time that night. Del would wait by the Graceland gate while Roy, riding his motor bike, would wait three blocks south from Graceland, in a side street, so that if and when Elvis rode by he could tag along at a discreet distance. Since it had now become clear to them that if Elvis was going out riding he wouldn't leave Graceland until after midnight, they waited until 11.30 to get into position.

It was shortly after midnight on September 18 when Roy tailed Elvis and two other motor cyclists for the first time. The three riders in front rode south from Graceland along Elvis Presley Boulevard then turned left into Shelby Drive. At Mill Branch Road, as Del and Roy had predicted, they sped up the ramp on to Highway 55 and headed south at speed. Roy, 200 yards behind all the way, decided not to bother to track them down the highway. Forty-five minutes later, just before 1 am, Elvis and his two buddies returned along Highway 55 and made their way back to Graceland by retracing the route they took earlier.

Two nights later, after one frustrating evening when Del and Roy waited outside Graceland until 2 am and no one entered or left, Elvis and one other rider retraced the exact same route. This pattern was repeated five times during the week that followed and on two rides out of the five Elvis took along only one companion.

'Elvis goes out with just one other guy about every second or third night he goes riding,' said Roy, studying his notebook. 'But there's no real pattern. I guess it's just whoever happens to be around.' Del nodded. They were in Roy's apartment and they'd been studying Elvis' nocturnal habits together for almost three weeks, painstakingly going over their notes together yet again. Del had explained his odd behaviour to Sandra by telling her that Roy had got him some part-time evening work doing security, and she hadn't suspected a thing.

'So we'll keep watch and the next night he goes out with just one other guy we grab him,' said Roy.

'If you say so,' said Del, grinning. 'It's do or die now buddy.'

The two friends shook hands, then Del left for his apartment.

At the beginning of October Del and Roy took off for the Kentucky Hills to the cabin they had rented for the first three weeks of the month. Del told Sandra that he and Roy were off on a hunting trip, something they'd done regularly in the past. The journey took them six hours, and on the way they bought sufficient provisions for a two-week stay, non-perishable food, drink, fuel and spare clothes and bedding as well as a hammock and two sleeping bags, all of which they stashed in the cabin. With a separate bedroom alongside the living area and kitchen, it was well off the main highway, about a mile and a half from the south side of Lake Cumberland, the ninth largest reservoir in the USA, constructed for flood control and the production of hydro-electric power. To reach the cabin required a four-wheel drive vehicle and a good knowledge of the surrounding area. Del and Roy knew it well. The last thing they did before turning in was to fix two strong sliding bolts to the bedroom door from the outside and fix a metal grill on the window, thus effectively turning the room into a prison cell. Satisfied that the cabin could accommodate them all for at least two weeks, they returned to Memphis the next day.

'Did you catch anything honey?' asked Sandra when Delmore got home.

''Fraid not babe,' replied her husband, kissing her on the forehead as he fumbled with the buttons on the front of her uniform. 'We're gonna go again soon, maybe one night next week after work. Maybe we'll catch something then.'

Chapter Three

(October 5 & 6)

On October 5, Elvis and Charlie West rode out of the
Graceland gates shortly after midnight and swung left
into Elvis Presley Boulevard, heading south away from
the centre of Memphis. The roads were deserted and the
steady rumble of their powerful bikes was the only noise
to be heard as they cruised through the lamplit streets. At
each intersection Elvis took childish delight in revving his
engine to hear his machine's purr become a roar. When
each light changed, he would accelerate fast and lunge
ahead of his companion. Charlie knew better than to try
and burn Elvis.

With a squeal of tyres, Elvis and Charlie turned left
at the Shelby Drive intersection and, as usual, headed
towards the Route 55 entry ramp. It was a route they knew
well, for they loved to ride on the freeway where they
could risk speeds over 90 mph, well above the legal limit
of 55 mph. They were both feeling relaxed, even a little
high at the prospect of a good run.

At that same moment Delmore Pandel and Royston
Kruger felt anything but relaxed. They had been stalking
Elvis for three weeks, planning their kidnap for five, and
they knew that failure tonight meant they would never
get another chance. But at the same time, the omens had
never been better. From their usual discreet distance they
watched the two riders emerge from Graceland, turn left
and continue along Presley Boulevard. The previous night
they had decided to strike the next time Elvis rode out
with just one companion for company.

Del and Roy noted that as usual one of the riders delighted in revving his engine. Roy tapped his helmet twice. It was their sign that Elvis was ahead. They were certain that Elvis and his co-rider would head for the freeway as they had done before. After following them at a discreet distance for a quarter of a mile they cut left, adopting their pre-arranged ploy to intercept Elvis close to the freeway ramp when he would least expect it. As they rode along the streets parallel to their prey they took .38 Special pistols from their belts and prepared to intercept.

Oblivious to the presence of two other night riders, Elvis and Charlie slowed to take the left corner leading up to the freeway and had almost reached the ramp when they noticed two other bikes approaching rapidly, apparently heading into their path. Their big mistake – which Del and Roy had counted on them making – was to check their own speed instead of accelerating away. The kidnappers were alongside them in seconds. Four riders were silhouetted in the gloom. Two of them held pistols above their heads. Charlie slowed to a stop and Elvis, figuring the intrusion to be some kind of stunt, followed suit.

'What the fuck… you know who this…'

Charlie's words were drowned out when one of the riders fired into the sky.

'Hey, man. What is this?' shouted Elvis. He was still feeling relaxed. The idea that someone might attempt an assault of some kind never occurred to him because it had never happened before. His defences were down, and what happened next took him completely off guard.

One of the riders fired into Charlie's front tyre. The impact of the bullet knocked Charlie off his bike, which keeled over on top of him. Charlie yelled in pain as the heavy engine and gas tank pinned him down. Roy swung off his bike and strode over to where Charlie lay. Holding the gun to his throat, Roy wrenched off his helmet.

'Move and you're dead, motherfucker.'

Charlie froze.

Rooted to the spot, Elvis could scarcely believe what was happening. Thrown completely by the violence, he was struck dumb, paralysed. He tried to gesture to the two riders. His words were drowned in his crash helmet. All he managed to say was, 'No, no, no. Oh, no.'

The second rider, also holding a pistol, turned to face Elvis but didn't speak. Keeping the gun pointed at Elvis' huge torso, he climbed off his bike, rooted in the saddlebag and produced a powerful flashlight that he switched on and aimed directly into Elvis' eyes. Blinded by the brightness, Elvis was on the verge of panic.

Finally, the rider with the flashlight spoke. 'Elvis... we won't harm you if you do exactly as I say. Dismount. Now!'

There was an authority to the voice that Elvis recognised as similar to the way his own thugs spoke when protecting him against unwanted intrusions. Now Elvis was on the receiving end, and he didn't like it one bit. He hesitated. Fear was a new experience for him; worse, he realised that for the first time in around 20 years he was in a situation that he couldn't control. Cushioned against reality for two decades, Elvis had no shield against spontaneous events, let alone a vicious attack like this. For someone who'd never had cause to defend himself personally, who'd lived a life surrounded by yes-men, even that most basic of human instincts, self-preservation, had been irrevocably eroded.

The rider with the torch strode over to Elvis and kicked his bike. It fell over, knocking the startled Elvis over too.

Elvis cried out in pain.

'Elvis, I said we won't harm you if you do exactly as we say. Get up... NOW!'

'You know who I am?' was all Elvis managed to say.

'Doesn't everybody?' said Delmore.

Elvis struggled to his feet.

'Take off your helmet.'

Elvis, nervous, too terrified by the suddenness of the attack to protest, his defences shattered, complied. His long black hair was ruffled. For the first time Delmore was able to see the most famous face in America close up. Gone was the haughty sneer, the rough-hewn handsomeness that had entranced a generation of women. In its place was a jowly and rather scared looking middle-aged man with long hair and sideboards who was perspiring heavily and seemed to have trouble gaining his breath. Elvis was in mild shock.

Ten feet away, Charlie had come to his senses. 'Run Elvis, run,' he cried. Elvis heard but remained rooted to the spot like a rabbit caught in headlights. He saw Roy's pistol butt come down on Charlie's skull. Charlie was knocked senseless.

Elvis, overweight, terminally unfit and encumbered by his leathers, was in no position to run anyway. Del, still wearing his crash helmet, approached to within a foot of his face.

'Do exactly as we say and we will not hurt you in any way. Now,' he said, indicating the dark, littered alcove beneath the expressway ramp, 'over there... move!'

Elvis walked away from his bike towards the underside of the ramp.

'Inside. Go inside as far as you can. That's right. Now, lie down. Face down.'

Elvis squatted then knelt down and finally lay flat on his stomach on the concrete. He had never been more frightened in his life, but something else was now mingling with the terror: a hideous feeling of shame. In the eyes of a million fans, he was a hero, but here in the dark gloom of a Memphis night, less than a mile away from his home, he was completely unable to defend himself. Bereft of his strong-arm mercenaries, his defences and his dignity crumbled. The reality was not just that he was no better than any other man when it came to handling himself in a tight spot, but that he was actually far worse, even impotent. All he knew or cared about was that he didn't want to die. Oh Lord, he prayed silently, don't let them kill me. Let me live.

Keeping his eyes on the prone figure of Elvis, Del walked back towards his bike, took a package from the saddlebag and returned to where Elvis lay. In less than a minute he'd tied Elvis' legs together at the ankles and his arms at the wrists behind his back. Next, he brought a cloth soaked in chloroform to Elvis' face and held it firmly against his mouth and nose.

Elvis knew then, as he smelt the chloroform, that he would not die tonight. His last thought before he sank into unconsciousness was one of immense relief. He struggled briefly against the urge to sleep but felt himself falling backwards into darkness and blacked out in seconds. Del then gagged Elvis with another handkerchief and placed a hood over his head. Like big game, Elvis was truly bagged.

Del and Roy next dragged Charlie West's inert body to the other side of the road and rolled him over into the undergrowth. They had counted on traffic being light at this time and were lucky that no inquisitive motorists came their way. As it was they had to hide twice in the darkness of the alcove before they could continue but each time the cars sped by regardless. As far as they were aware, no one saw them at all.

Roy tied Charlie's legs together and his arms behind his back, gagged him and put a second hood over his head. Then they rolled the bikes that Charlie and Elvis had ridden off the road and took the keys from each. They had gone over their routine with strict precision, and as soon as their captives were safely bound and the bikes hidden, Roy rode back to his apartment in Germantown, parked his bike, reversed Del's flat-bed truck out of his garage, wheeled the bike in and drove the truck back to where Del waited with Elvis.

Del, meanwhile, sat with his charges contemplating what he'd done. Trussed up and unconscious, Elvis was now his and his alone. Staring down at the huge body of the world's most popular entertainer, Del found it difficult to believe that this really was the Elvis Presley that Sandra had worshipped for nigh on seven years. Here he was, helpless as a kitten. Taking him had been simple, even simpler than they'd expected, Del thought. The so-called Memphis Mafia had been as easy to penetrate as a gang of kids; no problem for trained professionals like him and Roy.

It was just after 1 am when Roy arrived back with the truck. Together, they loaded Elvis into the front seat, then did their best to hide the two bikes that Elvis and Charlie West had ridden. Then they set off back to Germantown, Roy behind the wheel of the truck with Elvis unconscious at his side, and Del riding his bike. All that remained was for Del to ditch his bike in Roy's garage and jump into the truck. Then they headed off towards Kentucky on route 51 via Dyersburg and Mayfield, their booty between them, a dead weight slumped in the seat, the body with the most famous face in America.

Lamar Fike was not the kind of guy who panicked easily. He'd worked for Elvis since 1957 and in that time had handled situations that would have pushed other men to extremes of panic. Crowds, frenzied fans, Elvis' tantrums, last minute changes of plan, logistical nightmares on the road, he'd handled the lot with consummate calm. He'd been with Elvis in Germany and at his house in Bad Nauheim on the night when he was first introduced to Priscilla Beaulieu, never imagining for one moment the future role the 14-year-old schoolgirl would play in Elvis' life. Proud of an immense bulk that discouraged predators who might challenge Elvis, he was a professional in the kind of job that demanded extremes of professionalism.

It was almost 3.00 am when Lamar walked from the Graceland playroom to the kitchen to make himself a sandwich and got to thinking that Elvis and Charlie West had been out riding for longer than usual. He'd left at just after midnight and was usually back within two hours or less. He'd been gone for nigh on three hours now.

Graceland was silent. Vernon Presley was asleep in his room and Linda Thomson, who was visiting this week, was upstairs in the master bedroom, waiting for Elvis to return. Minnie and Vester Presley, the cook and gatekeeper of Graceland, were asleep in their quarters at the back of the house. The only other occupant of Graceland that night, Billy Smith, Elvis' cousin, was listening to records on earphones in the music room.

Lamar was halfway through slicing his ham off the bone when the phone rang. He picked up the kitchen extension.

'Yeah.'

'Lamar, it's Charlie. You won't believe this. Elvis is gone. Two guys took him.'

Lamar was momentarily speechless. 'What?' he sputtered. 'What are you saying? Where is he?'

'I don't know. They knocked me out cold on Shelby near the freeway ramp. I just came to. There's no sign of him or the two guys. I just walked to the nearest payphone.'

'Where are you?'

'I'm at Shelby and Mill Ranch.'

'Stay right there. I'll come and get you.'

Lamar replaced the phone and walked purposefully towards the music room where Billy Smith lay prone on a couch with headphones over his ears. Lamar shook him and Billy took off the phones.

'Hey, what's up, man?'

'Listen carefully,' said Lamar. 'There's been some kind of accident with Elvis. I'm going out to check right now. Stay here. Stay by the phone. Answer it if it rings but don't say nothing to nobody. Just tell anyone that Elvis is still out riding and that I've gone into town to see someone. Take messages.'

'What kind of accident?'

'I don't know yet. That's what I'm going to find out.'

Lamar left the den, walked through the hall and out the front door. There was a white Cadillac parked in the drive, its keys in the ignition. He slid into the driver's seat, then hesitated. He lit a cigarette, wound down the window, released the smoke from his lungs and stared out over the grounds towards the lights of Elvis Presley Boulevard.

'Holy shit,' he said out loud to no one in particular. He

was, of course, not a man to panic but this sounded like
big trouble. Sometimes, lying in bed at night, he'd tried to
imagine the worst scenario that could happen with Elvis.
He'd thought about what might happen if some crazy
fan, or someone with a grudge, ever got too close to Elvis
and tried to hurt him, even kill him. No way, he thought.
They'd never get that close. Elvis was surrounded by his
men friends, guys like Lamar, Joe Esposito, Marty Lacker
and the rest. But he'd never imagined a kidnap attempt, if
that was what had happened tonight. Goddammit! Why
hadn't more guys gone riding with Elvis tonight? Why
only Charlie, who wasn't the brightest of guys anyway?

Lamar started the engine and moved off through dead
leaves down the winding Graceland drive. There was
no one on duty at the gate at this time of night and he
had to get out of the car, open the big steel gates with the
wrought iron outline of Elvis on the front, get back in and
drive through, then get out again to close the gates behind
him. He was glad that at this time of night no fans were
lingering in the vicinity.

Charlie West was leaning up against the payphone
looking anxiously around when Lamar pulled up beside
him ten minutes later. Charlie wasn't looking forward
to seeing him. When the white Caddy stopped, he got
in at the passenger door and slumped down in the seat,
preparing for the worst. Lamar noticed the dried blood
on Charlie's forehead and realised he'd been hit hard. He
decided to be easy on him.

'I'm real sorry Lamar. I don't know what hit me. They
were just there, following us, and they jumped us and then
they hit me and I was out. They musta' planned it. I never
even saw them properly. They had black crash helmets
on.'

'Okay. Okay,' said Lamar. 'Keep quiet. We'll go into details later. Let's get back to the house.'

The two men didn't speak again until they reached the Graceland gates.

'When we get inside don't make any noise. I don't want anyone else to know what's happened yet. Don't even tell Billy, who's there manning the phones. We'll just go into the den real quiet and then you can tell me everything. Now open the gates.'

Charlie got out to open the gates and Lamar drove through, stopping to allow Charlie to get back in. Then they drove up the drive to the front door, got out and entered the mansion. Billy Smith was at the door. 'What's happening, man?' he asked. 'Hey, where's Elvis?'

'Billy, just stay in the kitchen while I talk with Charlie in the den. Just answer the phone if it rings. And don't come in yet.'

Lamar and Charlie headed for the den and sat down. Lamar closed the door, poured Charlie a beer and motioned to him to begin. 'Just tell me absolutely everything you can remember. Slowly now. Don't miss anything.'

'Well,' began Charlie. 'Me and Elvis just headed out the gates as we've been doing a lot lately at night. I guess it was around midnight. And we turned left and drove up EP Boulevard, Elvis in front, me behind. We stopped at a few lights, then turned into Shelby heading for the expressway so we could open up the bikes a bit, you know, like Elvis likes to do when it's quiet, and it was real quiet tonight.'

'No other traffic, you didn't see nothing following you?' asked Lamar.
'No sir. Maybe a car or two going the other way but nothing.'

'Go on.'

'Well, we headed into Shelby like I was saying and then we hears these other bikes coming in from a side road, like they almost knew we'd be there. And they came up alongside us real quick, and we slowed because of the noise to see what was happening. Then they was on to us. They had guns. They fired into the sky. One of them told us to get off our bikes and take off our helmets. Then he shot the wheel of my bike, knocked me to the ground and the bike fell on me. He was pointing a gun straight at me, man.'

'Then what happened?'

'The other guy knocked Elvis off his bike and then I got hit with a pistol.' Charlie rubbed his head where the bump still hurt. 'I don't know any more. That was it until I woke up.'

'Did they tie you up?'

'Yeah, but not too tight. They put a blindfold on me too, and gagged my mouth. And a hood. When I came to it wasn't too hard to wriggle free. Then I made for the payphone.'

'What happened to the bikes you were riding?'

'I don't know. Maybe they're still there somewhere near where it happened.'

'What time was it again when you were stopped?'

'I dunno for exact. It must have been around 12.15 I guess.'

Lamar looked at his watch. It was 3.30. That meant they'd had Elvis for over three hours. He could be anywhere by now, thought Lamar. Maybe out of the state. If the kidnappers had a plane, Elvis could be as far away as Mexico or Cuba.

'What was the last thing you saw Elvis doing?'

'Well, he'd stopped and was getting off his bike and taking off his helmet when the guy hit me.'

'Did Elvis say anything?'

'I can't remember. I don't think so... wait a minute, I think I yelled to him to run, to get the hell out of there. Then they hit me. Jesus, it hurt.' Charlie rubbed his head again and scowled. 'Oh yea, I remember now... our bikes are still by the side of the road where the attack happened. I saw them there when I came to. They took the keys. I think they must have been pros, Lamar. They were hard men, like tough army guys, cops, marines, security guys, something like that. They knew what they were doing, and they were real slick. We didn't stand a chance, man.'

'Okay, okay,' said Lamar. 'I guess I should blame you because you were supposed to be looking after Elvis but it seems like you were up against too much here.'

'Oh, man I know. Jeez! What's gonna' happen now Lamar.'

'Fucked if I know. Let me think.'

Lamar Fike sat in silence. As far as he was aware, apart from Elvis and the kidnappers, only two people in the world knew what had happened tonight, him and Charlie. The first thing he had to do, therefore, was to tell the rest of the household what had happened. They'd all start wondering where Elvis had got to as soon as they woke.

Billy Smith had sat in the kitchen for 20 minutes wondering what the hell was going on. Where was Elvis? Charlie had returned but there no sign of Elvis. He was the first to be told.

'Now, keep this quiet,' Lamar said when he'd finished repeating Charlie's story to Billy. 'Don't tell a soul. Now, go upstairs and see if Linda's awake. I'll tell her next.'

Linda Thompson had grown weary of waiting for

Elvis. Tired of reading, she had changed into pale blue silk pyjamas and fallen asleep beneath a sheet on Elvis' huge bed. She'd dimmed the lights. Billy entered the room on tip toe and shook her gently. She stirred, slowly.

'Mmm, hi Billy. Where's El?'

'He ain't here Linda. Come downstairs. Lamar wants to talk to you.'

'What's happened Billy?' Linda was quick to sense that something was amiss.

'Can't say. Just come downstairs quick.'

Linda jumped out of bed. She pulled on a bathrobe over her pyjamas and slid into a pair of slippers. Forgetting, for once, to check herself in the mirror, she rushed past Billy and headed downstairs.

Lamar was at the entrance to the music room. He put his fingers to his mouth and beckoned her inside.

'What's going on?' she asked.

'Well,' began Lamar. 'You'd better sit down first.'

Linda sat down on the nuagahide couch and noticed that Charlie West, whose forehead was covered in clotted blood, was watching her intently.

'What happened to you?' she asked, looking directly at him. 'You need to rinse your head.'

Charlie rose from the couch and looked himself in a mirror. 'Lamar will explain,' he said, heading for the nearest bathroom to clean himself up.

Lamar spoke slowly. 'It looks like Elvis may have been kidnapped.'

Linda swayed gently on the couch and gripped a cushion with both hands. 'Kidnapped?' she whispered. 'No!'

'Well, it kinda looks that way,' said Lamar. 'Charlie and Elvis were out riding and they were held up at gunpoint by two other bike riders. They knocked Charlie unconscious and when he came to Elvis had disappeared. We don't know any more.'

'Oh my God,' said Linda. 'Oh my. Poor El. Oh God.'

Charlie re-entered the room carrying a damp washcloth with which he wiped his brow.

'Do ya wanna drink?' asked Lamar. 'Charlie, get Linda a drink. Soda?'

'Scotch,' said Linda. 'Oh God.' Linda looked as if she might fall from the couch.

'Now don't panic,' said Lamar, trying desperately to be the voice of reason and keep the situation in control. 'You're only the second person we've told. We told Billy because he was up and Elvis didn't come home. Everyone else is asleep, but we've got to tell Vernon next.'

Linda took a gulp of her drink. Tears welled up in her eyes. 'I need a tissue. Oh God, what can we do?'

Charlie handed her a tissue from a box on a coffee table. Linda Thompson had been Elvis' most consistent girlfriend for most of the time since they met in the summer of 1972 and her position in the hierarchy of Graceland was dependent entirely on Elvis. With Elvis gone, she knew her status in the household would diminish. She had to try to show a cool head in the crisis, or at least be firm with someone. 'How could you let this happen? It's your fault,' she cried, glaring at Charlie. 'You dumb idiot. You were supposed to be protecting Elvis, weren't you?'

'Hey, these guys were tough. They meant business. They coulda' killed us,' said Charlie. 'They coulda' killed Elvis.'

'He might be dead now for all you know,' screamed Linda.

'Hey, you guys, quit hollering,' said Lamar. 'I don't think they've killed Elvis. If they wanted to do that, they could have done it on the spot. They've taken him some place. We don't know why or where yet. Screaming at each other ain't gonna help. I don't think...'

Lamar never finished his sentence. He was interrupted by a commotion outside, then Billy burst into the room. 'It's Vernon, he's awake...'

Vernon Presley, Elvis' 59-year old father, lurched into the room behind Billy in his yellow silk monogrammed dressing gown. 'What's all this yellin' about. It's four the morning, and where's Elvis? Sleeping?'

Lamar Fike stood up to face the old man. 'Vernon, we were just about to wake you. We've got some bad news. Just take a seat here, and I'll tell you.'

Vernon looked around the room at everybody present. 'Where's ma boy?' he asked. 'Where's ma Elvis?'

Lamar tried again. 'Please sit down Vernon. Please. I'll tell you everything. Charlie, go get Vernon a cup of coffee. Billy, you stay outside. I don't want Minnie May and Vester coming down too.'

Vernon Presley finally sat down on the couch near Linda.

'Now Vernon,' began Lamar. 'We don't know what's happened to Elvis. We don't know where he is. All we know is that two guys jumped Elvis and Charlie, knocked Charlie out cold and when he came to Elvis had disappeared. We don't know nothing else. He may have been kidnapped. He may come walking through the door any minute now, completely unharmed. We just don't know.'

Vernon turned to Charlie. 'You just let this happen? Why didn't you do something.'

Obliged to defend himself yet again, Charlie turned to Lamar. 'Tell Vernon everything as I told it Lamar. Vernon, I'm as sorry as everyone but it wasn't easy.'

Lamar Fike took a deep breath and repeated the whole of Charlie's story yet again for Vernon's benefit. The old man stayed silent, listening hard, occasionally glancing up at Charlie and pushing his fingers through his uncombed silver hair. Linda listened intently but did not interrupt. When Lamar finished Vernon leaned back and stared into the ceiling. 'We'll have to tell the Colonel,' he said. 'Tell the Colonel. Tell the Colonel,' he repeated.

'I know,' said Lamar. 'I'm gonna phone him now. And Priscilla. It's kinda early on the West Coast but I guess that don't matter anyhow.'

Vernon didn't appear to be listening any longer. Elvis' father, who looked much older than his 59 years, had lapsed into a trance and was mumbling something about the Colonel. 'The Colonel will take care of it. Tell the Colonel,' he seemed to be saying.

Lamar turned to Linda. 'Linda, why don't you take care of Vernon... take him back to bed? Give him a tranquiliser or something. I think he's in shock.'

Linda stood up and helped Vernon to his feet. 'Come on pappy,' she said. 'Let's go rest.'

'Tell the Colonel. Tell the Colonel,' was all Vernon could say.

At 4.30 am Pacific Coast time Colonel Tom Parker was sleeping soundly next to his wife Marie in the master bedroom of his large bungalow at Palm Springs, the desert resort two hours drive from Los Angeles in Southern California. His chest and sinuses had suffered through a constant diet of strong cigars that meant that he snored loudly but his wife Marie, now lame and confined to her bed, used ear plugs and slept soundly by his side as she had done throughout their long marriage.

When Elvis wasn't working the Colonel passed his days idly, unless there was a chance to harass his staff and RCA Records over sales and marketing of Elvis product. Right now there was no product and no shows and the Colonel had been kicking his heels in frustration. The Colonel hated inactivity. The previous night he'd gone to bed around midnight and he wasn't expecting to wake much before eight. When the phone rang at 4.30 he awoke with a start and grunted into the headset by his bedside.

'Hello. Who's that?'

'It's Lamar, Colonel. Lamar Fike.'

'Lamar? What time is it? Why you phoning me in the night? Whadda ya want?'

'It's around 6.30 in the morning my time Colonel. Must be around 4.30 your time. I'm calling from Graceland.'

'Well, whadaya want. Why're you waking me up like this?'

'It's Elvis, Colonel. He's disappeared. We think he might have been kidnapped.'

'What?'

'We think he's been kidnapped.'

'Is this some kinda prank Lamar... because if it is, I'm gonna...'

'No, Colonel. It's true. He was snatched last night. It's the real thing Colonel. It's an emergency. You'd better come out here fast.'

Colonel Parker, who'd been sound asleep not five minutes ago, came to his senses rapidly. 'Kidnapped, you say? How?'

'El and Charlie West were out riding their bikes late last

night when they were set on by two guys with guns, like ambushed. They knocked Charlie out cold and when he woke up Elvis had gone. We'd ain't heard nothing since.'

'What time was this?' asked Parker.

'Oh, round about half past midnight. Charlie came to about three hours later and called the house.'

'Who else knows?'

'Linda, Elvis' girlfriend, Billy Smith and Vernon. Minnie and Vester haven't woken up yet but we're gonna have to tell them when they do.'

'Have you called the cops?'

'No, not yet.'

The Colonel remained silent for a moment, weighing up the situation. Quick thinking was his speciality.

'Wait until I get there,' he said. 'I'll handle the police myself. Don't call them. What about Priscilla?'

'I haven't told her yet. I was gonna call her after I spoke with you.'

The Colonel hesitated again. 'Don't call her yet,' he said.

'What?'

'I said don't call her yet.'

'But, Colonel, she'll be mighty mad if she finds out we haven't told her straight away.'

'I'll call her.'

'You're gonna call Priscilla?' Fike sounded surprised.

'Yeah. Later today. Don't tell anyone else. No one. Not any of the guys if they arrive. Not Dr Nick. No one. Was Elvis expecting anyone else today, anyone coming to see him about anything?'

'Not that I know of.'

'Good. Don't do anything or tell anyone until I arrive in Memphis. I'll catch the first plane out of Palm Springs, probably change flights in LA. I'll call you back when I've spoken to Priscilla.'

'Whatever you say, Colonel. I won't speak to anyone.'

The Colonel hung up, got out of bed and walked to his kitchen where he filled a kettle and looked around for his cigars. Lighting up a six inch Havana, he made himself a cup of coffee and took stock of the situation. Elvis kidnapped, huh? Hell, this was something he could handle any which way. He'd always liked to be at the heart of things and if this was handled properly it could be the biggest news story to hit America in years. He poured himself another coffee. He'd have to get to Memphis to handle things. He'd have to call Priscilla. He'd probably have to call the police unless Elvis turned up real quick. He might have to call in a private detective agency. He might have to tell RCA Records. He would take charge, handle it his way. That was what he'd always done, ever since he signed Elvis to his exclusive management contract way back in 1955. That was why he'd offered to call Priscilla. He wanted her to know who was in charge.

Since taking over Elvis Presley's management, Colonel Thomas Andrew Parker had considered it his patriotic duty to keep Elvis in the highest possible tax bracket. When it came to maximising profits from Elvis he was a master, and he rarely missed a trick. Whether it was selling pictures outside a theatre at ten cents a pop or negotiating a million dollar movie deal, the Colonel operated with the kind of zeal that Croesus himself would have admired. Businessmen who'd found themselves sitting across a table from Colonel Parker had compared negotiating with him to doing business with a great white shark, or even the Devil himself. As a result, Colonel Parker had few friends in the music or film community or anywhere else for that matter. The only people he really knew either worked for him or

Elvis or for RCA or for the William Morris booking agency.
He was a solitary man by nature and he preferred it that
way. He didn't want anyone to know about his business
affairs, or even his real identity. Mind your own business
and I'll mind mine was his creed.

Colonel Parker had made millions of dollars from every
aspect of Elvis' career and life. Some estimated they had
generated over a billion dollars between them. It wasn't just
records, films and concerts that brought in the cash, it was
anything with Elvis' name on it and Parker never worried
too much about the quality of the product. The important
thing was the keep Elvis in the public eye; the takings, his
and Elvis' income, dropped when things were too quiet on
the Elvis front. He sometimes shuddered when he recalled
the doldrums period in the mid-Sixties when it seemed
Elvis was heading for stagnation. At the present time there
hadn't been a chart album since On Stage In Memphis
peaked in the Billboard LP charts at number 33 the previous
October. Two singles released during 1975 had stiffed
by Elvis' standards. It was another fallow time in Elvis'
kingdom right now and the Colonel saw no light at the end
of the tunnel. What was needed, as always, was more Elvis
awareness. Well, if this kidnapping turned out to be true
and news of it got out there'd be more Elvis awareness than
there'd ever been at any time in the last twenty years, he
thought, momentarily amused by the idea.

It was too early in the morning to call Priscilla, so
Colonel Thomas Andrew Parker, aka Andreas Cornelis
Van Kujik, took his coffee out on to the patio and sat
and watched the sun come up over the San Bernardino
Mountains. Gently puffing on his cigar, he just sat
and contemplated the situation for almost two hours,
occasionally wondering to himself just where his exclusive

management client might be right now, and how best to deal with this unexpected but not entirely unwelcome turn of events.

Priscilla Presley, the former Miss Priscilla Ann Wagner Beaulieu whom Elvis Presley had courted as a beautiful Lolitaesque schoolgirl, slept peacefully beside her lover, Mike Stone, in their duplex apartment in Beverly Hills. In the next room lay her daughter, Lisa Marie, the only acknowledged offspring of Elvis Presley.

Since Priscilla and Elvis were divorced in October 1973, they had become close friends again, and were now on better terms than at any time since the early years of their relationship. Mike Stone had entered her life in 1972 as her karate instructor, introduced to her by Elvis, and soon afterwards they'd entered into an affair, largely motivated on Priscilla's part by Elvis' declining passion for her. For reasons linked to his love of his own mother, he seemed unable, or unwilling, to make love to a woman who had given birth, and this included his own wife. Only rarely had she been able to coax Elvis into intercourse after the birth of Lisa, and her frustration led her into a brief liaison with a dance instructor, followed by the more fulfilling relationship with Stone. When Elvis calmed down after the shock of discovering that his wife was sleeping with her karate instructor, it had become an amicable separation. Indeed, after their divorce Elvis and Priscilla had left the courthouse hand in hand, and on top of a generous alimony settlement they'd agreed to share custody of Lisa Marie. Priscilla occasionally visited Graceland, taking Lisa with her, and although she strongly disapproved of the way Elvis lived his life, she knew there was nothing she could do to change it. She'd tried before and failed, and Elvis was no longer her responsibility.

When the phone by her bedside rang, Mike was the first to wake. He shook her gently. 'The phone, honey. Pick up the phone.'

'Hello,' said Priscilla, still half asleep. 'Who's that?'

At the other end of the line Colonel Parker was keenly alert.

'Priscilla... it's Colonel Parker.' He coughed discreetly and, without waiting for Priscilla to interrupt, continued. 'I'm sorry to disturb you at this time in the morning, but there's been an emergency. I'm calling from Palm Springs. I've just had a call from Lamar Fike who as you know is a member of Elvis' staff.'

'Is Elvis sick again?' asked Priscilla, jumping to the obvious conclusion.

'No,' replied Parker. 'It appears he's been kidnapped.'

'What?' Priscilla's voice registered shock, emotion and anger all at the same time. 'Kidnapped, you say?'

'Yes. It looks like that. All Lamar told me is that two men with guns held up Elvis and one of his men. They knocked the other man out and when he came to Elvis was nowhere to be seen. Our guess is that the two men just took him someplace, kidnapped him. I don't know any more. I'm gonna catch the first plane from Palm Springs to LA and then fly on to Memphis. Do you want to join me?'

Priscilla was still taking in the information. 'Yeah, of course. I've got to be there. I'll bring Lisa. Oh my God, poor Elvis. Does anybody else know?'

'Only the people at Graceland, and us.'

'Have you told the police?'

'Not yet. I'll tell them when I get to Memphis. I want to make sure it's handled properly by them.'

'Colonel, are you really sure he's been kidnapped? I

mean... really sure?'

'I don't know much more than you Priscilla. It's what I've been told and it's all we can assume right now. There's a plane out of LA to Memphis at 10.30. I'll aim to catch it and see you at the airport.'

'I'll have to bring Lisa Marie.'

'Of course. I must go now.'

The Colonel hung up rather abruptly, and Priscilla was left holding a dead phone. She turned to Mike. 'You aren't gonna believe this Mike but that was Colonel Parker calling to tell me that Elvis has been kidnapped.'

'What?' The incredulity in Mike Stone's voice was very audible. 'Kidnapped? You gotta be joking.'

'That's what the Colonel said. I've got to go to Memphis today. This is serious, Mike. Elvis could be in big trouble. No one knows where he is.'

'Jesus. Wasn't someone looking after him, like a bodyguard or whatever?'

'Yes but he was knocked cold. They must have been very professional kidnappers.'

'Who else knows?'

'Nobody. You must keep quiet about this Mike. For Elvis' sake.'

'Oh boy, the newspapers would kill for this.'

'Don't even think about it.' Priscilla kissed Mike on the forehead, slid out of bed and put on her robe. 'I'm going to take a shower, then I'll wake Lisa. Can you make me a coffee?'

'Sure.'

There was an en suite shower next to the bedroom that after discarding her robe and nightgown Priscilla stepped into. She turned the water jets up to maximum and felt her mind and body coming to full consciousness. She could scarcely believe what she had heard, but the Colonel wasn't the type to joke about something like this. She'd never seen eye to eye with the Colonel but, being a woman, her opinion was neither sought nor welcome when it came to Elvis' business. That was one of the many reasons why she'd left him.

Her life had been intertwined with Elvis since September 1959 when they'd been introduced in Bad Neuheim, the German spa town where Elvis was stationed during the last few months of his spell in the American army. The teenage stepdaughter of an American army captain, she was captivated by Elvis' boyish charm and she'd allowed herself to become enveloped by his world, a world in which Colonel Parker loomed as large as Elvis himself. Despite the misgivings of her sceptical parents she had moved to Graceland in 1963 on condition that she attended a Catholic girls' school, was chaperoned by Elvis' father and his second wife, and lived in their separate house on the estate. Another condition was that she and Elvis would eventually marry, in the event the only condition that was actually met.

Along the way Priscilla had developed a deep mistrust of Colonel Parker, a suspicion that increased as her marriage to Elvis faltered. Now that they lived apart, she was absolutely certain that Parker was siphoning off funds that by rights belonged to her ex-husband. Whenever she'd tried to inquire about Elvis' financial affairs in the past, she'd been fobbed off with trite answers and, it must be said, plenty of money of her own. Elvis had never denied her anything, but just how much money there was in Elvis' bank account was something she'd never been able to discover. Neither did she know for sure exactly how much Colonel Parker was making out of Elvis. Either way, it seemed to her that even though the Colonel clearly regarded Elvis as a goose that laid golden eggs, he didn't always care for the goose as well as he might, and he was always greedy for more and more eggs to be laid. Priscilla had long ago come to the conclusion that Parker placed the rewards of managing Elvis far above his client's artistic integrity. Elvis had often told her how much he despised the films he made after leaving the army, not to mention the songs they contained, but he seemed impotent in the face of his manager. She also believed Parker worked Elvis too hard in Las Vegas and on the concert tours and she could never understand why, unless it was because they needed the money. But then, hadn't the Colonel always implied that there was plenty of money in the kitty? Some day, Priscilla knew, she'd get to the bottom of it. In the meantime, Elvis was paying handsomely for her to live with the man she loved in the manner to which she'd become accustomed when she was his wife, and she had no real cause to complain.

After rinsing off the lather she stepped from the shower, wrapped herself in an enormous bath towel and took a sip from the cup of coffee that Mike had left by the washstand. Normally Priscilla would look long and hard into the mirror after a shower, and reflected back at her would be a young woman whose beauty had unquestionably ripened with age. Free of the cutesy clothes and gothic black beehive hairstyle that was demanded of the partner of Elvis Presley, she nowadays allowed her hair to grow naturally, used a minimum of make-up and wore casual clothes, jeans and t-shirts, instead of the restrictive garments that made her look like an early brunette Barbie Doll.

'What are you going to do?' Mike asked when Priscilla emerged from the bathroom.

'First, wake Lisa. Then dress and head for the airport. Mike... you'll have to call and cancel my appointments for today. I had a modelling job at noon, and I was meeting my sister Michelle this afternoon. Tonight we were dining with the people from that real estate place. Cancel that too. And everything else. You'll just have to wait by the phone and I'll let you know what's happening. Tell them I've had to go to Memphis to see Elvis because he's been taken sick again.'

Mike Stone accepted his reduced role in the situation without protest. He'd long ago realised that Priscilla and Elvis were bound together for life in many ways, principally through their daughter. While Priscilla selected an outfit from her extensive and sumptuous wardrobe, Mike went to wake Lisa.

Lisa Marie Presley was unaccustomed to being woken before 8 am and Mike had to shake her quite roughly to get a response.

'Hey, what's happening?' Turning over on the pillow, Lisa blinked and rubbed her eyes with her fingers. 'What time is it?'

'It's seven and you have to get up,' said Mike gently. 'You have to go to Memphis with you mum. It's your dad... there's been some kind of scene. Your mother will explain. She's getting dressed.'

'What kind of scene?'

'She'll tell you all about it when you're ready. Now get up and take a shower.'

Lisa Marie Presley, aged seven but mature beyond her years, was quite incapable of taking a shower at 7 am until she knew why. She leapt out of bed, marched past Mike Stone and out of the room, turned right and headed straight for her mother's room. Priscilla was ready for her.

'Lisa darling! Can you get ready as soon as possible? We

have to go to Memphis.'

'I know. Mike told me. What's going on?' she asked.

'I've just had a call from Colonel Parker. He says we have to go to Memphis today. I don't know the whole story myself yet.'

'Well, can't you just ring daddy and find out?'

'No.'

'Why not?'

'Because daddy's...' Priscilla hesitated. She didn't want to tell her daughter what the Colonel had told her. At least not yet.

Mike came to her rescue. 'Because daddy's not well. He's got sick again and he's in the hospital. He wants you and your mummy to go to Memphis to visit him.'

'Oh... is it serious?'

'I hope not,' said Priscilla. 'We won't know 'till we get there. Now hurry up and get ready to go.'

Lisa Marie dutifully left the room. Priscilla turned to Mike Stone and shrugged. It wasn't the first time she'd lied to her daughter about her father and it probably wouldn't be the last. As the white lies went, this one was more necessary than most.

An hour later Mike drove Priscilla and Lisa to LA International Airport. As the Colonel has informed her, an American Airlines flight to Memphis left at 10.30 am. Priscilla spotted him waiting in line at the first class ticket desk and rushed over. He agreed with her not to talk about the kidnap in front of Lisa and throughout the flight they kept up the pretence that Elvis was sick. Sooner or later, they'd have to tell her, but Priscilla needed to reach Graceland and find out precisely what was going on first.

At around the same time as the plane took off Elvis

Presley woke with a start in Del Pandel's truck. During the first half of their journey to Kentucky Roy had applied more chloroform whenever Elvis seemed to be waking so they wouldn't have to deal with a conscious prisoner while they were on the freeway. Now they'd turned off the main route, it made little difference. Anyway, Elvis was still trussed up, blindfolded and quite unable to move.

They'd driven on into the night until dawn, sharing the driving and maintaining a steady 50 mph. The last thing they needed was to attract a traffic cop. It took them a couple of hours to reach the Kentucky border. They wanted to leave Tennessee by the most direct route and they were skirting Mayfield when back in Memphis Lamar Fike heard from Charlie West that Elvis was missing. From Mayfield the journey east to Hopkinsville and then Bowling Green took them almost another two hours.

From Bowling Green they joined Route 65 until the highway swung north, then continued east to Glasgow and Columbia and on towards Somerset and the southern half of the Daniel Boon National Forest, a route that took them almost parallel to the northern Memphis state line. It was dawn when they cut down through the eastern reaches of Lake Cumberland on their way to the small town of Steubenville on the south side of the lake. They took the local road north back towards the lake and, half an hour later, unseen by anyone, pulled off on to the dirt track towards the cabin.

As the cabin and the hills came into view Del recalled his fishing expeditions with Roy in the past and chuckled to himself. 'Oh boy, we've hooked a big fish this time,' he said.

Roy smiled too. 'Sure have, partner. Sure have.'

Elvis had been in the hands of his kidnappers for ten hours.

Chapter Four

(October 6 & 7)

Elvis finally awoke at three o'clock in the afternoon of October 6. He'd been drugged and unconscious for almost 15 hours and he was ravenously hungry. His head ached, his stomach churned and his throat felt like dry cowhide. He was still bound hand and foot, gagged and the hood over his face had not been removed. He was able to breathe only through his nose. He was lying flat out on his back on what felt like a small hard bed, twisting his body and trying to call out through the gag. No one came and he heard no sound. He was completely alone.

Lying in the dark, Elvis tried hard not to panic and to gather his senses. He remembered being spoken to roughly and being told he was not about to be shot or even hurt. Kidnapped! That was it. He'd been kidnapped. He'd been out riding with Charlie – Goddam useless Charlie, what the fuck happened to him – when two men on motorbikes had stopped them. It all happened so quickly. They'd been overpowered very quickly, too quickly.

Elvis thought back to all the fight scenes he'd appeared in during his movies. Of course, he'd won virtually every one and always against men meaner than himself. He hadn't been in a real fight for years and when it happened he'd surrendered meekly. Some hero, he thought.

Elvis was also very scared. He tried to cry out through the gag but still there was silence. The room he was in felt damp but warm, and there was a musty, woody smell. He wished he could see. He wanted to know what time it was. He wished he could go back to sleep. Then he

got to thinking about what might be happening back at
Graceland. My, there'd be some fussing there, he thought.
Joe Esposito and Lamar Fike would take charge. They
were good men. They'd soon be on the trail, together with
half the State Troopers from the State of Tennessee. They'd
have told the Colonel by now, he thought. Oh fuck, that
wouldn't be easy; the Colonel always liked to complain
about the men who worked for him, overpaid layabouts
he called them. Gee, the Colonel would make a meal of
this one. And pappy. My, how pappy would take on.

Elvis tried one more time to shake himself free from
whatever it was that was holding him. In doing so he fell
off the bed and landed on the hard floor with a bump,
hurting his hip and crying out through the gag. Then
he heard what sounded like a lock being unbolted, the
squeak of a wooden door opening and heavy footsteps
coming into the room. He was no longer alone.

Del and Roy, who had been out on the cabin porch
smoking and drinking beer, had been alerted by the sound
of Elvis' fall and entered the bedroom.

'Gee, he's fallen off the fucking bed,' said a voice that
Elvis vaguely recognised from the previous night. 'He's
awake, too. Let's get him back up.'

'I'll take his legs, you take his shoulders,' said another
voice. The two men groaned as they took the strain of
Elvis' weight. 'Shit, he must weigh over 250 pounds.'

Elvis felt himself being lifted bodily off the floor and
placed back on the bed.

'Well, we'll have to feed him soon I guess,' said one
of the men. 'I think we'd better talk to him first, tell him
something, so he don't do nothing stupid.'

'Yeah.'

'Elvis,' began Roy. 'I know you can hear me even

though you can't see me and I want you to listen hard.
You've been kidnapped. Got that... kidnapped. We don't
intend to harm you and sooner or later we'll probably let
you go, but for the time being you ain't going no place
without us.'

Elvis remained motionless. He heard every word that
Roy said.

'It'll be easier on all of us if you just take it easy,'
continued Roy. 'We're some place where no one will find
you. We'll take off the blindfold if you just co-operate with
us, we won't hurt you at all. We'll look after you until we
decide what to do. We've planned this well and if all goes
according to plan you won't be harmed.'

Elvis shifted perceptibly on the bed and shook his
head. He wanted to say a thousand things but most of all
he wanted to say that these guys would never get away
with it, that he was friends with President Nixon, and that
he was a special agent in the FBI, and that once the police
found out about this all hell would be let loose and there
would be a thousand men combing the States looking
for him, that the biggest man-hunt in history would be
launched to find him. But for once in his adult life Elvis
could say nothing. He had to listen.

'You know, my wife is a big fan of yours, Elvis.' It was
the voice of the other man speaking now, Elvis realised.
'She really loves you, loves your records. We had tickets to
go see you in Vegas in August but the show was cancelled.
Too bad, huh? Well, who knows? Maybe you can make up
for that? Yeah?' Elvis felt an elbow dig him in the ribs.

'Now,' said the first voice. 'I guess you must be pretty
hungry. We're gonna take off the blindfold, so just take it
easy.'

Elvis felt a hand at the back of his neck untying the

loop that fixed the hood over his head. It was released
quite easily and suddenly the hood was pulled off.
Unaccustomed to the light, even though it was dim inside
the cabin, he blinked. He desperately wanted to rub his
eyes. He also wanted to look into a mirror. Still gagged
at the mouth, he looked up at his kidnappers for the
first time. They looked like tough, hard men, and one
seemed familiar to him from somewhere he couldn't quite
remember.

'Now, Elvis,' said Roy. 'We'll take off the gag, but
if you start hollerin' we'll just have to put it back on.
Understand? Ain't no use hollerin' out here anyway. Ain't
no one gonna hear you. There's no one but us for miles
around.'

Roy leaned forward and untied the handkerchief
around Elvis' jaw. When it was loose Elvis gulped for air
and started breathing heavily. Although he could speak
now he was still in a state of shock. He didn't know what
to say so instead of trying to speak, he just stared sullenly.
Finally, after about 20 seconds, he found his voice.

'Ah need ma medication,' were the first words Elvis
spoke. His voice, naturally deeper than most male voices,
was more urgent than normal and lacked the slow casual
Southern drawl that Roy and Delmore remembered
from seeing Elvis movies on TV. But it had a cadence to
it that was unmistakably Elvis, a voice that was known
throughout America, and it caused them both to stop
in the tracks for a second, to momentarily consider the
consequence of their actions. 'Holy gee, this really is Elvis,'
they both thought. 'Elvis fucking Presley.'

'I have to have ma medication.' The voice that sold a
billion albums now sounded a little petulant.

Roy stared hard at Elvis' face. 'Well Elvis, we've got

some food and drink here, and a few pills of one kind or another, maybe some aspirins or something, but nothing really special.'

'In my pocket... there's a bottle. I need a drink too. Water.' Elvis paused. 'Please.'

It was not often that Elvis Presley used the word 'Please' when speaking to men younger than him, and even he was surprised when he said it. 'My left jacket pocket.'

Roy leaned over Elvis' prostrate form and rummaged inside the pocket of Elvis' leather jacket. Inside he found two small bottles of pills, both of them labelled, two keys and a white silk handkerchief. Both bottles contained about two-dozen pills, red in one bottle, yellow in the other. 'Which ones?' he asked.

Elvis thought for a second. 'The red ones.'

Delmore poured out a glass of water from a plastic bottle and handed it to Roy. Then he took a red pill from the bottle. 'Uh, uh, two,' said Elvis.

Roy hesitated. 'One for now Elvis. We don't know how long we'll be here. We might need to conserve them. What kind of pills are they?'

'Painkillers,' replied Elvis. 'Morphine pills. I have a pain in my gut.'

'And the yellow ones?'

'Sleeping pills, tuinals. I have trouble sleeping.'

'Put out your tongue.' Roy placed a red pill on Elvis' tongue and held the glass to his lips. Elvis gulped, swallowing the pill and some water.

'You hungry?' Del asked Elvis when Roy had finished pouring water down his throat.

'Yeah.' Elvis nodded.

'Then we'll fry something up. When we do we'll untie

your hands. But if you try anything we'll just tie you up again. Understand?'

Elvis nodded again and lapsed into silence. For the first time he considered his surroundings. He was in a sparsely furnished room within a wooden cabin that contained two single beds and a table. Through the open door he could look out into another room that appeared to be L-shaped, and which contained a larger table, four simple wooden chairs, two windows, a bookshelf, a cupboard, a fireplace, a rifle rack and little else. Logs were burning on the fire and his kidnappers had rigged up some kind of simple barbecue apparatus nearby. They evidently intended to use the log fire as a primitive stove. There was one other doorway that Elvis assumed led to a bathroom and another that led outside. He wanted to go to the bathroom.

'Uh, uh,' Elvis coughed. 'Can I use the, er, bathroom?'

Del and Roy looked at one another. Roy left the bedroom, went into the bathroom and took a cursory look around. There was one window through which a slim boy might have been able to climb but Elvis stood no chance.

'Go ahead,' said Roy, re-entering the bedroom. 'Through that door.'

Elvis indicated the ropes around his legs.

'OK, we'll untie you. Del, watch him now.'

Del went outside and returned with a rifle that he trained on Elvis. 'Guess we gotta take these precautions for now, 'uh El?' he said, smiling. Roy untied Elvis' arms and legs.

When he was free, Elvis sat up and got up off the bed. He was unsteady on his feet and he sat down again before attempting to walk. Then, followed by Del and his gun, he walked slowly into the main room and towards the bathroom door. Once inside he closed the door behind him but there was no lock. There was a primitive bucket style toilet beneath a wide chair with no seat. It was unquestionably the least hygienic bathroom Elvis could remember using. After loosening his trousers he let them drop to his knees, sat down and passed some urine into the bucket. The smell was appalling.

Elvis squatted alone for about five minutes before he heard a knock on the door. 'You finished in there?' asked one of the two kidnappers. Unable to enjoy a bowel movement Elvis stood up and pulled up his leather pants. 'Ah'll be out in a moment,' he said.

Elvis emerged from the bathroom and walked back into the bedroom where he sat down again on the bed. Del retied his legs but left his arms free. Roy was frying some bacon and eggs on the primitive stove, and the smell wafting into the room served only to increase Elvis' hunger. A few minutes later Roy handed him a plate of four rashers of fatty bacon, two fried eggs, a pile of fried onions and a roughly cut slice of white bread daubed thickly with peanut butter.

'Chow down Elvis old boy,' laughed Roy. 'I guess you're used to better vittals than this most times, but this is all we got for now. Maybe we'll do some hunting and fishing tomorrow, bring back a fresh rabbit or maybe a fish or two, something a bit tastier.'

Elvis didn't answer. He ate his food greedily, wishing there was more. When he was through he put his plate on the floor and leaned back on the bed. Then he spoke.

'You guys must be crazy,' he said. 'Ah'm a friend of President Nixon. All the cops in Memphis will be after me soon. You'll never get away with this. Never.'

Del and Roy looked straight at him and then at each other.

'You know, it's a funny thing Elvis old buddy,' said Roy, 'but me and my buddy here were listening to the radio all the way as we drove here, and we've been listening some more while you were out cold. There weren't no mention of you being kidnapped on any of the news bulletins. I don't reckon many folks know what's happened to you yet.'

'They soon will,' said Elvis.

Del went out to the porch and returned with a battery-powered transistor radio that he switched on and tuned into a local AM station. 'Jive Talking' by The Bee Gees filled the cabin. 'Don't suppose you're much of a disco fan, huh Elvis?' asked Roy.

Elvis shook his head. 'If there's anything I hate more than disco music, it's disco music played by faggot white boys from England with high voices and girls' hair styles.'

Roy and Del roared with laughter. 'You know what El,' said Roy. 'I think you might be our kinda guy. I think we're gonna get along just fine.'

Elvis smiled in the presence of his captors for the first time. 'You guys from Memphis, huh?' It was more of a statement than a question.

'Well, wouldn't you like to know,' replied Roy, aware that it was unwise to tell Elvis too much about themselves. 'Maybe we is. Maybe we ain't. It ain't none of your business Elvis, so don't go asking no questions. We do the asking round here. So what's it like being as famous as you?'

Elvis hesitated before replying. He hadn't given an interview to the media for years, not since he went into the army, and even then he'd always answered in small talk; off the cuff humour that satisfied fans but would never have convinced a serious interviewer. He was trying now to gauge the seriousness of his captors.

'It ain't as much fun as you might think,' he eventually replied. 'It's kinda tough sometimes. Like now.'

Roy and Del started hard at Elvis. He seemed to be struggling for words.

'I mean,' Elvis went on. 'How'd you like to be taken away from your home and your loved ones like you've done to me?'

'Cut the bullshit Elvis,' said Roy. 'We meant what's it like being famous and a celebrity, having all that money, all that pussy chasing after you all the time. I guess you're missing that, huh?'

Elvis decided to ignore the sexual overtones. 'Sure. I miss my family right now. I miss my friends. I miss my girl. I ain't that different from you guys.'

'You sure as hell are. You're stinking rich,' said Del.

Elvis remembered the conversation he'd had with Colonel Parker over money, and the rows with his dad. 'I got money, sure. But I spend it, too,' he said. 'I give lots of it away to good causes.'

'I heard you bought cars for complete strangers. Is that right Elvis?' asked Del.

'Sometimes.' Elvis laughed. 'Yeah, I done that. I like to see the look on their faces.'

Elvis moved on the bed and winced. 'I need some more of my medication,' he said, matter-of-factly. Delmore produced one of the pill bottles from his jacket and handed Elvis another red pill and a glass of water.

'Why do you take this stuff?' he asked.

'I need it. It relaxes me.'

'Well, you're gonna be pretty relaxed here Elvis old boy,' said Roy. 'You ain't going nowhere for a while.'

'What are you guys gonna do to me?'

'That,' said Roy, 'is the $64,000 question right now. For the time being, nothing. Now it's getting late and me and my partner here didn't get much sleep last night thanks to you. If I were you I'd try and sleep too Elvis.'

'Then I need a yellow pill as well.'

Del handed Elvis a yellow pill and a glass of water, then closed the door to the bedroom. Elvis heard the bolts sliding. Del and Roy planned to use the sleeping bags they'd brought on top of a couple of old mattresses they had left in the cabin on an earlier visit, but before turning in they went out on to the porch and, gazing out over the beauty of the forest, listened to an AM station on the radio. There was no mention of Elvis' kidnapping on any news bulletins.

Inside the bedroom Elvis could just make out the sound of the radio newsreader. He could tell from the reaction of his kidnappers that his plight wasn't mentioned. Even with the yellow pill he couldn't sleep as he'd slept all day so he tried to imagine what was going on at Graceland. He couldn't help wondering how many people now knew what had happened to him.

Those that did know what had happened to Elvis had gathered in the early afternoon in the ample sitting room at Graceland where the mood was tense. Assuming a senior role that as yet went unchallenged, Colonel Parker presided over the gathering. Sat around him were Priscilla Presley, Vernon Presley, Linda Thompson, Lamar Fike, Charlie West and Billy Smith. Lisa Marie Presley was upstairs playing with Vester Presley, Vernon's brother. She'd been told that her daddy was in the hospital again but might be home soon. Vester and Minnie-Mae, Graceland's senior citizens, had been told the truth and, like everyone else, sworn to secrecy by Fike. Minnie, as ever, was preparing food in the kitchen. There was talk of calling Joe Esposito in Los Angeles, Dr Nichopoulos and other members of the Memphis Mafia, but Parker decreed that the fewer people knew about the kidnap the better. If any of the guys called up Lamar was instructed to tell them that Elvis was back in the hospital and their services weren't required at present.

When he and Priscilla had arrived at Graceland Parker had stormed inside and hurled a tirade of abuse at Lamar Fike and Charlie West. Priscilla, who had known Fike and West as long as she had known Elvis, had joined in the shouting, accusing them of rank incompetence and threatening to fire them on spot. Their principal, shared, contention was the stupidity of allowing Elvis to ride out at night with only one other member of his staff to protect him in the event of an emergency. For once, it seemed, Parker and Priscilla were on the same side, but as the meeting wore on it became clear to Priscilla that Parker was shifting his support to the Memphis Mafia guys. But even she had to concede that firing them now would be futile; they might tell the press what had happened.

Linda Thompson shared Priscilla's rage at the ineptitude of Elvis' so called bodyguards. At first she had been the only one in the household to unleash abuse on Charlie West but now she had Priscilla to back her up. Of all those present, Priscilla and Linda seemed the most concerned about Elvis' predicament. West felt remorse, Fike a bit guilty that he hadn't gone out riding with Elvis, and Vernon Presley, out of his depth in any crisis, was simply befuddled, eternally indecisive about everything.

Parker's attitude, however, seemed to be shifting from belligerent to nonchalant as he listened to everyone's point of view. It was as if something had occurred to him that he did not wish to share with any one else. Finally, he shifted awkwardly in his armchair and leaned forward to address the meeting. 'Well,' he began, 'the way I see it is this. We ain't got no idea where Elvis is and we ain't got no chance of finding him unless whoever took him gets in touch. There really ain't a lot we can do right now. I've been thinking things over since last night and I think we should just wait until the kidnappers get in touch.'

'That's right,' said Charlie West. 'There ain't nothing we can do.'

'Sure there is,' said Priscilla Presley. 'We can call the police. And you keep out of this Charlie. It's your fault Elvis was kidnapped in the first place.'

'We can't really blame Charlie,' said Lamar. 'It could have happened to anybody.'

'That's god dammed rubbish,' said Linda Thompson. The two women in Elvis' life, who thought as one in their condemnation of West, weren't afraid to voice their feelings. It made the men very uncomfortable. 'If you guys had guarded Elvis properly, all this would never have happened. It was damn stupid to allow Elvis out with just one another guy. You guys think you're so god dammed tough. What about poor Elvis? Who knows where he is right now or what they're doing to him? I think we should call the police right away. What do think pappy?'

Vernon Presley, tired through having been awake much of the previous night, was quite unable to make an appropriate contribution to the discussion. 'Well, I just don't know,' he said. Then, after a pause, he scratched his head wearily. 'Maybe we should tell the newspapers. That way everyone in America will be looking for our boy.'

'That's crazy,' said Priscilla. 'If this gets out, the

kidnappers might just kill Elvis.'

'Well, call out the National Guard then,' said Vernon. 'I could call the White House if you like. Elvis and that President Nixon know one another... I bet he'd help if he could. Hell, he's the President of the United States.'

'Pappy,' began Priscilla who knew from long experience that Vernon Presley was rapidly heading towards premature senility. 'President Nixon is no longer President. It's President Ford now. And we just can't tell all those people because the more people that know what's happened, the more likely it'll be that the news gets out and that'd be dangerous for Elvis. Don't you understand?'

Vernon didn't understand much when he was dog tired, but Priscilla's argument won out. 'Then we don't tell no one,' he said, folding his arms and sitting back like a wise old Indian chief.

Colonel Parker leaned back in his chair and relit his cigar. Vernon's original suggestion, foolhardy though it was, actually appealed to him in many respects, not least because the publicity would send the sales of Elvis' records soaring. Every radio station in America would play Elvis' records non-stop until he was freed. The royalties would be enormous. And if he wasn't returned... well, they'd still buy his records and still play them on the radio. He'd already decided that his next port of call would be New York where he would inform Rocco Laginestra, the president of RCA Records, about Elvis' kidnapping. Rocky was his kind of man, the kind of guy who put profits before everything.

Parker was just about to speak when Lamar Fike, the voice of reason, sided with Priscilla and Linda. 'I think the girls are right. We should tell the police, maybe the FBI even. They'll know best how to deal with it all. Hell, they must have dealt with this kind of business before.'

'Lamar's right,' said Billy Smith, who'd kept quiet until now. 'We can't deal with this ourselves, and if we tell any others the word will get out fast, and then the newspapers will be on to it. I vote we call the police now.'

'Okay everybody. Who wants to bring in the police?' asked the Colonel, whose only objection to this plan was that the police would almost certainly insist on absolute secrecy.

Priscilla, Linda, Lamar and Billy Smith raised their arms. Vernon wavered. Charlie kept his own counsel. It was clearly the preferred course of action, whether Parker liked it or not.

Lamar Fike, whose wide range of contacts included a couple of plainclothes lieutenants at Memphis Central, lifted the receiver and dialled.

Detective Lieutenant Al Shriver was drumming his fingers on his desktop trying to figure out the best way to write up an incident report involving a fight between two drunks outside a downtown bar when the phone to his right sprang to life.

'Yeah,' he said, lifting the receiver.

'Is that you Al?'

'Yeah, Lamar? Lamar Fike?'

'Yeah, that's me. How ya doing Al?'

'Me. I'm fine. How's the Big E? I heard he was sick but the newspaper says he's getting better.'

'Yeah, he's getting better now,' lied Lamar. 'Listen... I need to talk to someone in the detective department about something... er, I need some advice on something to do with security but I don't wanna talk over the phone. Could you meet me some place, maybe even get around to

Graceland here.'

Al Shriver had been to Graceland only once before, to talk with Joe Esposito and Lamar about a complaint regarding one of the boys in the Memphis Mafia. Some girl had complained that a guy who worked for Elvis had assaulted her in a bar, and the case had been due to go to court until Shriver intervened, suggesting the girl had led him on in the hope of being introduced to Elvis and that when this didn't happen she'd concocted the story to get even. Thanks to Al the matter had been successfully hushed up and he had received a very nice boxed set of autographed Elvis albums the following week. He saw no reason why he shouldn't take an hour out to visit Graceland for a second time. This time he might even get to meet Elvis. 'Sure, I can get round there Lamar,' he said, delighted that one of Elvis' staff should wish to consult him. 'I'll be there in half an hour.'

'Okay Al. Listen... don't say nothing to nobody until after you've talked with us, huh? It'd be better that way, believe me.'

'Sure, Lamar. Bye'

Al put down the phone and lit a Marlboro. Inquisitive by nature, like all good detectives, he was doubly intrigued and not a little flattered by the call from Lamar Fike. So Elvis Presley's men wanted his advice on security. That was something to tell Kathy when he got home. He couldn't wait to get down to Graceland but he didn't want to appear over eager, so he took his time leaving the office, then chatted with the front desk duty man about baseball before driving uncharacteristically slowly down Elvis Presley Boulevard to Graceland. At the gates he was met by Vester Presley who ushered him through. For the fans outside it was no surprise to see a police car enter the grounds of Graceland. Al parked his car beneath the columns at the front entrance and rang the doorbell. It was answered by Lamar Fike.

'Good to see you Al. Thanks for coming down at short notice like this. Come this way.'

Lamar ushered Al into the sitting room and motioned for him to take a seat. 'You know the Colonel?' he asked, pointing out Parker, 'and Priscilla?'

Al, who had never met either, was duly introduced. He realised instantly that whatever it was that had brought him here was more serious than Lamar had originally implied. 'Hi, pleased to meet you,' he said to the Colonel and Priscilla. 'Where's Elvis?'

'Well,' said Colonel Parker slowly, 'that's the problem.'

Frankie Wilson had spent over 20 years building up his contacts in and around Memphis, and the phone on his desk at the Memphis Press Scimitar often rang with tip-offs about Elvis from casual acquaintances. Most such tip-offs were a waste of time and there were always crazy fans like that stupid woman who called him a few weeks ago to complain about Elvis cancelling his last Vegas season.

But Frankie nevertheless encouraged callers and the day after Elvis' kidnapping two calls in particular preyed on his mind.

The first was from an advertising salesman on the Scimitar who just happened to be passing through Memphis International Airport that morning and who'd called Frankie to say that he'd recognised Colonel Parker waiting for his baggage in the arrivals lounge. Wilson knew that Parker did not often fly into Memphis these days and therefore whatever had brought him here might be serious. The second was from a friend of his wife's who worked at the Avis Car Rental desk at the Airport. She rang in to tell him that Priscilla Presley, accompanied by her daughter, had arrived at the airport and rented a luxury car that morning. Also, Priscilla's other passenger was Parker.

Priscilla, Frankie knew, was a regular visitor to Memphis so there was nothing unusual in this, except that normally someone from Elvis' staff would have met her at the airport. Also, she'd probably have flown in on one of Elvis' private planes and been driven straight from the plane to Graceland. Frankie reasoned that she'd probably come at short notice.

It was obviously more than a coincidence that both Colonel Parker and Priscilla should arrive in Memphis the same morning, so Frankie called his friend Charlie West. Charlie's wife Gail replied.

'Hi Frank. No Charlie ain't here. I think he's at Graceland... stayed there all night. He called in a while ago to say he was real busy with Elvis and couldn't get home. No... I've no idea why. But you never know with Elvis do you... anything can happen when he's around. One time Charlie went off to Graceland for the day and ended up in Hawaii. Didn't come back for a week. I'll tell him you called.'

Frankie called another member of the Memphis Mafia but there was no reply. He made a mental note to keep trying then went off for his lunch.

'Jesus H. Christ!' Al Shriver prided himself on keeping a cool head but the story he'd just been told was as fantastic as any he'd heard in his days in the police department. Well, the implications were at any rate. Lamar Fike and

Charlie West had finished telling him of the events of the previous night and Colonel Parker was addressing him for the first time.

'Lieutenant Shriver. We called you because Lamar knows you and we believe we can trust you to handle this discreetly. What do you propose we do?'

Shriver looked Parker directly in the eye and paused before answering. 'Nothing,' he said.

'Nothing?' repeated Parker.

'Nothing, for the time being. I'll have to discuss this with my senior officers. Maybe even the FBI. This is a major kidnap, perhaps the biggest celebrity kidnap of the century. I cannot handle this alone.'

'We appreciate that,' said Priscilla. 'But we are afraid that if the news of this gets out, whoever has taken Elvis may harm him.'

'I understand your concern ma'am,' replied Al, adopting a tone of courtly respect when speaking to the ex-wife of Elvis Presley. 'But a Police Captain must take charge of this matter. I can't command the resources... the men, the cars, choppers maybe...'

'That's just the point,' interrupted Priscilla. 'We don't want hundreds of policeman crawling all over Graceland and talking about the case to everyone they meet. We don't want helicopters flying overhead attracting attention. We don't want anyone to know what's happened. We want this kept quiet. You start a full scale investigation and it'll be on CBS news tonight and on the front page of every newspaper in the world before we know it.'

'Then why did you call me?'

'Because we wanted to tell someone in the police and ask for some advice,' said Lamar Fike. 'We had to tell someone but only someone we could trust.'

'Then why didn't you call a private detective?'

'Maybe we should have done just that.' Colonel Parker had decided to try to re-establish his control. 'Maybe we will. But we brought you along so you could offer us some advice. What do you propose we do?'

'Wait,' said Shriver.

'Is that all?' asked Lamar Fike.

'What else can y'all do? Elvis could be anywhere right now. He could have been smuggled out of the country. If the guys that kidnapped him have money, he could be in Europe, South America, anywhere. From what you tell me, they seem like professionals and it's unlikely Elvis will be able to escape. We don't know where he is and there isn't a trail to follow. I could go snooping around near the freeway where you say the kidnap took place, but I doubt I'm gonna find nothing there to help me. No one was around to see where they went with Elvis. Charlie was out cold and didn't see the faces of the kidnappers and in any case they wore crash helmets. The trail's cold, stone cold, and until we hear from the kidnappers there's nothing we can do. So all I can tell you is you're just gonna have to wait.'

'So even if you did tell the captain or whoever, they couldn't do much either?' asked Lamar.

'That's right.'

Colonel Parker stood up. 'Then don't tell him,' he said. 'Keep this to yourself. Pretend you never heard what we've told you.'

'I dunno whether...'

'Do as I say and you won't regret it.' Parker fixed Shriver with a steely glare, the kind of look he used while negotiating Elvis' movie contracts.

'Yes, sir,' Al found himself saying. 'But I'm gonna stay in touch with y'all and if anything happens, you make sure you tell me about it first.'

'We will,' said Parker. 'We will.'

'What did Elvis have on him when he was taken?' asked Shriver, taking a notebook from his pocket and writing down the answers to his questions.

'He was wearing his leather biker's outfit,' answered Charlie. 'Black leather. Black boots. He didn't have much on him, maybe some keys. His crash helmet was left by the roadside.'

'Any cash,' asked Al?

'Elvis never carries cash,' said Lamar Fike.

'Anything else?'

'I think he may have had some pills on him,' said Lamar. 'He doesn't often go any place without some medication.'

'What kind of medication?'

'Tuinals. That's a sedative,' said Lamar. 'Probably some pain killers too.'

'Prescription?'

'Sure. All of his Elvis' medication comes on prescription.'

'Anything else?'

'No,' said Charlie. 'We were only going to ride for an hour or so and then return straight back to the house. There was no reason to take anything.'

'Then why'd Elvis take the pills?'

'Like I told you,' said Lamar. 'No matter where Elvis went, ever, or for however long, he always took his medication with him. There could have been an emergency.'

'Well, he did right,' said Al, packing away his notebook.

'There was an emergency.'

The room fell silent. 'Just let me know if anything turns up, if the kidnappers get in touch... whatever. I'll make some discreet inquiries of my own, see if I can turn anything up. I'll give it 24 hours before I tell the Captain.'

Al stood up and was shown to the front door by Lamar Fike. When Lamar returned, Parker was addressing the whole room.

'I've gotta go to New York to do some business, but I'll be in touch and I'll be back soon. Lamar, if anything happens, you make sure you tell me first, before that policeman. Okay?'

'Sure.'

'Charlie, you go home, get some sleep,' continued Parker. 'Don't tell anyone what's happened, not even your wife. Tell her Elvis is sick again. Whatever... Priscilla, I think you'd better stay here... and you're gonna have to tell Lisa what's going on... tell her something at any rate. And that doctor, Dr Nichopoulos, if he calls tell him Elvis has gone away someplace. I don't want him to know about this. I don't trust him.'

Priscilla, who also harboured doubts about Doctor Nichopoulos, found herself in agreement with Parker yet again, but she still wasn't sure about his motives.

When Charlie West arrived home later that day his wife told him that Frankie Wilson had called, wanting to know how Elvis was. Charlie shuddered.

'He ain't too good I'm afraid Gail,' Charlie lied. 'He took sick again but he's still at Graceland. That's why I had to stay over. I'm beat. I'm going straight to bed.'

'What should I tell Frankie if he calls?'

'Just say I was up all night with Elvis, nothing else. And

tell him I'll call him back tomorrow.'

Colonel Parker left Graceland in the late afternoon and headed for the airport to catch a seven o'clock flight to New York. His plane banked right after take-off, then settled into a north-eastern route almost directly over the cabin not far from the shores of Lake Cumberland. Down below, inside the cabin, Elvis was growing increasingly restless. After the meal in the early evening his two kidnappers had tied him up again, locked him in the bedroom and gone to sleep in the cabin's main room, evidently deciding not to use the empty single bed next to the one where he lay.

When Del and Roy awoke the following morning they cooked some more bacon and eggs, taking a portion into Elvis who was dozing on the bed. Then they announced they were going off hunting for most of the day, but that they would return before dusk. Elvis had pleaded with them not to tie him up again, and they relented by handcuffing his right leg to the bed on which he had slept. They left him some magazines and a few well-thumbed paperback books, also a loaf of bread, a pitcher of water, some cheese and two of his red pills.

'And don't bother shouting for help, Elvis,' one of his two kidnappers had told him before bolting the bedroom door. 'There ain't no one for miles around and you don't wanna hurt your throat.'

Locked in a room within the cabin with no plausible means of escape was a unique experience for Elvis. He had never known before what it was like to be truly alone. Forever surrounded by family and flunkies, he'd become so accustomed to having others within his orbit that he felt strangely insecure after Roy and Del left the cabin. For as long as he could remember he'd always been accompanied by others: his parents, his school friends, his bands, his army buddies, his staff, his management, his girlfriends, his hangers-on... there was always somebody around with whom to pass the time, more often than not someone to dance attendance on him. Only in his sleep was Elvis ever truly alone.

Never a reader apart from obscure religious texts, Elvis ignored the magazines and lay on the bed staring into space. He was still trying to recall where he'd seen one of his kidnappers before. Elvis thought back over recent events. On the day of the kidnapping he'd awoken at four in the afternoon, spent an hour in the bathroom, then emerged to find a plateful of bacon fried to a crisp, mashed potatoes, gravy, hamburger buns and bananas awaiting him. He'd guzzled away for an hour or so, then gone to his private gym where he'd sparred listlessly with his cousin Billy. Later in the evening, with Linda by his side, he'd watched a video of Monty Python's Flying Circus on his wide screen TV in the den and devoured another meal similar to the first. It was shortly after midnight when he and Charlie had decided to head out for what had now became their regular nightly motorbike ride.

He remembered leaving Graceland through the music gates, and recalled that as ever there were a few fans assembled at the bottom of the drive, and that he'd waved to them as he sped through the gates.

It was then that Elvis realised where he's seen the kidnapper before. 'That's it,' he said to himself. 'That guy was hanging around the gates a few weeks back.' Come to think of it, Elvis thought, that same guy had been there a few times recently. Of course, no one had thought twice about him then because many fans on a visit to Memphis from out of state came night after night in the hope of catching a glimpse of Elvis.

It pleased Elvis that he'd remembered where he'd seen his kidnapper, but the knowledge did him no good at all in his present situation. He took another of his Morphine tablets and a yellow sleeping pill, washed them down with a glass of water and fell into a restless asleep.

Late in the afternoon Frankie Wilson called Charlie West's house one more time. Gail West was out shopping and the phone startled Charlie who was dozing on the couch in their living room.

'Yeah. Who's that?' he asked.

'Did I wake you Charlie?' asked Frankie. 'It's Frankie Wilson. Sorry. I'll call back later.'

Charlie gulped. He wasn't prepared. 'Could you do that? I'm bushed.'

'Sure,' said Frankie and hung up.

Two hours later Charlie called again. Gail answered.

'I'll just get him. He's up now.'

'Hi Frankie. What can I do for you?' asked Charlie when he got on the phone.

'Sorry about waking you earlier Charlie. I was just wondering... I got a report that the Colonel was in town and Priscilla too. Is that so?'

'Yeah, they both stopped by to see Elvis,' said Charlie, who by this time had concocted a reasonable story. 'The Colonel had some papers that Elvis needed to sign and he's left for New York now. Priscilla brought Lisa Marie to see her pappy now he's out of the hospital.'

The story sounded reasonable enough.

'Kind of a coincidence for them both to be here at

once,' suggested Frankie.

'Sure was... that's why I was up most of the night,' said Charlie.

'So how is Elvis? Getting better?'

'Yeah, he's better than he was,' said Charlie. 'But he's still not real good, though. I guess it'll take a while.'

'Yeah.'

The conversation petered out and both men hung up after a promise to stay in touch.

But something about the way Charlie spoke nagged at Frankie. He decided to keep an eye on Graceland himself.

Back in his office at the Memphis Police Department, Lieutenant Al Shriver was pondering over what he'd been told at the meeting at Graceland. The knowledge he'd gained worried him. Priscilla Presley was right. If Elvis Presley really had been kidnapped, and this seemed more than likely, if it became public it would be the biggest news story to hit America in years. Like many police officers who had risen in the ranks he was a team player, disinclined to stand out or attract media attention. If the news of Elvis' kidnapping were to break, then media attention would fall on him and the department, and this was not something he relished. Others in the department might feel differently and enjoy the publicity, perhaps seeing it as a means of advancement. Shriver, on the other hand, felt that a low profile was best for policing, that a good detective did his job best when undercover.

Now aged 38, Shriver had joined the police department of his home town when he turned 23. At college he'd studied law and physical education, but after flunking his bar exams he'd opted to become a detective, a job where he could put into practice what he'd learned about the law and use it to catch criminals. He was good at his job too, hence his rapid advancement; brighter than most cops who drove patrol cars or walked the streets, and certainly more flexible than most when it came to assessing the mindset of criminals. He admired thinkers more than tough guys, Sherlock Holmes more than Kojak, Lieutenant Columbo more than Dirty Harry. He fervently believed that brains were more important than brawn when it came to apprehending crooks, and he was mindful that a dishonest lawyer with a briefcase was as dangerous as a desperate man with a gun.

From his meeting at Graceland he deduced that whoever had kidnapped Elvis had done their homework and left few, if any, clues behind. He didn't hold out much hope of finding them or Elvis until after they'd issued a ransom demand, if that was their motive. In the meantime he decided to sit on it, perhaps question that Charlie West at greater length without others present, perhaps mooch around in the area by the ramp to the freeway where Elvis had been snatched. Sooner or later he'd have to tell his captain about it, but for the time being he's do a bit of research, read up on the kidnappings of Patty Hearst and John Paul Getty III to see if these high profile cases offered any pointers as to be how to proceed. He though it unlikely.

By the shores of Lake Cumberland a mile or two from the cabin where Elvis sat handcuffed to the bed, Del and Roy crept through the tall grass with their rifles by their sides. They were stalking rabbits to kill and cook for supper.

'So what do we do now buddy?' asked Del.

'Nothing,' said Roy, echoing Al Shriver's advice to the

residents of Graceland. 'I guess you could go get Sandra if you want. Drive to Memphis, pick her up but don't tell her what's in store at the cabin. I can't wait to see the look on her face when she sees Elvis.'

'Me neither,' replied Del. 'Oh boy.'

The two men shot a couple of rabbits, then fished in the lake for an hour without success, and took them back to the cabin, arriving back earlier than they – and Elvis – expected. Their captive looked sullen and when they unbolted the bedroom door he petulantly kicked his leg so the bed to which it was attached rattled and shook.

'Now Elvis, temper temper,' said Roy. 'We got a nice fat rabbit here and it'll be rabbit stew for dinner tonight.'

Among his entourage Elvis was known for his sudden mood swings and his present experience seemed only to exacerbate them. Meekly, his voice almost a whimper, he said, 'Please let me go. Please. I ain't done nothin' to harm you guys. What do you want me for anyway?' Then, with a great surge of emotion, Elvis started to sob. 'I can give you anything you want... I'll give you cars, jewellery, money, jobs. I can give you anything. Just let me go.'

Del and Roy were startled by Elvis' about turn. So this was the macho guy, the great star who turned women on by the truckload. Really, deep down, he was just a mamma's boy, a cryin' softie.

Elvis was sobbing uncontrollably now. Tears streamed down his puffy face and over the greyish stubble that in the last 24 hours had appeared on his chin. He looked pathetic. His uncombed hair was a wild thatch of untidy black needles and his leather cycle outfit was creased and scuffed. Despite his huge size, he adopted a foetal position on the bed, and cried into his pillow. The bed shook. It was almost as if he was keening, like he'd keened for his dead mother Gladys all those years ago.

Del, moved by the scene, sat on the metal bedstead and tried to comfort Elvis. 'Hey, come on man. We ain't gonna harm you.'

'Then let me go,' said Elvis.

'No.' Roy remained unmoved. 'You're just gonna stay here until we decide to let you go. Now pull yourself together. Behave like a man for fuck's sake. My God... and girls fall over themselves to touch you.' He stepped out on to the porch and Del followed.

'I'm gonna fetch Sandra, right now,' said Del. 'We gotta do something man... I can't just sit around with that pathetic wreck. You look after him. I'll be back as soon as I can. I'll get something to eat at a truckstop. Shit, Roy, this'll be one fucking present she ain't never gonna forget, that's for sure.'

'Get him a change of clothes while you're at it, before he stinks the place out. Maybe some overalls or jeans and t-shirts, extra large, maybe super extra large.'

Del grinned, jumped into his truck and gunned it into life, then steered it away from the cabin in the direction of the highway. Roy watched as the tail lights disappeared then stepped inside the cabin to where Elvis lay immobile on the bed.

'Well Elvis old boy, looks like it's just you and me having rabbit stew for supper. So tell me, how many of those hot little numbers in your films did you fuck? All of 'em or just a few?'

Elvis grinned. The emotional outburst was forgotten. 'All of them,' he replied. 'Every single one.'

Chapter Five

(October 7 & 8)

As the President of RCA Records, Rocco Laginestra presided over the affairs of one of the biggest and oldest established major record labels in the world. From his office high up above Sixth Avenue in Manhattan, he could make or break the careers of those artists signed to the label but deep inside he was acutely aware that the fortunes of RCA were nowhere near as propitious as those of his main rivals, Columbia and WEA. The principal reason for this was the innate conservatism that had prevented the company from embracing rock music with the enthusiasm and know-how of their rivals. As a result RCA was slipping and its owners, NBC, were on Rocco's back to do something about it.

In England the company was unusually excited about their glam-rock star David Bowie but Rocky couldn't see this fey British boy, who admitted he was a faggot, capturing America with the ease with which he'd captured Europe. And Bowie's manager, Tony Defries, had squandered a fortune of RCA's money on tour support and funding his huge and flamboyant entourage. In Rocco's opinion John Denver, the guitar-playing hick from Colorado who sang songs about the Rocky Mountains, was a much safer bet. His albums were shipping gold right now, which was more than could be said for Bowie. Then there was Elvis.

In what was without doubt the boldest move in the company's history, RCA had paid Sun Records chief Sam Phillips $35,000 for the exclusive recording rights to Elvis

Presley way back in 1955, with an additional $5,000 bonus
for Elvis that he'd spent on a pink Cadillac for his mother.
At the time this seemed like an awful lot of money but
the investment was unquestionably the shrewdest move
RCA had ever made. Elvis proved to be far and away the
biggest selling recording artist that emerged in the first
phase of the rock'n'roll era, which made him the biggest
selling singer in the world, and throughout most of the
Sixties – despite intense competition from The Beatles
and their successors – he remained a top seller. Then,
just as sales were starting to dip in the second half of the
decade, Elvis re-emerged after the 1968 Singer TV special
and began a new career as a Las Vegas performer, the
hottest ticket in town. Naturally, his new-found success
on stage translated into record sales and for the next few
years Elvis was rarely out of the Top 100 on the Billboard
listings.

In 1972, when sales of Elvis' Records began to dip
again, RCA and Colonel Parker reached an agreement that
from Elvis' point of view was a betrayal of monumental
proportions. After a bit of horse-trading, the Colonel
consented to a deal in which he and Elvis would
relinquish all future royalties on Elvis' back catalogue
sales up to that point in exchange for $5 million dollars
in cash that was split 50/50 between them. Clearly still
oblivious to the merits of the records Elvis made in
the Fifties and early Sixties, Parker justified this deal
by suggesting that 'the old stuff don't sell any more'.
Naturally Elvis paid tax on his share – leaving him with
just over $1 million for his life's work, a paltry sum in
view of its significance and heritage. From RCA's point of
view, however, this deal was as sweet as they come – they
now owned Elvis' back catalogue outright – and for Parker

the deal provided a handsome nest egg for his eventual retirement.

Laginestra and Colonel Parker enjoyed what could best be described as a relationship based on mutual respect, though a shade more respect went in the Colonel's direction. Laginestra was wary of the Colonel's ways but also well aware that his and Elvis' fortunes were tied up with RCA for the duration. There was no way that any other record company could poach Elvis. He was – and would always remain – the jewel in RCA's crown.

Colonel Parker's flight had arrived in New York shortly after nine o'clock the previous evening and an RCA car was waiting to take Elvis' portly manager straight to the suite he had booked at the New York Hilton. Tired after being aroused early in the morning in Palm Springs and the events in Memphis, he went straight to his room, undressed, climbed into bed and was soon asleep. The following morning he breakfasted on bacon, sausages, eggs, fried potatoes and toast, all of it washed down with sweet black coffee. By 10 am he was on his way to RCA's offices on Sixth Avenue, sitting in the back of a black limousine smoking his first cigar of the day.

On a previous visit to RCA's offices in New York Parker had famously become stuck in the lift doors that refused to open sufficiently to allow him to leave. When he'd stabbed the button to open them he'd become trapped, with half his immense bulk inside the lift and half outside while the doors repeatedly slammed against him. Some saw this strange incident as an augury, a sign that the RCA behemoth was somehow avenging Parker's shifty greed, but no such unbecoming calamity befall Parker on this visit.

Rocco Laginestra ushered Colonel Parker into his office and dismissed his secretary. It was most unusual for Parker to come to New York for a meeting at such short notice and he was eager to learn the reason. All he could think of was that Elvis' health was worse than anyone was letting on, and that his life was in danger as a result.

The two men sat opposite each other across a coffee table strewn with music trade magazines. Parker relit his trademark cigar and settled back into an armchair. Laginestra waited. There was little need for pleasantries.

'Are you sure we can't be overheard?' asked the Colonel.

'Quite sure,' replied the company man warily.

'Very well... first I must have your word that everything I am about to tell you is in the utmost secrecy, that for the time being you will not repeat any of this to anyone, no one at the company, not your wife, not your mistress, no one.'

Laginestra winced. How did the Colonel know he had a mistress? 'Very well,' he replied. 'You have my word.'

'Well then,' said Parker, lowering his voice for effect, 'Elvis has been kidnapped.'

'What?' Laginestra's voice registered the same shock and disbelief that had afflicted Lieutenant Shriver the previous day.

'You heard me... kidnapped, abducted, whatever you want to call it.'

'You're joking.'

'No. I am being absolutely serious. Elvis was kidnapped two nights ago while riding his motorbike. The man who was with him was knocked unconscious and didn't see the kidnappers. Eventually he came to and returned to Graceland with the news. We haven't heard a word since from whoever took him, or from Elvis of course. We have no idea where he is.'

'How could this happen?'

'That's what I wanted to know... lax security, stupidity.'

'How many people know?'

Colonel Parker went on to tell the RCA president everything he knew, including the visit of the police lieutenant to Graceland, the presence of Priscilla and how they were attempting to keep a lid on the story.

'If the press got hold of this....' began Laginestra.

'Exactly,' interrupted the Colonel, cutting him off to allow his imagination to run wild.

When Laginestra had fully absorbed what the Colonel had told him, the pair discussed the situation at length. Like Parker, Laginestra was quick to realise that if the news were to be made public, then sales of Elvis' records would skyrocket overnight. Neither wanted to be the first to mention this. Eventually the RCA man broached the subject. 'What, if, let's say, the news were to leak out or Elvis were to... er, come to some harm... heaven forbid.'

'Heaven forbid... that would be terrible,' replied the Colonel.

'Terrible.'

'Maybe it might not be a bad idea to press up some extra Elvis records... er, just in case… a precaution…. To cater for potential demand in the event…'

The RCA man considered the suggestion. 'Well, maybe we could do just that. It might arouse some suspicion at the pressing plant but no harm in taking sensible precautions. Staff might assume that we stockpiling records in the event that Elvis doesn't recover from his present illness.'

'Yes, that would explain it. No harm in pressing them

up at all... sound commercial sense.'

'And if, er, for some reason or another, news of the kidnapping were to become public, then there might be a demand for more records too.'

'Yes, but the police have strictly forbidden it... and Priscilla... you know,' said the Colonel.

'Of course...'

'But if it were to leak out accidentally...' said the Colonel, an idea forming in his mind.

'It won't come from me,' said Laginestra hurriedly.

'No. But if something like that does happen, I would expect to be able to renegotiate our previous royalty agreements.'

'I think we could come to some arrangement there,' said Laginestra, who had already anticipated such a request. 'Let's wait until things play out.'

'Yes,' said Parker. 'We'll just have to wait and see.'

Their meeting over, the two men rose from their seats and shook hands. Laginestra's secretary showed Parker out and escorted him to the elevator.

When Parker left RCA's offices he went back to his hotel and called Graceland, only to learn from Lamar Fike that no one had been in touch with regard to his missing client. Then he took a cab to La Guardia Aiport and flew back to Memphis where he checked into a Holiday Inn near the centre of town. He didn't want to stay at Graceland where Priscilla and Linda and everyone else would nag him for results – but he needed to be close to the action. When he got to his room he called Lamar Fike at Graceland again to tell him where he was and settled down to get some rest. It had been another long day.

Delmore drove steadily back to Memphis, retracing

the route that he and Roy had used after abducting Elvis. Along the way he stopped to eat at a roadside diner and called Sandra from a payphone.

'Hi honey, I'm on my way home,' he told her. 'I should be back by morning.'

'You catch anything?'

'Sure but it's a surprise. Look, I need you to take some time off work, maybe even quit that job.'

'What for?'

'It's another surprise. Listen, when I get home I'll be dead tired so I'll sleep all day while you're at work. Then when you get home we'll take off again.'

'Where to?' asked Sandra, her curiosity aroused.

'Back into the hills where I've been with Roy. It's beautiful there and you need a break. Anyway, me and Roy have been talking, making some plans about the future, but I wouldn't do anything without you.'

'Del... what's this about?'

'I can't tell you now,' said Del. 'Just get the time off. I'll see you when you get home from work. Don't call me during the day – I'll be asleep.'

'Okay honey but I sure am curious about what's going on, what you two are cooking up.'

'I know – but don't be worried. Everything's gonna be alright.'

Delmore replaced the phone and strode back to his truck. Then he drove back through the night to Memphis, keeping a wary eye on his speed and listening to the radio. He switched stations a lot. No news stations mentioned Elvis.

Frankie Wilson's reporter's instinct continued to nag him. Charlie West's explanation as to why Parker and

Priscilla had been in Memphis together seemed plausible
enough, but there was a slightly nervous hesitancy to
his voice on the phone that suggested something wasn't
quite right. He knew from long experience that everyone
connected with show business told lies in order to put
a positive spin on an unpleasant truth. Show biz PRs
were forever glossing over the indiscretions of their star
charges, telling lies about their ages, love affairs and
personal habits. Experts in the art of spin, they could
lie with such consummate skill that even hardened old
timers like himself were often taken in. But Charlie West
was different. He wasn't a show biz PR – he was a good
ol' boy who just happened to have lucked into the Elvis
gig through having lived nearby when Elvis was at high
school. And he'd ridden that luck for almost 15 years
without having learned much at all, only that showing
absolute loyalty and obedience to Elvis guaranteed him
$200 a week, a car and plenty of paid travel.

Late that afternoon, while the Colonel flew back to
Memphis, while Elvis was trussed up in the cabin and
while Del and Roy were returning from their day tracking
rabbits, Frankie decided to pay a discreet call to Graceland
himself.

He arrived about five in the afternoon and parked
his car within walking distance of Elvis' home. Then he
strolled back towards the gates and mingled with the ever-
present gaggle of fans that was waiting around. None of
them recognised him as Frankie Wilson from the Memphis
Scimitar, which was unlikely anyway, and after a while he
began to ask a few questions.

'Do you like Elvis?' he asked a girl young enough to be
his daughter.

'Sure do mister,' she replied.

'Been here all day, have you?'

'Yeah, since the morning.'

'Have you seen Elvis go in or out yet?' asked Frankie, as casually as he could.

'No I ain't,' replied the girl. 'I ain't seen no one go in or out today. I was here yesterday and lots of cars went in and out. Even a police car.'

Frankie tried to act nonchalant. 'A police car?' he repeated.

'Yeah... the cop stayed for an hour, maybe an hour and a half and then left. Then a little later another car left and someone told me he thought it was Colonel Parker inside, you know Elvis' manager.'

'You don't say,' murmured Frankie, nodding.

'You like Elvis mister?' asked the girl.

'I sure do,' said Frankie.

'You know...,' said the girl, hesitating, '... I'm kinda worried about Elvis. All this business about him being sick and that. I sure wonder sometimes what he's thinking up there in that big house of his, what he's doing, who he's with. I just hope everyone's taking good care of him.'

'So do I,' said Frankie. 'You sure he's in there?'

'Well, I don't know for sure for I ain't seen him but this morning Vester, his uncle, you know, was here at the gate and he said Elvis was resting, still recuperatin' from his illness. Ain't no reason for Vester to lie to us fans is there?'

'No,' said Frankie. 'No reason at all that I can think of.'

Frankie smiled down at the girl and wandered off. He crossed the road and went into the small coffee shop that sold Elvisburgers and ordered a cup of coffee. Then he sat down at a table, lit a cigarette and stared out across Elvis Presley Boulevard, up towards the mansion on the hill. Something was wrong in Graceland, he thought. Or at the very least, something wasn't right. In his mind he was already writing a story.

Half an hour later Frankie got up, paid his cheque and walked back to his car. Then he drove home. His wife Grace greeted him and he told her he wasn't hungry and needed to work in his den. Once inside he shut the door and made a phone call. Then he sat down at his desk where his old portable typewriter sat waiting. He put in a crisp new sheet of white paper and began to type: 'Elvis Mystery,' he wrote, suggesting a headline.

'*Reports from Graceland suggest that Elvis Presley's release from the hospital six weeks ago may have been premature. Although the singer is reported to be recuperating at his home, the identity of certain visitors this week suggests that the singer's health is still far from good.*

'*The visitors include Colonel Tom Parker, Elvis' long serving manager, who arrived yesterday at the same time as Priscilla, the singer's former wife, who flew in from California with Lisa, their seven-year-old daughter. It is unusual for both Parker and Priscilla to be at Graceland at the same time, which perhaps indicates the seriousness of Elvis' condition.*

'*According to fans milling around outside Graceland, the police were also called to Graceland late yesterday afternoon. Following their visit Colonel Parker left, apparently on his way to New York. The same fans report that Elvis hasn't left his home for over 48 hours or even been seen in the grounds.*

'*A spokesman for the Memphis Baptist Memorial Hospital denies that Elvis has been re-admitted, or even that they have been consulted with regard to his medical condition since he was discharged six weeks ago.*'

When he'd finished typing Frankie tore out the sheet

of paper, folded it neatly and placed it in his inside jacket pocket. He needed more information before he could submit it to the Scimitar so he settled down to dinner with his wife, watched television and went to bed.

Roy had never been much of an Elvis fan so the prospect of spending several hours in his company wasn't the novelty it might have been for millions of others. Looking through the door towards the dozing hulk on the bed, Roy was idly wishing that he and Del had chosen instead to kidnap some glamorous actress from the movies or TV. Although he didn't know it, in reality he had much in common with the famous singer, for both had come from the wrong side of the tracks and knew what it was like to feel hungry when there was insufficient money to put food on the table.

Neither of them would go hungry tonight. Roy and Del had caught a couple of fat rabbits on their hunting expedition and Roy had spent the last hour skinning them outside on the deck and preparing them for dinner. He washed them and, using the same sharp hunting knife he used for skinning, cut pieces of meat from the bones and dropped them into a pan of boiling water. Then he threw in some salt and pepper, some gravy powder and waited for his stew to cook.

The smell of cooking woke Elvis who pulled himself up on the bed and leaned against the headboard. He called out to Roy.

'I need my medication again,' he shouted.

'Sure, Elvis. Red or yellow?' replied Roy.

'Red.'

Roy walked into the bedroom and handed Elvis a red pill and a cup of water to wash it down. 'Why do you need so many pills?' he asked.

'I been sick, you know. Real sick,' said Elvis.

'Yeah, I know. You cancelled some shows. What was wrong with you?'

'I get pains in my stomach. I can't sleep.'

'You're too fat, man. You need some exercise.'

Elvis considered Roy's diagnosis for a moment before replying. It occurred to him that no one, not even Colonel Parker, had ever told him he was too fat before. None of the Memphis guys that he employed would have dared to say such a thing, and his girlfriends were too polite, though Priscilla might now that they were separated. It also occurred to him that Roy was right.

'Maybe,' said Elvis, hesitantly. 'But I do exercise.'

'Like hell you do,' said Roy. 'I bet you just sit around guzzling food and pills.'

'I do karate,' said Elvis.

'So how come you didn't put up a fight when me and my buddy got you two nights ago?'

'You had guns.'

'You think we might have shot you?' asked Roy.

'Yeah.'

'Why would we wanna do that?'

'I dunno. Maybe you didn't know who I was and just wanted to rob us.'

'We knew who you were all right,' laughed Roy.

'I guess you did.' Elvis faltered before continuing. 'Ah saw you outside my home, you know. Ah saw you waiting there by the gates. Ah knew I knew you from somewhere and it came back to me after I awoke yesterday. You was spying on me I guess.'

Roy looked hard at his captive and saw no reason to deny it. 'You even waved at me Elvis,' he laughed. 'Yeah, we did our homework.'

'Why'd you do this?' asked Elvis. 'You need money? I got plenty of that.'

'There's more to it than that,' replied Roy. Elvis looked quizzical. 'Y'see my friend's wife is a big fan of yours and they had tickets to see you in Las Vegas a while back, the show you cancelled when you was sick. Anyway she was real, real disappointed, got depressed and lost her job. They'd been saving up for months to make that trip. They lost a load of money, plane fare, hotel. He's gone to fetch her now and he wants you to sing for her.'

Elvis was stunned. 'You mean you two guys grabbed me to perform for one of your wives. Just because of those cancelled shows? That's it?'

'Sure is Elvis.'

'You're crazy.'

'I know we are, so you'd better watch it around us. And you'd better put on a decent show when my friend gets back with his wife. 'Cos then we'll have to decide what to do next.'

Elvis lapsed into silence while Roy checked the rabbit stew.

'You like rabbit Elvis?' asked Roy, matter of factly.

'I could eat anything right now, I'm so god dammed hungry.'

'I guess you ain't used to waiting, huh?'

'No, I guess not,' replied Elvis. 'But I ain't got much choice here, do I?'

'No, you don't,' laughed Roy, throwing some vegetables into the pan, along with more thickening powder. 'Be about ten minutes. You wanna beer?'

'I don't drink. It ain't good for you,' said Elvis.

'Neither are all them god dammed pills you take. You

mean you ain't ever had a beer?'

'Yeah I tried it. Didn't much like the taste though. I tried champagne too.'

'Well maybe I'd have tried champagne if I'd been in your shoes.'

The small talk between the two men didn't last and Roy busied himself with the rabbit stew. When he served it up Elvis seemed pleased with the result, wolfing it down like he hadn't eaten in days. When he'd finished he looked up at Roy.

'You sure cook well considering you ain't got no real stove.'

Roy smiled. 'Thanks Elvis,' he muttered.

'Ma grandma does all the cookin' at Graceland,' replied Elvis.

'I never knew my grandma, or my grandpa,' said Roy. 'Didn't know my pa either.'

Detective Lieutenant Al Shriver was frustrated at having to keep the news of Elvis' kidnapping to himself and after one largely sleepless night he decided to become proactive rather than passive. He'd read up everything he could find about Patty Hearst and John Paul Getty III, and in both cases it seemed the kidnappers held the upper hand. So it was with Elvis. The only real lead Shriver had was Charlie West, so he opted to interrogate him further. Maybe, just maybe he surmised, Charlie was in on the job. That would at least explain the ease with which Elvis appeared to have been snatched.

So the next day Al called Lamar Fike and told him he wanted to talk to Charlie again, alone this time. Lamar called Charlie and told him to get down to the precinct house where Al worked. He didn't want anyone to see another police car entering Graceland, not two days running.

Al took Charlie for a ride in his car and, once they'd reached the outskirts of town, pulled into a shopping mall parking lot and switched off the engine. 'I didn't wanna talk in the office as I haven't told anyone about Elvis yet,' said Al.

Charlie nodded. 'I don't know what else I can tell you.'

'Did you notice anything unusual when you rode out of Graceland on the night that Elvis was kidnapped?'

Charlie thought for a moment. 'No… nothing unusual at all.'

'Were there fans hangin' around?'

'Yea… there's always fans hanging around.'

'Every night?'

'Yea… every night.'

'How many?'

'It varies,' answered Charlie. 'Sometimes two or three, sometimes more than ten. They get to know when Elvis is home and when he's away. Vester, Elvis' uncle tells them. If the word gets around that Elvis is home, more fans arrive and they tend to linger in the hope of seeing him. If he's away then they just take a photo by the gate and leave.'

'Do they ever hang around real late?'

'Well, the later it gets the less fans there are – but there's usually some that stay until we get back if we've been out ridin'.'

'And how late might that be?'

'One in the morning, maybe even a bit later.'

'Do you think that these fans recognised Elvis when he went out on his bike late?'

'Yes... oh yes. Elvis often revved up his bike for them,

just showing off like.'

'And those fans who knew he was out might stay until he returned, just to see him again?'

'I guess so, but most go home.'

'Do you get the same fans night after night or are they always different?'

'Well, I don't pay too much attention to them really.'

'Are they male or female.'

'Mostly female.'

'And did you or Elvis acknowledge them at all.'

'Not really... like I say, Elvis might rev up and maybe burn a little rubber as he sped off.'

Al thought for a moment. An idea was forming in his mind.

'Charlie I want you to think hard for a moment. Was there a pattern to Elvis' night riding activity? Like... did he ride every other night, or did he sometimes ride out with one rider one night of the week and two the next because there was a duty roster.'

Charlie smiled. 'There was never a pattern to Elvis' life, let alone his bike ridin',' he replied. 'Elvis just did what he felt like whenever he felt like it. I don't think anyone ever knew what he was thinking of doing at any particular time, except when he had concerts to do of course.'

'So anyone who might have been watching Elvis, observing his habits, wouldn't have been able to plan this attack?'

'Not really... but we went out most every night over the past two or three weeks, so if anyone was watching they could pretty much work out when we went out and where we went.'

'So,' said Al, 'was there anyone watching?'

'Gee, I dunno. There could have been.'

'Think Charlie. Did you see the same person hanging around late, night after night, at Graceland?'

Charlie hesitated. 'You know... there might have been.'

'Might?'

'Well there was this guy. I never saw his face really, but I seem to remember him being there when we left and when we came back on quite a few occasions. It was too dark to see and there might have been times when he wasn't there, but he could have been in a crowd of fans or even across the road in the diner that stays open real late.'

'Would you recognise him again?'

'Maybe... he was stocky. Not too tall. He had his collar up, as if he was maybe trying to hide his face. But of course it was always dark when we went out.'

Al let out a deep breath. This seemed like the first lead. 'Was he always alone?' he asked.

Charlie seemed lost in thought. 'You know Lieutenant, now I come to think about it, there may have been two guys on some nights, like he was with another guy, and what's more we might even have been tailed on our bikes for a short way before the night they got Elvis.'

'What do you mean?'

'I mean that, looking back, I think I might have heard other bikes near ours, behind us or on the next block, in the nights leading up to this. I mean... I can't be sure and they could just have been other road users, but... I don't know. It's just guessing really. Of course, I didn't think anything about it at the time.'

Al had already guessed that the kidnappers must have done a pretty thorough yet discrete surveillance job beforehand. What Charlie was suggesting merely confirmed his opinion.

'Anything else you remember about them?'

'They looked like they could have been soldiers, you know, straight-backed, heads held high.'

'That makes sense... Charlie... I don't want you to say anything about this conversation to anyone. It's a lead but there's not much to go on really. It's obvious the men who took Elvis knew what they were doing and had probably followed you before. I need to think about it some more.'

Al switched on the ignition and drove back into Memphis. 'Where can I drop you?' he asked.

'Anywhere near Graceland,' said Charlie. 'Oh... and there's one other thing. A newspaper reporter called Frankie Wilson has been calling and asking about Elvis. Do you know him?'

'Everybody knows Frankie.'

'Well, he's like the Elvis correspondent on the Scimitar and all the guys know him, even Elvis. He was calling to ask about Elvis' health but I got a feeling he was suspicious about the goings-on at Graceland. I didn't tell him nothin' of course but all the same I just felt he might know something, or have put two and two together.'

'I'll take care of him,' said Al, who had absolutely no idea whatsoever how he might take care of Frankie Wilson.

In his room at the Memphis Holiday Inn Colonel Parker was restless. Ever a man of action, the idea of doing nothing at a time like this was anathema to him. So he decided to call Lamar Fike at Graceland.

'Lamar, it's the Colonel. Any news?'

'No... nothing. Priscilla's still here with Linda and Lisa-Marie. The little girl's getting a bit concerned, so they're gonna have to tell her something real soon. Vernon's taking it badly... he's going crazy and I'm worried he might do something stupid, like call the newspapers or something. The copper, that Lieutenant, he wanted to talk to Charlie again.'

'Did he?'

'Yes, Charlie went down to the police HQ to meet him.'

'I wanna talk to that cop again, too.'

'Al Shriver?'

'Yea… call him and get him to call me here. I wanna talk to him alone.'

Shriver was at the hotel within an hour.

When he arrived back in Memphis the first thing Del did was to head for the centre of town and buy a Polaroid SX-70 Land camera and a cheap acoustic guitar that he asked the man in the shop to tune for him before stashing it in the back of the truck wrapped in a blanket. He didn't want Sandra to see it, not at first anyway. Then he shopped for an extra large pair of denim overalls, two plain white t-shirts, two pairs of undershorts and some socks, also extra large. 'You don't need to buy them this big,' said the girl in the store, admiring Del's trim physique as she wrapped the garments.

'They ain't for me honey,' he replied as he paid in cash. 'They're for my cousin who eats far too many cheeseburgers.' The girl smiled. She was flirting with him but Del had no time for her and headed homewards, went inside and collapsed on the bed. He was asleep within minutes.

It was early evening when Sandra arrived home and she was relieved to see Del asleep in the bed. She shook him gently and he came awake. 'Hi honey,' she said. 'What's all this about… I'm going crazy.'

Del wiped his eyes and held his arms out to Sandra

who fell into them. 'I can't tell you, not yet. But trust me, just trust me. Can you fix me something to eat while I take a shower?'

'Please tell me. I'm so…'

'Honey, trust me. You'll know soon enough. I just don't want to spoil the surprise. Did you get off work for a few days?' He began to kiss her neck.

'Yes,' replied Sandra, pulling a face and extracting herself from his arms. 'Later perhaps,' she said, sensing his need. 'You need to shower first.'

Back in the bedroom Del was towelling himself when Sandra walked in. She had changed from her Howard Johnson's waitressing uniform into shorts and a t-shirt. 'Food's on the table,' she said, kissing him on the cheek and putting her arms around his neck. 'At least you smell better now. Please tell me, at least where we're going and what I need to pack.' She playfully grabbed the towel and tossed it aside, then kissed her naked husband hard on the lips. 'Please,' she whispered, moving her hand down to between his legs. 'I'll do anything…'

Unable to resist his wife's shameless display, Del sat down on the bed and tugged at her shorts until they were around her ankles. She kicked them off and they tumbled into an embrace on the duvet. 'Tell me,' he said between kisses. 'Tell me what you'll do…'

After they'd made love Del was still reluctant to tell Sandra much about his plans though he did suggest she pack sufficient clothes for three or four days, something warm too, and that they'd be heading north, into the mountains. As an afterthought she threw in the nightdress she'd bought for their trip to Las Vegas.

Once they'd eaten, Del packed some fresh clothes for himself while Sandra cleared the table. Then they locked up their home and got into the truck. Del took the wheel.

'Where are we going again?' asked Sandra as they pulled away.

'Up into the Kentucky hills,' said Del.

'We're having a vacation?'

'Sort of... why don't you just curl up and fall asleep while I drive.'

'I am sleepy. I don't sleep well when you're away.' Sandra yawned and made herself comfortable, letting her head rest on Del's shoulder for a few moments before closing her eyes.

Del turned on the radio and flicked through some local stations. Sandra heard the snatch of a song and told him to stop.

'*We can't go on together… with suspicious minds… We can't build a dream…*'

By the time the song was over she was fast asleep.

Al Shriver thought he was a good judge of men and knew all types but he had never met anyone like the Colonel before. With his beady eyes, steely gaze and arrogant manner Colonel Parker reminded him of a reptile, and a large one at that. The conversation in the Colonel's hotel room had started badly and gone downhill from there.

'So, Sergeant, how's the investigation going?' asked the Colonel, omitting any small talk whatsoever and deliberately confusing Al's rank.

'It's Lieutenant, Mr Parker.'

'And it's Colonel Parker to you. I asked how the investigation was going.'

'I have certain ideas and a few leads and I'm following them up as best we can.'

'What can you tell me that I don't already know?' asked Parker.

Al took a deep breath and began. 'I believe that the kidnappers have been watching Graceland for several weeks and charting Elvis' movements, especially at night when he went out on his bike rides. This suggests the kidnappers live locally or have been staying locally. I believe there are two men involved and that both of them were involved in the reconnaissance operation. Like Elvis they rode motorbikes and I believe that on occasion they even followed Elvis and his friends to find out where they went at night. I suspect they waited until an evening when Elvis went out with just one other rider for company. From the manner in which he was taken I suspect that both men were physically fit, very fit indeed, probably even combat trained, which suggests they were in the military, maybe together. I think Elvis has been taken to a secure location where he is being kept, alive, while the kidnappers make up their mind what to do next. That is all.'

'It's not much is it?'

'It's all I can tell you for now. I could add that Frankie Wilson, the newspaper reporter, is sniffing around the story, probably because he's seen, or been told about, unusual comings and goings at Graceland.'

This news seemed to lighten the Colonel's mood. 'Should we tell him?'

'No,' said Shriver. 'I would advise against that at all costs, but if he finds out too much he must be silenced.'

'Lieutenant Shriver,' replied Colonel Parker, rising to his feet and fixing the policemen with a cold glare, 'as you know I was in favour of calling in a large scale manhunt which involved the police forces of all the states surrounding Tennessee, utilising the press and generally raising a hue and cry of colossal proportions but I was persuaded against this, not least by yourself, in case it jeopardised the safety of Elvis. As far as I am concerned Elvis' safety is already in jeopardy. And in my opinion the publicity that will arise from a press conference on this will terrify the kidnappers into releasing our boy unharmed. It's my belief that if they did harm him and were caught later, then they would run the risk of being lynched by Elvis fans. Even if they weren't hung for murder their lives would not be worth living, especially in jail.

'However, in deference to your wishes and to those of Mrs Presley and Elvis' girlfriend Linda Thompson I have refrained from taking this course, but I must warn you that unless some progress is made soon I will do just that – call a press conference and announce to the world that Elvis has been kidnapped.'

Shriver cleared his throat before answering. 'In my opinion, if you were to do that you'd never see Elvis again. The kidnappers would almost certainly panic and then kill Elvis, bury his body anywhere in this vast country of ours and that'd be the last we'd ever hear of it.'

'How do you know?'

'Because I'm a policeman.'

'OK. You've got 48 hours before I instruct my staff to call that press conference.'

Shriver left the Colonel in his suite and made two decisions, the first to speak to the Captain of Memphis Police, the second to silence Frankie Wilson by enlisting his help.

In the truck that left Tennessee and sped through Kentucky with Del at the wheel, Sandra awoke after about two hours feeling very stiff and announced she was hungry, so they stopped at the next roadside diner, grabbed a bite and some provisions from the shop at the gas station next door and got back into the truck.

'How much longer to go?' she asked as Del headed back out on to the highway.

'Three hours, maybe a bit longer.'

It wasn't long before Sandra had fallen asleep again, but she awoke with a start when Del pulled off the road and drove down the rough track that led to the cabin. It was just after three in the morning as Del pulled the truck to a halt beside the wooden hut and climbed out. There was a dim light from one of the windows.

'Where are we?' whispered Sandra as they walked towards the cabin.

'Up in the mountains. Wait here. Please... just stay right here. Don't come inside yet.'

Del knocked lightly on the door and in the darkness Sandra could just make out Roy opening the door for his friend.

'Roy,' she called out, but Del turned and repeated his request for her to stay put. Then both men disappeared into the hut. Elvis was sleeping in the bedroom, a blanket over him. Del took in the scene instantly.

'Anything happened?' asked Del.

'Nope. We had dinner, rabbit stew, talked a while. I gave him another pill and he's been sleeping like a baby for four or five hours. I nodded off myself too. Does Sandra know?'

'No, not yet. Wake Elvis.'

'Now?'

'Yep, now. Now's the time for him to sing for his supper.'

Roy went into the room where Elvis slept and shook him, gently at first, then with more force. Elvis twitched, then opened his eyes.

'What the…'

'Wake up Elvis. You're gonna perform.'

'What…'

'We want you to sing some songs.'

Del looked across at his friend and the King of Rock'n'Roll, took a sharp intake of breath, turned on his heel and went to fetch his wife and the guitar.

Outside Sandra was impatient.

'What's happening in there? Can't I go inside? It's cold out here.'

'Just one more minute honey.'

Del reached into the back of the truck, grabbed the guitar with one hand and took Sandra round the shoulders with the other.

'Why have you got a guitar?'

Instead of replying he put the guitar down on the ground and fastened a crude blindfold around his wife's eyes. 'Just don't say nothing Sandra,' he assured her. 'Tonight, you're gonna get the surprise of your life.'

And then he ushered her into the presence of the King.

Chapter Six

(October 8)

In the hours while Del was heading for Memphis, Roy
grew tired of talking to an unresponsive Elvis and took a
stroll through the woods, leaving their captive alone in
the locked bedroom and handcuffed to the bed. Unable to
sleep, Elvis had little else to do but dwell on his situation.
He had reached the realisation that his kidnappers were
not hardened criminals but skilled amateurs who'd
used expertise they'd probably learned in the army to
intercept him and Charlie, overpower them and spirit
him to this cabin, obviously somewhere remote, though
he had no idea where he really was. From the view out
of the window it looked like mountainous country. Luck
had favoured them thus far but once the motive for the
kidnap – this absurd idea that he would sing for one of
their wives – had been accomplished, what then? What
will they do with me, thought Elvis. Will they harm me,
let me go, ransom me… the possibilities flickered through
Elvis' mind as he lay on the bed staring up at the wooden
ceiling, his mind all shook up.

It had not been the best of years for Elvis. His
health was deteriorating, with a distended abdomen, a
malfunctioning liver and poor muscle tone due to overuse
of laxatives. As well as the medicine prescribed by his
personal doctor, Dr George Nichopoulus – Dr Nick – he'd
acquired other drugs from random doctors in Memphis
and Los Angeles, some of which had been intercepted
in the mail by his staff who had expressed concern over
his intake to the extent that confrontations ensued. His

relationships with the men closest to him – the 'good buddies' in the Memphis Mafia – were permanently on a knife-edge over his capricious ways.

A recording session in March had yielded little in the way of usable material and it was only at Colonel Parker's urging – a suggestion that a benefit concert for victims of a tornado in Mississippi would be good PR – that he resumed touring at the beginning of the year. The Las Vegas season that followed in March was below par, though he'd gone through with it. An onstage spat with bass player Duke Barnwell resulted in Barnwell quitting, and his relationship with Kathy Westmoreland, a member of his Sweet Inspirations vocal backing group, once close, was irredeemable due to his thoughtless behaviour. Then there was the quarrel with Parker over A Star Is Born, the movie that Barbra Streisand and her hairdresser boyfriend Jon Peters wanted to make. Streisand and Peters had met with Elvis in his Las Vegas dressing room in March, offering Elvis the starring role, which flattered him enormously. Then Parker, who wasn't present at the initial meeting, had raised objections. A week later he'd received an offer but Parker had asked for double the money, along with other unacceptable demands, and by the end of April the deal was off. Elvis, who longed for a serious acting role, was furious with his manager but, as ever, complied meekly with the status quo.

Girls had entered and left his life at an alarming rate. When Linda expressed a desire to move to Hollywood and launch an acting career he'd bought her a house there, and while she was away he'd taken up with a model and former Playboy cover girl called Sheila Ryan who soon left him for the actor James Caan. A succession of models and hostesses – Mindi Miller, Melissa Blackwood and Jo

Cathy Brownlee – all came and went, much like last year's flame Ann Pennington. Linda, meanwhile, remained at his beck and call, abandoning Hollywood for Memphis when he was sick, the other girls slipping into the background when she arrived and reappearing on demand but sooner or later they became unwilling to endure his neediness, time clock and idiosyncratic behaviour.

His spending habits had escalated during the year, leading to confrontations with Parker and his father like the one in Las Vegas before the season was cancelled. Although he'd earned almost half a million dollars from touring during the year so far, his spending on jewellery, cars and planes had reached enormous levels. In July he'd given away 13 Cadillacs in one spree alone and over the course of the year, inspired by what he read about planes acquired by other performers, his outgoings on three separate planes had amounted to almost $2 million.

Elvis tried to block these thoughts from his mind but they kept straying back. Now, to cap it all, he'd been kidnapped. Nevertheless, although he was loath to admit it, Elvis wasn't feeling any worse physically for his ordeal. His stomach pains had receded and his head was clear. In the 48 hours since he'd been snatched he'd taken fewer pills and eaten far less than he normally would, and although he longed for a shave and a shower and to see himself in a mirror, he was feeling more in control of himself than he'd felt for a long time. His kidnappers hadn't mistreated him unduly, and didn't seem to bear him any ill will. There was even something about them that he warmed to – they were his kind of people, proud southern men raised on the wrong side of the tracks, skirt-chasers, loyal, the kind of men that Elvis might himself have befriended if circumstances had been different. Indeed,

Elvis thought that these two men would have made admirable recruits to the Memphis Mafia.

Being unable to sleep was a common enough state of affairs for Elvis and as he lay awake he shut away the problems of 1975 and allowed his mind to drift back to the good times in his extraordinary life. He wasn't able to recall much from his childhood, other than that his little family was dirt poor, that his pa had spent time in prison for something to do with money and that they'd had to skip his birthplace Tupelo in a bit of a hurry so pappy could find work in Memphis. He remembered being picked on at school because he was different, and that he'd always felt different to everyone else, as if his singular life was somehow pre-ordained for him, that music was a calling from God or whoever, and he had no choice but to follow.

The first music he remembered hearing was in church, hymns praising the Lord, often sung by black folks whose devotion to God he shared. He'd joined in with the gospel signing as a child and those around him had noticed the cadence in his voice, an instrument that they told him was gift from the Lord. So he had always respected God and had no cause to doubt His existence. After church music came country music, followed by rhythm and blues, all heard on the family radio. Living in Memphis, he was at the centre of the blues, the music of the poor black man bemoaning his lot. He was apart from Nashville, the country music capital of America, but not too far away to avoid its effect. Somehow he'd been able to combine all of these influences into a whole and develop a singing style all of his own. He didn't mean to excite young girls in the way he did by shaking his hips, it just sort of happened, and when some folks called it ungodly he was hurt more than anyone knew. He was just expressing himself.

He never knew quite why he felt the need to dress differently from the rest of his classmates, to grow his hair into a quiff and wear pink jackets, even before he was famous. He just knew he needed to stand out, and dressing like he did was the means to do so. His best memories were of the early years, when fame was beckoning, when he and Scotty and Bill would play the one-nighters around Memphis, gradually widening their reach to Louisiana, Alabama, Kentucky and Texas, the three of them packed into a car with just their instruments for company, driving through the night, hopping up on one godforsaken stage after another, bopping away as he sang and watching the reaction as their music started to take a hold on the audience.

Then there were the girls. Man, Elvis had never known anything like it. At his high school the girls had looked down on him like he was some freak but out on the road, after the shows, they had thrown themselves at him night after night, wanting him to touch them in their secret places, and Elvis had not disappointed. No sir. Elvis had taken these girls in the dressing rooms, in cheap motels, in the parking lots, in the back seats of cars across two thousand miles of America stretching from Florida to New Mexico. It was like he had some power over them, like he was a hypnotist, and he often wondered how many little Elvis' might be out there, all of them ignorant as to the identity of their father.

Yet, the more famous Elvis became, the more he was obliged to curb fooling around with girls on the road. The Colonel warned him that a scandal could finish him, and Elvis took note, reluctantly for sure. He wouldn't want to do anything that might upset his mamma, that might

shame her. The first thing he did when the money started
rolling in, after he'd bought his first pink Cadillac, was to
buy her a new house and to make sure she never had to
work again. Gladys Presley, or Satnin' as he called her, was
the real love of his life. Elvis often felt the tears welling
up when he thought of his mamma. What would have
happened to him, he thought, if she'd lived longer than
she did? He knew she was unsure about Colonel Parker
but his dad had fallen hook, line and sinker for Parker's
patter.

Elvis turned over in the bed. Now, sooner or later,
he'd find himself face to face with another woman, this
one the wife of one of his kidnappers and he'd better not
disappoint. His life might depend on it.

Elvis tried to make himself comfortable on his
makeshift bed, hoping in vain to fall asleep. The last thing
on his mind before he eventually did drop off was that he
needed a change of clothing.

Back in Memphis, in the offices of the *Memphis Press-
Scimitar*, Frankie Wilson was reading again the story
destined to appear on the following morning's front page
headlined ELVIS MYSTERY. He had rewritten the first draft
he'd prepared at home the previous evening.

*'Mystery surrounds the state of Elvis Presley's health since
his release from the hospital six weeks ago. Reports from
Graceland suggest his release may have been premature.
Although the singer is believed to be recuperating at his
home on Elvis Presley Boulevard, the identity of certain
visitors to Graceland this week suggests there is deep
concern for the singer's wellbeing.*

*'The visitors include Colonel Tom Parker, Elvis' manager,
who flew into Memphis yesterday morning at the same*

time as Priscilla, Elvis' estranged wife, who arrived from California with Lisa-Marie, their seven-year-old daughter. The Colonel and Priscilla both drove straight to Graceland but it is unusual for both parties to be there at the same time, which perhaps indicates the seriousness of Elvis' condition.

'According to fans milling around outside Graceland, a police officer has also visited the singer's home. Following his visit, Colonel Parker reportedly left Memphis on a flight bound for New York. In the hours since, there have been various comings and goings at Graceland, the police and Colonel Tom Parker among them. Confusingly, according to fans, Elvis was last sighted three nights ago riding out on a motorcycle, his health apparently much improved. These same fans report that there have been no further night-time excursions, which is unusual as they occurred almost nightly until now. So has the singer's health taken an unexpected turn for the worst in the past 48 hours?

'A spokesman for the Memphis Baptist Memorial Hospital denies that Elvis has been re-admitted, or even that they have been consulted with regard to his medical condition since he was discharged six weeks ago.

'If the King is so ill that he has been bed-ridden for the last three days, then surely he would have been re-admitted to the hospital? If he's not in the hospital, then where is Elvis Presley?'

Satisfied with his work Frankie ripped the sheet of paper from his typewriter and placed it in the in-tray for the night editor to read. Then he went home and tried to put two and two together. It didn't make four. Instinct told him something wasn't right.

Al Shriver had requested an immediate audience with the Captain of the Memphis Police after his last meeting with Colonel Parker but as he wasn't immediately available he had to kick his heels for two hours. This at least gave him time to consider how he would explain the situation to his boss, and how he might best suggest his plan of enlisting the reporter Frankie Wilson's help in tracking down Elvis and, at the same time, securing his silence.

Captain Jim Magill, a tough cop of Irish descent who'd worked his way to the top of the police ladder from the lowest rung, was a man of action, in many ways the opposite of the cerebral Shriver. He believed in confrontation, in taking on criminals face to face, and asking questions afterwards. He wasn't an Elvis fan. Indeed, he had little time for entertainers of any kind aside from the more conservative country singers like Roy Acuff, Porter Wagoner and George Jones. Shriver was aware of this as he was ushered into the presence of his boss.

'What is it Al?' asked Magill.

'Well Captain, it's like this.' Shriver took a deep breath. 'Elvis Presley has been kidnapped.'

Magill looked up from his desk with the kind of expression a man might adopt if he'd seen an elephant take flight. Like everyone else hearing the news for the first time he was dumbstruck. 'Whaaaaat?' he replied, extending the single syllable so that it came out as a word that neither man would recognise again.

'Elvis has been kidnapped,' Shriver repeated.

'I heard you. Is this some kind of joke?'

'No, sir.'

'Well, you'd better take a seat and tell me about it. But first of all, how many others know?'

'Very few, sir,' said Shriver, drawing a chair up his boss'

desk. 'Elvis' manager, Colonel Parker, his former wife and his current girlfriend, some staff at Graceland and, of course, the kidnappers, of which I believe there to be two.'

'No one else in our department?'

'No, sir.'

'How long have you known about this?'

'Just over 36 hours sir. I was called by the head of Elvis' staff at Graceland, and put in the picture. We all decided to keep the lid on it.'

'That was quite right Lieutenant. Now tell me the whole story, everything from the beginning to the moment you walked into my office two minutes ago.'

Shriver sat back and told the Captain everything he knew, repeated the conversations he'd had with Colonel Parker and Charlie West, the suspicions of Frankie Wilson and the results of his investigations so far. When he'd finished Magill remained silent for abut 15 seconds, then rose from his seat and walked towards the window of his office. Then he turned around and addressed the Lieutenant.

'Al, you don't need me to tell you this has the potential to be the biggest news story since Neil Armstrong walked on the moon. If it were to be released the world's press would descend on Memphis in their thousands, reporters, TV crews, the lot, as would fans of Presley. We would be placed in a position of having to give press conferences on a daily basis and, what's more, to come up with results. The FBI would want to get involved, maybe even the CIA. The White House might even be calling me.

'If this were to happen and we failed to get Elvis back alive, we would look like fools. My position as the Chief of Memphis Police would be untenable. I must insist therefore than under no circumstances can the media get hold of this. At all costs it must be kept secret, at least until Elvis is safely returned. Do I make myself clear?'

'Yes, sir.'

'Very well then. Tell no one, no other police officers, no one. The fewer people that know about this the better. Deal with that newspaper reporter any way you like. I won't ask questions. And if that Colonel Parker looks like he might cause trouble for you in this regard, refer him to me. Now go and do what you've been doing for the last day or two. Make discrete inquiries, stay in touch with the folk at Graceland. And let me know the minute anything develops.'

'Yes, sir.'

After his last meeting with Lieutenant Shriver Colonel Parker took a taxi to Graceland where the stress was beginning to tell on all its occupants, not least Vernon Presley who had locked himself in his bedroom and refused to come out. 'He thinks the kidnappers will come after him next,' Linda Thompson explained to Parker when he arrived. 'He's barricaded himself in, Colonel. He ain't comin' out, not for nobody.'

The Colonel seemed unruffled by this development. 'He'll come to his senses when he's hungry.'

'He hasn't eaten anything since yesterday morning. Don't you wanna talk with him? Try and calm him down a little?'

'I have better things to do.'

'I just thought...'

'You thought wrong,' replied Parker, fiddling inside his front pocket. He pulled out a cigar, lit up and blew out the smoke with great deliberation. Settling into an armchair in Graceland's sitting room, he asked Linda to fetch Priscilla but just as she walked in the phone rang.

Linda picked it up. 'Colonel, it's for you,' she said.

'Who is it?'

'Lieutenant Shriver.'

With considerable difficulty Parker hauled himself free from the chair and left the room to take the call. The chair remained hollowed out before rising ever so slowly back into shape.

'Colonel?' Al's voice sounded strained.

'Colonel Parker, yes. What have you got, Shriver?'

'I have just come out of a meeting with Captain Magill, the chief of Memphis Police. I need to convey to you what he told me. Can I come on over? I don't feel comfortable on the phone.'

'Why not?' asked Parker. 'Nobody knows anything I hope? 'Cos if they do, there'll be trouble.'

'No, nobody knows nothing Colonel. It's just that the longer this goes on the more likely it is that there'll be a leak. That reporter Frankie Wilson…'

'What about him?'

'I think he's on to something.'

'Right, get over here then. Immediately.'

'Yes, Colonel, of course, right away, Colonel,' Al found himself saying, appalled by his own subservience.

Shriver arrived at the Graceland gates twenty minutes later and drove slowly up towards the entrance, well aware that he faced the formidable task of convincing Elvis' manager that secrecy was still paramount, that the investigation was advancing rapidly, that they had some idea of where Elvis was being held and that they were on the trail of the kidnappers. He felt increasingly uneasy as he took a seat in the living room where five pairs of eyes blinked in his direction.

Colonel Parker twiddled a cigar between his thumb and forefinger and stared hard at the Lieutenant. The others in the room, Priscilla, Linda, Fike and West, looked on expectantly.

'So this police captain of yours insists on absolute secrecy does he,' said Parker after Shriver had told him of the captain's wishes.

'He does, yes.'

'That's good,' said Priscilla. 'I agree with him.'

Linda Thompson nodded.

'Well, for now I guess we'll have to go along with what he says. But I may pay a call on him myself if we don't get somewhere soon.'

'He'd welcome that,' said Shriver. 'But to get back to the investigation, I'm pretty sure that Elvis has been taken out of the state, probably somewhere fairly remote.'

'So, what you mean is, you're guessing he's out of state.'

'Well now, Colonel, that's not quite fair. You see, we can't act on the information that we have until we've received word from the kidnappers.'

'What information?' sneered the Colonel. 'And why not?'

'The kidnappers may be dangerous. Acting without due care may put Elvis' life at risk.'

Priscilla and Linda nodded.

'Yes, so you say,' replied the Colonel.

Lieutenant Shriver squirmed.

Linda began to cry affectedly and Priscilla left the room, unsympathetic to such displays and beside herself with worry for her daughter's father, though she would never admit it.

'Captain Magill understands the situation, and if you wish to speak to him he'd be happy to confirm this. He is adamant that we keep a lid on it.'

'Anything else?'

Shriver hesitated for a moment before replying. 'Yes, Colonel. I think we may have to consider the likelihood that whoever kidnapped Elvis will sooner or later demand a ransom. It might therefore be sensible to have easy access to a sum of money in cash. I don't know how much but I would suggest something over a million dollars.'

Parker spluttered and was about to interject but Shriver continued without letting him. 'If this does happen we will need to have a go-between, that is someone who will deliver the money to some location. He or she will need to be absolutely trustworthy and, of course, in on the situation. I have someone in mind that will effectively kill two birds with one stone.'

'And who might that be?' asked Parker.

'Frankie Wilson of the Scimitar. Bring him into our confidence and he'll

stop snooping. That way we'll kill two birds with the same stone.'

Priscilla re-entered the room just as Shriver mentioned Wilson.

'You wanna tell the press... absolutely no, no, no, and I thought your Captain Magill...'

'I will talk to him first. We would have to insist on Wilson's silence until Elvis is returned unharmed of course.'

'But what if we tell him and he doesn't agree?' asked Priscilla.

'That's a chance we'll have to take but I think he'll take the bait,' said Shriver. 'If we promise him an exclusive afterwards, tell him the whole story, it'll be the scoop of a lifetime. He won't turn that down, especially if he plays a role in it. Also, he'll be on our side. Either way, he won't want to jeopardise the relationship he's built up with Elvis and the Colonel over the years.'

Parker, who had remained silent during this exchange, surprised everyone by agreeing with Shriver. 'That's an excellent idea, but we'll insist that Wilson stays silent until the whole business is resolved,' he said. In his mind he saw the newspaper headlines that would follow Frankie Wilson's 'exclusive' and how they would translate into record sales. He would need to speak to RCA about this, of course, renegotiate a deal so his and Elvis' income from those sales was assured, but it would surely dwarf the ransom he might have to pay to get Elvis back.

Priscilla was still sceptical. 'I don't know…' she began.

'Wilson wouldn't double-cross us,' said Shriver. 'There's too much at stake for him… his long relationship with Elvis, the scoop, the money he'd earn from it.'

Parker nodded. 'I agree Lieutenant… now go and do your work.'

Realising the meeting was over Shriver stood and left the room.

'Thanks detective,' said Lamar Fike as he left the room. 'Keep up the good work.'

'Show him out, Lamar,' said the Colonel, claiming the last word as usual.

Elsewhere at Graceland, Lisa-Marie Presley, still unaware of the fate that had befallen her doting father, was becoming restless, running from room to room in the way that spoilt children do when they are bored to tears with the company of adults. She appeared at the doorway of the living room just as Fike was showing Lieutenant Shriver from the room.

'Lisa, come in here please,' said her mother, rising from her seat. 'There's something we need to tell you. It's about daddy.'

Lisa Marie quietened down immediately. 'What's happened to him?' she asked.

Priscilla turned to the men in the room. 'Colonel, Lamar, Charlie, leave us alone please. Linda, you can stay.'

When the two women were alone with the little girl Priscilla began to speak. 'Your daddy is missing and we don't know where he is. We think some men have taken him somewhere against his will but we don't know for sure. He's probably alright but we are keeping the whole thing a big secret because as you know daddy is very famous. So we can't say anything to anybody. We have asked the police to help find him and they are doing their best.'

Lisa Marie began to sob. 'Will he be alright? Will he come home soon?'

'Of course he will darling,' replied Priscilla, taking her into her arms. 'And you have to be a brave girl in the meantime. Now promise me you'll be brave and be a good girl.'

Lisa Marie nodded. Linda Thompson left the room, leaving mother and daughter alone and thinking how well Priscilla had dealt with telling her daughter. Linda was due back in Hollywood the following day for an audition but had called to cancel. Not only didn't she want to be the only person in Los Angeles who knew what had happened to Elvis but she wanted to remain in Graceland while the investigation was continuing. She felt Priscilla needed an ally, another woman in which to confide.

Outside, in the hallway of Graceland, Colonel Parker was reading that day's Press Scimitar with its ELVIS MYSTERY headline. 'Shriver was right about Frankie Wilson,' Parker told Linda. 'He needs to be curbed.'

Linda glanced at the story. 'What if the kidnappers see this and think we've leaked something to the press?' she said, handing the paper back to the Colonel.

'That's possible,' replied Parker. 'But I doubt it. I'm more worried that other news media might read this story and follow it up themselves.'

Priscilla joined them and read the story herself. 'They might... God forbid they might... well, who knows what they or the kidnappers might do? Christ, I wish this whole darn business was over, it's driving me crazy. I just want Elvis back here where he belongs so he can be a daddy to Lisa Marie again.'

Priscilla turned to Linda and the two women went back into the room where Lisa Marie was playing. 'I'm glad you're here,' said Priscilla. 'I know Elvis was with other women while he was married to me, and I somehow accepted it, being as he was the man he was. But you came later, so I don't bear you any ill will. I know you love him and have his interests at heart.'

Relived that Priscilla had accepted her, she hugged Elvis' former wife. 'That means a lot a lot, thank you Priscilla,' she said.

'We have to work as a team, you and, me and make sure Parker doesn't get his way and tell the media.'

'I know. I don't trust his motives.'

'I never have,' replied Priscilla. 'Now why don't you go and see if you can persuade Vernon to leave his room and come down and eat something?'

Realising she'd effectively been dismissed Linda headed for the stairs.

'So, what do we do now?' Priscilla asked the Colonel, who entered the room as Linda left.

'Nuthin' we can do,' he replied. 'Maybe we just gotta sit tight, like the policeman says.'

'What do you mean?' retorted Priscilla. 'That can't be the end of it. The press certainly won't let that be the end of it. They won't leave us alone now, and it won't be long before the national news gets a hold of the story. We're going to have to deal with this reporter somehow. We can't let him write any more stories like this in the paper.'

'Well, we might just have to pay Frankie Wilson a visit like the Lieutenant said,' said Parker. 'In the meantime I need to go and make sure I have at least a million dollars I can get to in a hurry, and I might need to visit New York again. Lamar,' he called to Fike who was still standing by the open front door, 'can you drive me to my hotel?'

Back at his hotel, Parker placed a call to Rocco Laginestra in New York. 'Rocco, I'm coming back to New York in the next 24 hours. I want you to arrange for $1.5 million in cash to be made available to me. I don't care how you do it, just do so. In the meantime make arrangements to press up at least a million Elvis albums, Greatest Hits, Memphis, Sun recordings, Blue Hawaii, all the best sellers, and I want a new contract with a 20% royalty or I'll start talks with Ahmet Ertegun for a new deal for new records. This story will blow but not until after Elvis has been released. It'll be the biggest story since Kennedy was shot.'

'Are you sure?' Laginestra asked. 'I mean sure the story will blow.'

'Yes but not until Elvis is released. I may need the money to pay a ransom if we get a demand, and the police are certain we will and soon. Don't worry. You'll earn it back ten times over when this story becomes public.'

Parker replaced the receiver, lifted it again and redialled. 'Shriver, did you speak with Wilson?

'Yes, he'll meet us in the bar at your hotel at eight.'

Lieutenant Shriver drove straight to the police station and requested another meeting with Captain Magill. Ushered into his office moments later he handed the captain a copy of that day's Memphis Press Scimitar, drawing his attention to the ELVIS MYSTERY story. Magill read it attentively and put it down.

'This man must be silenced,' he said. 'At least for the time being. I haven't yet set a time limit on the news blackout, but if nothing happens… well we might have to revise out strategy. In the meantime though… we need to deal with this Wilson guy.'

'I agree captain,' said Shriver. 'And I think I know how to go about it.'

'It's a risky strategy but I don't see we have any other course of action,' said Magill after Shriver had outlined his plans for taking Frankie Wilson into their confidence. 'The sooner you meet with him the better. And let me know what he says. If he threatens to blow the whistle I think I know how to silence him. We have ways,' he added menacingly.

Frankie Wilson was in a state of extreme apprehension as he made his way to the Holiday Inn where Parker was staying. His story in that morning's Memphis Press-Scimitar had evidently touched a nerve with those surrounding Elvis – as he knew it would – but he was surprised that the call to arrange a meeting had come from a police lieutenant. He made his way to the bar, ordered a soft drink and sat down at a table well away from any other customers. He didn't have long to wait.

Colonel Parker and Detective Al Shriver made their way across the room at precisely eight o'clock. He'd met the Colonel on several occasions over the years and, like almost everyone else who came within orbit of Elvis' Machiavellian manager, was deeply intimidated by him. He recognised Shriver, although they'd never been formally introduced.

Wilson stood to receive them and all three sat down.

'Colonel, detective, how can I help you?' asked Wilson.

'Well,' said Shriver. 'We didn't like what we read in the paper this morning, that story you wrote.'

'I was only doing my job.'

'I appreciate that but it would have been better if before you wrote about the police and the Colonel here visiting Graceland, you asked us for a comment first.'

'I didn't think I'd get a response. Is Elvis still very ill?'

The question was directed at Parker who after lighting a cigar joined in the conversation for the first time. 'That's neither here not there,' he replied. 'As it happens Elvis is getting better, as far as we are aware.'

'I don't understand. If you don't know for sure…'

'The thing is,' said Shriver, 'if anything like that makes its way into your paper again, you might find that Elvis and the Colonel won't extend the hand of friendship any more.'

'I see,' said Frankie. 'OK. I won't write any more speculative stories like this so long as you tell me how Elvis really is. All I want to do is report the truth about his health. I've always been a friend to Elvis.'

'We know that,' said the Colonel. 'And we'd like you to

write stories that are true as well. Up to a point.'

'How do you mean?'

'What if we told you that Elvis wasn't here in Memphis at all, that he was missing, that we don't know where he is?'

'You've lost me,' said Frankie.

'What we're about to tell you is in the strictest confidence, do you understand?'

Wilson was becoming more curious by the minute. 'Of course,' he said. 'I might be a reporter but I know when to hold back on a story.'

'Good,' said Shriver, 'because this may well be your biggest story ever. Colonel, do you want to tell him?'

Parker shifted in his seat and blew out a cloud of cigar smoke that made Wilson recoil in his seat. Through the smoke he watched Parker's face. The famous manager seemed to be struggling for words, but eventually decided not to beat about the bush. 'We believe that Elvis has been kidnapped,' he said, staring intently at the reporter to see the effect of his words.

'This is a joke, right?' said Wilson. But he could tell by their faces that it was no joke.

'It's no joke,' said Shriver, and he was about to continue when the Colonel interrupted him.

'Lieutenant, let me finish,' he said. 'Mr Wilson, before I say anything more I want to say again that what we are about to tell you is in the strictest confidence. I want your solemn word that what we tell you now won't be repeated anywhere, at least not until after Elvis is released.'

'You have it,' said Wilson.

'And if you break that promise we cannot be responsible for what might happen to you,' said Shriver.

Wilson swallowed hard. He had no wish to end his

days in the Mississippi River.

'Well,' began the Colonel. 'It's like this…' and for the next 10 minutes he related the story of Elvis' abduction to the increasingly astonished newspaper reporter. Wilson was too stunned to speak, simply staggered. His newspaperman's instincts told him that this was the biggest newspaper story since the assassination of President Kennedy, bigger even than Neil Armstrong taking one giant step for mankind way up there on the moon. A scoop like this could make him a household word, like Bob Woodward and Carl Bernstein of the *Washington Post* who'd blown the Watergate affair. They might even make a film of it, with Dustin Hoffman or Robert Redford playing him in a starring role. Eventually the Colonel stopped talking.

'Why have you told me this?' he asked.

'We want you on our side. We want to enlist your help in finding Elvis.'

'How can I do that?'

'First of all by not writing any more stories that draw attention to Elvis right now. We think that other newspapers or media outlets might pick up on what you've written and start making inquiries of their own. We want Elvis' illness to have a low profile from now on. Maybe you can write a story that says he's still up at Graceland but his doctors have told him to take it real easy. You can quote me as saying he won't be playing shows again until at least December, like it's an 'exclusive' interview with Elvis' manager. Write just such a story and it'll take the heat off, cool things down.'

'OK, I can do that,' said Wilson.

'And there's another thing,' said Shriver.

'What's that?'

'You're good at snoopin', aren't you?'

'Yes, I'm a journalist. It's what we do.'

'Exactly, so you're good at snoopin'. Hang around the Graceland gates, talk to people, see if you can pick up any information. Someone might have seen something. You could help in that way.'

'OK, I'll do that,' said Wilson, eyeing the Colonel.

'So, we'll forget this matter of the story in the paper today, like it never even happened, if you are willing to offer your services.'

With Wilson's willingness to co-operate now assured, the Colonel wrapped up the meeting. 'No more stories like this, nothing more on Elvis, expect maybe something along the lines of he's resting at Graceland, getting over his illness.'

The reporter took a deep breath. 'OK, I'll write a story along those lines and make sure it gets in the paper tomorrow, and I'll see if I can sniff out anything from fans or anywhere else. But remember your side of this bargain. I get the exclusive when it's all over. Agreed?'

'Agreed,' said the Colonel, extending his hand towards the reporter – but like Priscilla Presley, Frankie Wilson didn't trust him any more than he'd trust a coyote that hadn't eaten for a week.

Chapter Seven

(October 8 & 9)

Blindfolded, Sandra stood before the man she had idolised since her teens. Incredulously, she heard Del's voice saying, 'Elvis, this is my wife Sandra. Maybe you could sing 'Love Me Tender' for her.'

Del removed Sandra's blindfold; she blinked. There, sitting on the bed, rumpled, dishevelled and unshaven, overweight and dressed in a scuffed black all-leather outfit, his unruly hair unlike she'd ever seen it before, was – unmistakeably – Elvis Presley, and her husband was handing him a guitar.

'Come on Elvis, sing,' said Del, raising his voice slightly.

'What the...,' cried Sandra but her words were silenced by a voice she knew well. The man of the bed cradled the guitar, struck a chord and began to sing the title song from his first movie. '*Love me tender...*'

Sandra couldn't believe what she was seeing and hearing. 'Oh ma go-ad, oh ma go-ad, oh ma go-ad.' She was shrieking now, barely able to look.

'Hush,' said Del, taking her hand. 'Elvis is singing for you.'

Sandra stopped screaming and gazed on disbelievingly. Roy looked on from the corner of the room, Del smiled and Elvis sang, his confidence increasing as he found his way into a song he'd sung hundreds of times before.

Elvis strummed the cheap guitar, the chords were far from perfect and the tuning was imprecise but there was something in the performance, his distinctive vocal style, that unmistakable three-octave range, that melted Sandra's heart. She was awestruck. As Elvis reached for the chorus she leaned against Del and gripped his hand tightly. It was a song of immense yearning, as tender as it was stately, and when Elvis reached the final line Sandra burst out crying, sobbing like a child whose soft toy was lost, great convulsions in waves that shocked the three men in the room.

Elvis put down the guitar and rose from the bed. He tried to walk towards her, shuffling like a man twice his age, deeply unsure of himself, but was held in check by the handcuff around his ankle and the bed leg. Sandra glanced up at his face, still handsome but bloated now, and a bit wary. She took a pace forward and stopped, trying to pull herself together. Then Elvis leaned towards her and touched her shoulder. 'Ah'm real sorry I cancelled that show back in Vegas ma'am,' he said in his inimitable southern drawl. 'I was sick, real sick. But I hope I can make it up to you now.'

Then, seemingly inspired by the occasion, he sat back down on the bed, picked up the guitar again and hit another chord. '*Well, it's a one for the money…*'

Sandra said nothing. She was 15 again, watching the Singer special on TV, only this time it was happening in front of her, Elvis in person singing just for her. Twice she pinched herself to make sure it wasn't a dream and as Elvis reached the punch line – '*Well, you can do anythang, but lay offa my blue suede…*' – she came to her senses and realised the implications of what she was seeing. It was beyond believable.

Elvis was about to begin the second verse of 'Blue Suede Shoes' when Sandra could take no more. 'Stop! Hold it there!' she yelled, throwing her husband's hand away.

'Please... just stop!'

Elvis brought the song to an abrupt halt and put down the guitar. 'I don't mind singing for you ma'am,' he said.

'Thank you,' she managed to say, before turning to Del. 'But this isn't how I wanted it to be, Del! I didn't want this.'

'But, honey...' he repeated, grabbing her arm.

Sandra struggled free of his grip and turned to face him. 'Just what in hell do the two of you think you're playin' at? What's going on here? How come Elvis is here? Did you kidnap him for me?'

Del smiled. 'Yes, sort of.'

'Oh no. Are you out of your mind? I cannot believe you kidnapped Elvis goddam Presley just to have him perform for me, like this. Just look at him. He's a wreck.'

'I did it for you,' said Del, simply.

Elvis looked on silently as Sandra dried her eyes. In truth, she didn't know what to think, to be angry at her husband for the foolishness in what he had done or grateful for the risk he had taken in a seemingly wilful, potentially disastrous, attempt to make her happy. 'Look,' she offered at last, nearing her husband. 'I am real happy, honey, I'm real flattered that you'd do this for me, I really am. But I still think this is the craziest thing in the world.'

'That's just what I said when Roy suggested it,' said Del.

'That's true,' said Roy. 'It was my idea, to make up for the disappointment of the cancelled show in Vegas.'

'You were right Roy, it is crazy. But I... I just don't know what to think. I'm speechless,' she added, leaning towards Del and squeezing his hand. 'Why don't we just go outside to talk alone?'

Once outside, she asked, 'So tell me, how did you do it? I want to know everything.'

'Well,' Del began, 'as I said, it was really Roy's idea. It

all started back at the end of August, after we'd got back from Vegas. You remember a night when I was late home, said I'd been at Roy's 'cos he wanted to show me a letter and some pictures from some old army buddy? Well, I wasn't telling you the truth. That was the night Roy came up with the idea and I went along with it…'

For the next half hour Del went into the details of how he and Roy had planned the kidnap, how they'd watched Graceland night after night, succeeded in snatching Elvis and brought him to the cabin, and how the whole thing was really so that they could get him to sing for her, to somehow make up for what he knew had been such a huge disappointment for her. She was flattered, of course, but she still thought she'd married a madman.

'Y'know he's not like I thought he'd be,' she said when Del had finished his story.

'What do you mean?'

'He's not as attractive as I thought he'd be. He's very overweight.'

'Real life never is. The Elvis you loved was a fantasy. In any case, he hasn't had a change of clothing for about 48 hours, or a wash.'

'I know it was a fantasy, but you've shattered it for me.'

'I didn't mean to.'

'I know you didn't, and it doesn't really matter. The fantasy was shattered when he cancelled that show. But what do we do now?' she asked.

'I guess we let him go.'

'Just like that?'

'Maybe Roy and me need to think about that. Let's go back inside.'

Inside the cabin Elvis and Roy were sat on the bed laughing.

'Y'know,' said Roy to Sandra, 'me n'Elvis, we're getting to be good buddies. Remember when I said I didn't much like him. Well, that's all changed, hasn't it El?'

'You never told me you didn't much like me?' said Elvis, smiling.

'Oh, that was before I knew you.'

The two men had evidently bonded while Del had been in Memphis collecting Sandra, and the change in Elvis was noticeable. Strange thought it might seem, he appeared relaxed, as if the change of air had done him good. He'd had to swallow some pride and act humble, and for 48 hours he'd been treated not as the King of Rock'n'Roll but as simply another human being, albeit one held captive. He was also very tired, as were his kidnappers. Dawn was approaching.

Del and Sandra opted to share two sleeping bags joined together on the mattress on the floor, while Roy would sleep out on the porch in a hammock they had rigged up. They checked on Elvis and as they closed and bolted the bedroom door behind them they noted that their prisoner was snoring lightly; evidently the exertions of the previous 24 hours had the same effect on him as the sleeping pills he downed so greedily in the past. Then Roy went outside with a can of beer and a lit cigarette, leaving Del and Sandra alone in the cabin together.

Lying snugly beside one another in their sleeping bags in the next room to Elvis, Sandra squeezed Del's hand and kissed him lightly on the lips. 'I wish we were really alone,' she whispered in his ear.

'Elvis is asleep,' said Del, kissing her back and manoeuvring his hand so that it rested between her legs. She was wearing a white t-shirt over loose-fitting linen trousers. Del deftly undid the top button and zip, and slipped his hand inside, seductively inching downwards towards the warmth of her centre.

'We can't... not with Elvis so close,' whispered Sandra, but her resolve soon faded as Del continued to kiss her and gently drew aside her underwear. Sandra turned on to her back and kissed him back, more urgently now, and responded to his caress, opening her legs so that his fingers might more easily find their way into her wetness. Del was adept at pleasuring his wife and Sandra soon became exquisitely aroused, moaning softly to herself as he continued to kiss her neck and probe her sex, and she was reaching a point of no return when in the room next to them they heard Elvis grunt and turn over in his sleep. The noise brought her to her senses. She reluctantly reached down and pulled Del's hand away. 'No... not now,' she murmured. 'Elvis can hear us and Roy might come back inside.'

'I thought it would turn you on to do it with Elvis asleep in the next room to us.'

'Oh, you know I love it when you touch me there and I wanted you to really... you know that... I was so turned on... but not now,' said Sandra. 'Not like this. Tomorrow we can get away from Elvis and be alone somewhere. I love you... I truly do.'

Del kissed Sandra again. 'I love you too,' he said as she turned over so that they lay together with her back pressed against him. She felt a reassuring hardness as Del put his arms around her waist and hugged her tightly. The last thing she heard before drifting off to sleep was snoring coming from the bedroom. So even Elvis snores, she thought to herself as she drifted off.

They slept late and made breakfast from the provisions

that Del had collected in Memphis. Elvis was sullen and uncooperative, last night's performance evidently forgotten. He asked to use the bathroom and was in there for almost 15 minutes before Del knocked on the door.

'You OK in there?'

'I'm sick. I need my meditation.'

Del opened the door ajar and passed Elvis the bottle of red pills and a mug filled with drinking water. Two minutes later Elvis emerged and sat back down on the bed.

'We brought you a change of clothing,' Del told Elvis after he'd retrieved the package from the truck. He took out the blue overalls, t-shirts and undershorts and placed them on the bed next to Elvis. Then he unlocked the handcuffs so that Elvis could undress and change.

'I don't wear denim jeans,' said Elvis. 'Only in my films. They're working man's clothes, poor man's clothes, and I ain't no poor man no more.'

'Well, it's all we got and you need to get out of those leathers. We got you the biggest size we could. It ain't easy to shop for clothes for a man as big as you.'

Elvis glanced down at the overalls on the bed. 'Elvis don't wear overalls,' he said, trying to sound defiant.

'In that case you don't get no breakfast,' said Del, turning on his heel and leaving the room, closing the door behind him.

It took about five minutes for Elvis to change his mind and his clothes. He took off everything he wore and put on the undershorts, a t-shirt and a clean pair of socks then finally stepped into the overalls, fastening the suspenders on each side. He was grateful he couldn't see himself in a mirror for he knew for sure that he looked like a farmhand in the kind of life he'd vowed to leave behind. It was humiliating for him to dress like this, and as he looked down at the shapeless, baggy jean trousers he made another vow to himself, that he would somehow escape from this mess and find his way home.

Elvis called out to his captors and all three entered the room.

Sandra gasped, and the two men found it difficult to hide their smiles. The transformation was stunning. No one spoke. Roy reaffixed the handcuffs around Elvis' ankle to the bed leg.

'Will you feed me now?' asked Elvis, as humbly as he could.

Sandra left the room and returned with a plate of bacon and eggs that she placed on the bed. Elvis ate hungrily while his captors watched and when he'd finished he turned to them. 'What are you going to do with me now?' he asked.

'That's for us to decide,' said Del. 'You'll know soon enough.'

When they too had eaten, Del, Roy and Sandra went out on to the porch. They brought with them Elvis' leather outfit, doused it with gasoline and ceremoniously burned it.

'Listen,' said Sandra as she watched the flames rise up and then die, 'how about you boys go out and talk about where we go from here? I'll clean up this place and make sure Elvis gets something more to eat and a decent rest while you're gone.'

'We'll go shooting again,' suggested Roy. 'Maybe try to catch a fish or two.'

Del hesitated. 'You think we should leave Sandra alone with him? Is that safe?' Well, at least his wife didn't seem to find Elvis as attractive in the flesh as he thought she would.

'He's still handcuffed to the bed. He won't try anything.'

'OK, let's do it then,' said Del. 'I think we can trust him.' Then he turned to Sandra, and kissed her hair. 'Watch him, watch he doesn't try something.'

Roy went back into the cabin bedroom and addressed Elvis. 'We're going on another hunting expedition. Sandra will stay here to look after you, but don't try anything. If you do you'll regret it.'

Then he checked the handcuffs and, satisfied, went outside to where Del was unloading more provisions from the truck. The two men left with loaded guns and two fishing poles, leaving Sandra to attend to domestic duties, watched by the man she had idolised since she was a teenager.

His right leg still chained to the bed leg, Elvis sipped water and watched through the bedroom door as she busied herself with clearing away the plates, sweeping the floor and washing down the table and chairs. She knelt down by the fireplace and cleaned the hearth, sweeping away ashes, and spread kindling before placing a couple of logs on top. He couldn't help but notice her gracefulness; she was evidently no stranger to hard work. As she bent down and rubbed the back of the chair with a cloth, she stopped suddenly, concerned.

'How long did you say the boys had kept you in here?' she called out, knowing that Elvis would hear her.

'I didn't,' he replied.

'Oh.'

'Well, the days sort of merge together when you're, you know...'

'No, I don't know,' she said.

'No, I don't suppose you would,' he mumbled, then, in an effort to make conversation. 'What did you say you did for work?'

'I didn't,' she echoed.

'Oh.'

'I've never done anything glamorous, so I wouldn't expect you to be interested. Actually, I do waitressing mostly, in Memphis.'

It was the first indication to Elvis that his kidnappers were from the city in which he lived. He'd already guessed as much but confirmation was welcome. 'I wasn't born this way, you know,' he said. 'My ma and pa were real poor folk.'

'I know.'

'I'm sorry I made you lose your job.'

Sandra walked into the bedroom and looked down at Elvis. He was sprawled on the bed. 'How did you know about that?'

'Your husband's friend told me. I am real sorry, though, ma'am.'

'You can call me Sandra.'

'Sandra,' he repeated. 'I like that name.'

It amused Sandra Pandel to hear Elvis Presley speak her name. And when she stepped out of the cabin and on to the porch outside, closing the door behind her, it amused her even more to realise that he was her prisoner. Hanging up damp cloths to dry and shaking the broom so that the dust blew up and away into the forest, she thought about the things she might have done with Elvis years before if only she'd had the chance, and laughed at herself now for having that chance and refusing to act on it.

They were wicked thoughts, those that occupied her

mind when she first saw him on that TV show back in December of 1968. He was so handsome then, just the most beautiful man she had ever seen, so much more desirable than the rock stars of the same era with their long, shaggy hair, patched jeans and shapeless t-shirts. She couldn't understand why her friends preferred them to Elvis who looked like a man to her, a real man. After she'd heard him sing and watched him move his hips in that black leather outfit, there really was nothing that she wouldn't have done for him then, and if that meant lying down beside him and letting him have his way with her, then she would have allowed it to happen, eagerly and without any hesitation on her part. The thought of Elvis taking her virginity was so exquisite that in her bed that night, after she'd undressed and bathed, she had caressed herself and brought herself to orgasm for the very first time, imagining Elvis whispering into her ear as she opened up for him and felt him enter her, and afterwards, as her teenage body settled down and the excitement subsided, she had fallen into a sleep so deep that in the morning she awoke feeling more alive than ever before. It wouldn't be the last time she thought about Elvis as she satisfied herself alone in bed, but later, after she had encountered real men, especially Del, she had ceased the habit, and now that Elvis, the real Elvis, was a few feet away from her, she shied away from any such thoughts and turned on her heel, retracing her steps back to the cabin where Elvis was waiting.

Closing the door behind her, she entered the bedroom. Her captive glanced up at her and was about to say something when she interrupted him.

'Do you remember that TV Special you did in 1968?' she asked,

'Yeah, I sure do,' replied Elvis. 'It saved my career. Man, I was so nervous. I was shakin' all over.'

'You didn't appear nervous to me. I watched it. I loved you in it. I've been a fan ever since that night. I was too young when you first started, and I didn't much like those films you were making, but that TV show was something else.'

'I nearly didn't do it,' said Elvis. 'Not the way it turned out. It was supposed to be a Christmas Special with me singing carols, maybe even dressed as Santa Claus.'

'Really?'

'Yeah. My manager thought that was best. The producer of the show had other ideas and I agreed with him. I needed to get back to signing and playing properly after all those movies. I was getting sick of them.'

'I saw some, after I'd seen the TV show,' said Sandra. 'I didn't like them much. Then a friend who was older told me to watch your early films, like Loving You and King Creole. They were good. I liked those. And Jailhouse Rock.'

'I wanted to be a real actor. Then the army got in the way.'

'Why did you join the army?'

'I had to. I was conscripted.'

'Yes, but you… surely you could have got some deferral, some kind of special assignment.'

'My manager said it was the right thing to do. He thought my fans would admire me for it.'

'Did you agree?'

'Yes, no… I don't know. I didn't really want to go. I was having too much fun. The army wasn't fun, not really. I went to Germany, that's where I met Priscilla.'

'I know. She was just a teenager. Do you still love her?'

'Yes… I, er, I still do. But she couldn't handle my

lifestyle. I guess it's not easy being Mrs Elvis Presley.'

'No, I don't suppose it is. I've seen some film of you performing before you went into the army, on TV shows. I loved you when you were young, but the army seemed to do something to you, to take your life away, if you know what I mean.'

Elvis hesitated before continuing the conversation. During his entire career he'd never given a serious, considered interview, never talked with anyone much about his inner feelings, let alone a newspaper or magazine interviewer. Now this girl, whose husband had kidnapped him, was asking the kind of questions that he'd avoided answering all his adult life. Colonel Parker had always fobbed off interviewers with trite remarks or made excuses, telling Elvis that this was the way to retain his mystique. That might have been the case at first but now it had backfired with the result that many thought he was a weirdo, a recluse, like some sort of fossilised dinosaur. Sooner or later, he thought, morbid curiosity would expose his demons to the world.

'You saying the army killed me?' he eventually said.

'In a way, yes,' replied Sandra.

'Well, maybe you're right,' admitted Elvis. 'I made all those lousy films because that was the best way for me to make money. I guess I... er, I lost my way.'

'What changed?' asked Sandra.

'Lots of things. I got married. The films stopped making money. I saw what else was happening in the music world. I needed to reassert myself. There was more money to be made from playing concerts and touring. The TV show was the best way to make a comeback.'

'If it wasn't for that TV show I wouldn't have seen you and become a fan.'

'Then if it wasn't for that TV show, I wouldn't be here right now.'

'I guess not,' said Sandra, smiling.

'Will you sit next to me on the bed?'

Sandra did as Elvis asked but kept her distance, even as he leaned towards her and touched her hand. 'I'm real lonely most of the time,' he said, lowering his voice so that it appeared to Sandra almost as if he was making a confession. 'Oh, I'm surrounded by people all the time in my house, and when I'm performing there's thousands of fans cheering at me, but inside my soul I'm desperately lonely. I don't know what to think half the time… this life of mine. I hate to be alone. I get angry with people, bored easily. I buy things for people, cars, jewellery, so they'll like me, so they'll love me, but I don't know whether they do or not. They think I'm strange, that I'm stupid, uneducated. I'm like a caged animal. And I don't mean here, chained to this bed in this place… I mean all the time, like I can't get out.'

'Would you want to?' asked Sandra. 'Would you want a normal life? Your voice… would you change…?'

'My singing?' interrupted Elvis. 'I think maybe this gift I have to sing means I was specially chosen by God to do something special on this earth, to do something more than just entertain but I don't know what that is and the temptations get in the way. So I'm alone inside myself thinking about it and it drives me to do things that I know are wrong.

'Sometimes I wanna… I just wanna be normal. I just want to do normal things, like walk down a street, walk into a shop, buy something, or eat in a restaurant, with no one staring at me, no one making a fuss. Being famous like I am is like being a beautiful woman that everyone stares at… the men because they desire her and the women because they envy her, and I'm like that beautiful woman except that it's the other way around, the men envy me and the women desire me. So I'm not a person any more, I'm… I'm like a work of art, a statue. I want to be a person, just an ordinary person. But I know I can't. I'm Elvis and I can't stop being Elvis and I never will.'

Elvis paused. He hadn't opened his heart to anyone like this in years, not even Priscilla, but this girl Sandra, this fan whose husband had kidnapped him, had somehow brought something out of him that he'd never felt before. There was no stopping him now. 'All these people depend on me,' he continued. 'I can't stop. I'm on a permanent roundabout, making records, making movies, playing shows. I can't switch off, ever. Even at home, at Graceland, I have to be Elvis, the singer, the King of Rock'n'Roll. And in the middle of it all I'm real lonely. Everyone wants to talk to me but I don't have anyone to talk to, not really talk. It's, 'Yes Elvis. Whatever you say Elvis, of course Elvis.'

'And now here I am dressed in these overalls like a common working man which is something I never ever wanted to be, and something I vowed never to be again, like my pa was. So I suppose in a way, being here has fulfilled that dream, to be normal. I don't like it, I really don't. I feel like a fool in these clothes, like some country bumpkin.'

Sandra gazed at his bloated face, realising that she was as close to discovering the soul of Elvis as anyone ever had. 'Surely there are advantages to being Elvis,' she said.

Elvis laughed. 'Yes, I'm rich, but the more money I have the more I spend, the more money I need. I have my own planes but I'd rather have someone who loved me for who

I am and not what I am.'

'You have a wonderful voice. That voice melts hearts.'

'Yes, I can sing, I know. I love to sing. I'm paying the price for my voice.'

'Can you sing for me again?' asked Sandra.

'But I thought you didn't want me to. Last night you told me to stop.'

'That was last night. I was in shock. I've changed my mind.'

'I can't sing like I used to.'

'Yes, you can, and I know you need a band to back you up, but I love your voice, and I want to hear you sing again.'

'Well, I guess so.'

'Can you sing 'Suspicious Minds'? It's always been one of my favourites.'

'Mine too.'

Elvis took up the guitar and cleared his throat. This time, however, he looked nervous, unaccustomed to the intimacy of such a tiny audience. He strummed the opening chords, somehow conjuring up the tension of Mark James' tale of romantic paranoia and deceit, and began to sing to Sandra who got down from the bed and sat on the floor opposite him, closed her eyes and leaned back against the bedroom door.

'We're caught in a trap... I can't walk out...'

Elvis sounded nervous, unsure of himself, as if he realised that the words of the song might refer to his present situation. His voice faltered over the next line.

'Because I l-love you too much baby...'

Sandra opened her eyes. It seemed to her that Elvis's tripping over the word 'love' revealed an underlying insincerity. Elvis continued, striving to rescue himself, and sang with all his heart. Indeed, the words were more meaningful to him in his present situation than they had ever been before.

'Why can't you see, what you're doing to me, when you don't believe a word I say?'

Sandra didn't believe him. To her, he was trying too hard and the result was a pale imitation of a great icon, her cherished idol. She closed her eyes again and tried to imagine herself in a concert hall with Elvis up on stage.

'We can't go on together, with suspicious minds, and we can't build our dreams, on suspicious minds...'

Somehow Elvis found his way back into the song as the verse moved into the chorus. Sandra felt it too, relaxing into a dreamlike state, again overwhelmed by the sensation of having Elvis Presley sing to her and her alone. With her eyes closed she didn't notice that although Elvis was still singing he had stopped playing the guitar. And then there was black...

Sandra slumped down onto the floor as Elvis leaned over her, holding the guitar in the air above his head ready to deliver a second blow if the first failed to render her unconscious. There was no need. Blood oozed from the side of her head and she lay still. Elvis despised himself for what he'd just done. He pushed Sandra's comatose body aside and hauled himself back onto the bed, and with all his strength dragged the bed across the room with his chained leg, angling it so it would go through the door, into the main room and over the short distance to the fireplace where he'd seen a small axe used for chopping wood. It took him about five minutes to hack through the chain between the handcuffs and the bed leg, and though he bruised his ankle in the process and had to walk away with the link still around it, he was free at last.

Elvis Presley staggered out of the cabin, sucked in some fresh mountain air and ran up the dirt track that he assumed would lead to a road with cars and people. It was a long climb and at the top of the track there was another ridge, too steep for him to climb. Elvis realised he was probably going in the wrong direction, so he retraced his steps for ten minutes and took another path that led away from the valley and, he hoped, towards a highway, cars and freedom.

About three miles away in the opposite direction Del and Roy trudged down the Kentucky mountainside, Roy swinging a bunch of dead but still-warm rabbits over his shoulders and Del carrying a pair of bass and a rainbow trout.

'I don't like leaving Sandra with Elvis,' said Del, not for the first time.

'We should get back.'

'You worried he'll try something on with her?' said Roy, smiling. 'Don't you trust her with Elvis?'

'Oh, I trust her alright. It's Elvis I don't trust.'

It took them another hour to reach the cabin and when they did they were puzzled to see no wood-smoke rising from the chimney. Lowering their voices to a whisper, concerned that an intruder had discovered Elvis and Sandra, they approached the doorway cautiously. Del entered first, opening the cabin door, his rifle cocked. The half-light fanned out into the empty room. They found Sandra on the floor in the bedroom, her golden-yellow hair matted on one side where it was stained with blood.

'Sandra!' called Del, rushing towards her. 'Quick, Roy, get some light in here!'

Del cradled Sandra in his arms and she began to

murmur faintly. 'Her head's bleeding,' he said. 'Wake up, honey, come on, tell me what happened.'

Del moved Sandra to a sitting position as Roy brought a damp towel over to rinse the cut over her left eye.

'Honey, talk to me.'

Sandra opened her eyes slightly.

'Ow.'

'It's ok, we're gonna clean it up. Tell me what happened.' He was dabbing her forehead with the towel, wiping away the clotted blood.

'It was all those bright colours, Del. It was wonderful.'

Her husband looked confused. 'What are you talking about?'

Sandra opened her eyes fully and looked around.

'Oh.' She seemed surprised to see the two men. 'I just had the weirdest dream about Elvis Pres... about Elvis... it wasn't a dream, was it?'

'No, honey, it wasn't, now tell us what he did to you.'

'Did to me? Who?'

'Elvis, honey, tell us what Elvis did to you.'

'Well, nothing, I mean he sang to me, that was all.'

'I know he sang to you, we were all here,' said Del.

'She's concussed, buddy,' said Ray. 'I'll get some more water for her head.'-

'No,' Sandra insisted, 'it was just me and Elvis.'

'What do you mean, it was just you and Elvis?'

Del's response jolted Sandra back to her senses.

'Nothing,' she quickly added. 'It was just a dream. I was dreaming just now, dreaming about Elvis.'

'So, tell us what he did.'

'He must've hit me. Real hard. He hit me with the guitar.' Sandra flinched at the shock of the cold water touching the wound as her husband gentled dabbed it.

'Yeah, well, we're gonna get that fat son of a fuckin' bitch for that,' said Roy.

'He could be anywhere by now,' said Del. 'He may even have been picked up.'

'How long ago did it happen?' asked Roy.

'I have no idea,' replied Sandra. 'Two hours, maybe three.'

'Well, it's a long way back to any major routes,' said Roy. 'Besides, it'll get dark soon, so no point in looking for him tonight. We'll have to go after him at first light tomorrow.'

As I happened, at the precise moment that Del and Roy reached the cabin Elvis was hopelessly lost in the hills of Kentucky, tired, cold and hungry with no prospect of sleep, warmth or food.

He couldn't remember the last time he'd had to sleep rough, unless it was in his army days back on manoeuvres in Texas or Germany, but at least the army had given him a tent and sleeping bag and something to eat. Having assumed wrongly that he was close to a highway, he'd lost his way in the twilight and strayed from the track, then settled down in a clearing, leant up against a tree and stared up at the starlit sky, unable to relax. The noises of the forest spooked him. Every so often he'd hear the sound of some animal calling to another, or a bird in flight or something moving in the undergrowth. He was hoping that nothing too dangerous was out there.

In fact Elvis was surrounded by squirrels, rabbits, raccoons, bobcats, wild turkeys, foxes and otters. Deer and elk were also close at hand, and in the sky above were waterfowl of all types. He'd never been remotely interested in wildlife, nor had to fend for himself in the situation he now found himself. As the night descended he wished he'd stayed in the cabin and deeply regretted hitting the woman over the head with that guitar, not least because the chances were pretty strong that the two men would come looking for him in the morning, and probably find him and wreak revenge.

He remembered the conversation he'd had with the woman, how he'd opened himself up to her. He hadn't meant to lull her into a false sense of security that would enable him to overpower her in the way he had. It just happened that way. When she closed her eyes he couldn't stop himself from hitting her with the guitar and escaping. Now he wasn't so sure it was such a good idea.

Elvis was fortunate that it wasn't cold in Kentucky in September, and he was relieved when dawn finally broke. He was ravenously hungry. He decided to try and retrace his steps to the cabin.

Around about the same time Elvis had made his break for freedom, the RCA Records executive Lear jet carrying Rocco Laginestra touched down on the runway at Memphis airport. Laginestra took a taxi downtown to the Holiday Inn where Colonel Parker was staying and where his secretary had booked him a suite that adjoined the Colonel's. They had important business to discuss.

It took Parker about five minutes to explain to Laginestra where things stood, that Elvis was still missing, that a reporter was snooping around and that the only way to silence him had been to bring him into their confidence with a promise that he would have the exclusive story once Elvis was freed and back at Graceland. From their point of view, it didn't really matter whether this happened before or after Elvis was released, assuming that he was eventually released of course. When the story broke Elvis would be in the headlines all over the world and record sales would soar. Stocks therefore needed to be high.

'We can rescind any previous agreements and offer you, sorry Elvis, an extra 50 cents per album,' said Laginestra.

'We want an extra $2 an album,' replied the Colonel. 'And we want $1.5 million up front. I need it in cash in case we have to pay off a ransom. I ain't paying it myself.'

'One and a half fucking million,' spluttered Laginestra. 'How do you know the kidnappers will ask for that?'

'We don't. But it's a nice round sum, and it can't be far off the mark.'

'I might need to speak to the board.'

'Bullshit Rocco. You can raise that much tomorrow if you want.'

'I don't know about the two dollars an album. That won't leave us much.'

'Yes, it will.'

'How about one dollar?'

The Colonel thought for a minute.

'One dollar on the first million sold and two dollars 50 cents thereafter?'

'Two dollars and a quarter thereafter?' countered Laginestra.

'Worldwide.'

'Done.'

Negotiating with Colonel Parker was like negotiating with a great white shark, though Laginestra, not for the first time.

'Get back to New York tomorrow and make the arrangements. Draw up the papers for me to sign on this new agreement, get the money in cash and talk to your production people so the pressing plant can start rolling,' ordered Parker.

Laginestra, who was more used to giving orders than taking them, nodded his assent and returned to his own suite where he spent an uneasy night before taking the Lear jet to New York the following morning.

As Parker concluded his negotiations with Laginestra, Frankie Wilson was
typing up his latest story on Elvis.

'Reports that Elvis Presley's health is deteriorating may have been premature. According to Colonel Tom Parker, Elvis' personal manager, the singer is recovering his health at Graceland but has been warned by doctors to take it easy which is why he hasn't been seen in the grounds at any time during the past week.

'Elvis is recuperating well,' Colonel Tom told me in Memphis last night. Speaking exclusively to the Press-Scimitar he said: 'I have been following Elvis' progress closely, visiting him in Memphis, along with Priscilla, Elvis' former wife, who has brought their daughter Lisa Marie to spend time with her father while he gets better. I am confident he'll have recovered in time for a season of shows in Las Vegas in December that will make up for the cancelled shows in August.'

'Colonel Parker, who rarely gives interviews, seemed cautiously optimistic that a full recovery was on the cards for his famous client. 'Elvis has been working hard, recording here at his home in Memphis, doing shows and it was getting on top of him,' he told me. 'Now that he can relax it'll help him to get better. His doctors are in attendance daily, and nurses from the Baptist Hospital have been visiting to check

on him. He'll be up and about very soon.'

'Colonel Parker stressed that fans who bought tickets for the cancelled shows in August would be able to exchange them for tickets for the December shows at no extra cost. 'Elvis wants to make it up to those fans who were disappointed by the cancellation,' added the Colonel. 'He hates to let fans down and I can promise some great shows come December.'

After he'd written the story Wilson headed over the offices of the Press Scimitar to hand it in to the subs desk in time for it to appear in the following day's edition. Then he headed out down Elvis Presley Boulevard to fulfil the second part of the bargain he'd struck with Parker, still unsure whether he could trust him but at the same time realising he had little choice.

Wilson parked his car near the cafes opposite Graceland. He ordered a drink in a bright and bustling bar in the parade of stores and restaurants opposite Graceland. It was a popular hangout for Elvis fanatics to meet up and discuss anything and everything Elvis.

He took his drink to a vacant table near the window. On the adjacent table were two girls chattering, eating Elvisburgers and drinking strawberry milkshakes. They were evidently excited by having just seen Elvis in the grounds, up on the hill near the pillared entrance, playing with his daughter Lisa Marie.

'Hey girls,' said Wilson, making his move. 'Did I hear you say you'd seen Elvis at Graceland?'

The girls turned to stare at him.

'You sure it was Elvis?' he asked, knowing perfectly well that no one would have seen Elvis at Graceland for at least three days.

'Yeah, sure I am. He's gone back inside now, though,'

said one of them. 'But he was out with a nurse just a few moments ago playing with his little girl. He seemed pretty weak, but he waved to all us fans.'

'We're going back out there when we've eaten!' said the other.

'Are you here often, mister?' asked the first girl again.

'Every week, I s'pose,' said Wilson. 'When I get enough time in my lunch break.'

'Oh, yeah? What d'you do?'

'I'm a... mechanic.'

'Why ain't you in your overalls, then?'

'I've got the day off today – actually, I've got a week's holiday.'

'That's cool.'

'You girls from round here?'

'Nah,' said one who was seated on the other side of the table. 'We're from Nashville. 'We make it up here when we can. We work in the office of a country music publisher.'

'Hey, mister, what's yer name?'

'Fr-Freddie,' said Frankie.

'Wanna hang out at the gates with us, Freddie? Would be nice to hang with a Memphis guy.'

'Oh, I dunno, I have some things I need to do,' said Frankie, not wishing to sound too eager.

'Aw, please mister?'

'Well, alright,' he added. 'Maybe for a while, then.'

The girls smiled.

Inside Graceland Charlie West stepped out of the black leather outfit and took off the sunglasses and Elvis wig he'd been wearing. 'How long do I have to keep up this charade?' he asked Lamar Fike.

Chapter Eight

(October 10)

Arriving at the RCA offices in New York by mid-morning the following day, Rocco Laginestra, as the head of the company, had little difficulty extracting one and half million dollars in cash from the accounts department. A call was made to a bank and two security guards with the required ID sent to pick it up. Rocco then instructed the company's in-house lawyers to prepare contracts that reflected his newly negotiated royalty deal with Colonel Parker for future Elvis Presley record sales. Like all accountants and lawyers they were discrete and did not question the reasons for these demands. Then he contacted his production manager and instructed him to press up three million Elvis records, the best-selling hits compilations, the albums recorded in Memphis in 1968 and the Blue Hawaii film soundtrack, his own personal favourite. When the production manager, who was less discrete than the company lawyers, inquired why so many records were to be manufactured Rocco explained that Elvis' poor health indicated that it was wise to have plenty of stock.

'Is Elvis going to die?' asked the man at the production plant.

'We will all die sometime,' replied Rocco, 'and so will Elvis. I can say no more.' The message was duly conveyed.

When Rocco left the office that night he took the money home with him to his flat in Manhattan, locked it in his personal safe and called a delighted Colonel

Parker to tell him all was in order. Parker assured him he would be on the first flight to New York the following day.

Back in Memphis that morning, Lieutenant Al Shriver got his first stroke of good fortune. He was in his office when the phone rang; an internal call from the sergeant on the front desk who told him that a member of the public had walked in off the street to report a suspicious incident. As luck would have it, Shriver was the only detective available. 'Send him up,' he told the sergeant.

Shriver flipped open his notebook and stared across the table at a well dressed man who at first refused to give his name. Asked to make a statement, he shifted uneasily in his chair and told Shriver that four nights ago he'd witnessed a series of odd events in Memphis and that instead of keeping it to himself had finally decided to report it to the police.

'So what did you see?' asked the Detective.

'Well, I was walking near the Shelby Drive freeway ramp,' he replied. 'It was late, after midnight, maybe getting on for one or so.'

Shriver's antennae began to hum. 'You were parked up?'

'Well, no, I was taking a stroll,' the man half-whispered.

'A stroll?' repeated Shriver. 'Near the freeway?' He sat up taller. 'So, let me get this straight. You were taking a stroll near the freeway after midnight when you were witness to something strange?'

'Yes, sir,' replied the man cautiously.

'Were you alone?'

'No.'

'Who was with you?'

'I'd rather not say.'

The detective scribbled some notes in his pad and surveyed him. He looked culpable somehow, as if coming in to make this report was not just against his better judgement but also a strain. 'Could you explain why you were on foot near the freeway at that time of night?' he asked.

'I believe that's my business,' muttered the man cagily, averting his eyes to the floor. 'I ain't done nuthin' wrong.'

'I didn't say you had. And someone was with you?'

'No. I mean, yes,' he hurriedly corrected himself and leaned in towards the detective. 'You see, I'm a married man,' he said, lowering his voice. 'I was with a woman friend.'

Shriver nodded and decided not to pursue this line of questioning in case the man clammed up. 'OK, but you should have reported this sooner. You needn't have worried, we're very strict on confidentiality, you know?'

'Yes, it was wrong of me.'

'Anyhow, it doesn't matter now. Just tell me everything.'

'Well, we was walking along the left side of the road just before the freeway ramp, minding our own business, when I heard some motorbikes tearing towards us real fast, engines revving like hell. It was dark, though the moon gave a little light, and I could make out two bikes riding side by side and another two closing in on them. Soon, the ones closing in swerved in front, forcing them to stop.'

Al Shriver tried to hide his excitement as he continued to take notes.

'Did they see you?'

'No, I don't think so. We hid behind some bushes nearby and kept real still.'

'Good. And...?'

'And that's when it got rough.'

'Rough?'

'There was a gun shot.'

Shriver felt his heart beat faster. Elvis might have been shot. 'Was anybody...' he hesitated... '... hit?'

'It seemed to me the shot was fired into the air.'

'You sure about that,' asked Shriver.

The man nodded. He couldn't fail to notice that the detective was unusually excited by what he'd been told, and that he was hanging on to his every word.

'Go on, what happened next?'

'Er... it's hard to remember exactly but there were raised voices and then there was another gunshot and one of the riders went down.'

Shriver turned pale as chalk: 'Down?'

'I think they shot at his bike. It fell over with him on it. Then the other attacker shone a flashlight at the second rider. He was a big fat guy...'

'Who?' asked Shriver. 'The guy with the flashlight or the guy on the bike?'

'The guy on the bike, and there was more shouting and the attacker kicked the bike over, and knocked the fat guy over too. Then the fat rider took his helmet off but it was too dark to make him out, and that's when the attackers made him walk under the freeway ramp. I couldn't see what was happening, but before long they came out without the fat guy then rolled the other biker into the undergrowth. I think they'd knocked him unconscious.'

'And you were still hiding in the bushes?'

'We had no choice. We had to wait there. If we'd left the bushes we would have been seen. They might have shot us. We weren't willin' to risk it.'

'OK.' Al scribbled some more.

'Then one of the attackers rode off and about 20 minutes later, about one o'clock I guess, he pulled up again, only this time in a truck.'

'You waited around for 20 minutes?'

'Like I said, we couldn't move without being seen by the guy who stayed behind.'

'This truck... what colour was it?'

'White... a white flat bed truck, a Ford I think. The back was empty.'

'Good... and what happened next?'

'Next, they hid the two bikes in the bushes, bundled the fat guy into the truck and it headed back towards the city. One guy was driving it and the other guy followed on his bike. And later, maybe about ten, 15 minutes we saw the same truck heading back towards the freeway again. I swear it was the same truck. They took no notice of us walking on the sidewalk.'

'Did you catch any conversation earlier?'

'Oh, not really, the wind was blowin' and there was traffic passing on the freeway. I only caught the odd word.'

'Such as?'

'Well, 'motherfucker' was one of them.'

'Who said that?'

'The guy with the gun.'

'Who was he shouting at?'

'To the guy on the bike. The one they knocked unconscious. He was threatening him.'

'Anything else you remember?'

'No. Expect that I think they shoved the fat guy into the truck, like they were taking him somewhere.'

'Mmm,' said the Detective, his brain whirring. 'Don't tell anyone else about this, and tell you girlfriend to keep quiet about it too.'

'Oh, she won't say a word,' said the man. 'She got a husband too. That's why I didn't report it earlier. She didn't want me to say anything at all to anybody. 'Ain't no good gonna come of this if you go telling anyone,' she said. She's scared of her husband. He's a bully and a drunk.'

Shriver finally persuaded the witness to give his name and address and a phone number, took down the details and showed him out. It was unlikely he'd need to interview him again, or his companion. Wasting no time, he went to investigate any recent reports of white Ford trucks speeding along Route 55 North two nights ago. There were none.

At Graceland, the word had spread among fans outside the gates that Elvis was back at the house, and they were gathering in their numbers, keen to catch a glimpse of him and reassure themselves that he was recovering his health. The latest Memphis Press Scimitar article by Frankie Wilson had been widely read among fans and both Priscilla and Linda were concerned about the ever-increasing numbers outside the gates. It didn't help that Lisa Marie had persisted in racing her golf cart around the mansion grounds while Charlie, given the unenviable task of keeping her away from the gates, was preparing for a reappearance as Elvis in the grounds, this time with his hair dyed black.

'Does this stuff wash out easily?' Charlie asked

Priscilla as he stared at his reflection in the mirror. His normal light brown hair was now jet black, but with the slight purple tint that invariably occurs with black dye.

'No,' she replied. 'It'll need to grow out.'

'How long will that take?'

'As long as your hair takes to grow. Get it cut short after Elvis returns and you'll be back to your regular colour in no time.'

After Elvis returns, thought Priscilla as she rinsed Charlie's hair with cold water and then blow-dried it, puffing it up into a thick glossy mane. When will that be? And where was he now? And how was he coping?

Amongst those close to Elvis, no one knew better than Priscilla how helpless he really was. Unaccustomed to the real world, dependent entirely on his support mechanism and hopelessly adrift amidst normality, Elvis simply didn't relate to situations, to people and things, like others. He'd lived in a goldfish bowl since the mid-Fifties, rarely leaving it except when he was in the army and even then he was separated from reality, as serving soldiers so often are. With all of his needs catered for by others, Elvis was the very opposite of self-sufficient, whatever that was; simultaneously the neediest man she'd ever encountered yet at the same time in need of nothing. Elvis was a paradox, reared on a diet that had left him as helpless as a child when he wasn't surrounded by his courtiers.

Then there was his temper. Elvis could fly off the handle at the slightest provocation as she had cause to discover on many occasions. He could be selfish and manipulative, determined to get his own way and prone to riding roughshod over anyone who disagreed with him. He disliked negativity and being told what to do.

He moulded individuals into creatures that suited his purpose, none less so than herself whose image he had personally created; a living doll whose clothes, make-up, hairstyle and personality were carefully sculpted by him. During the early years of their relationship, any deviation from this model on her part was met with either an outburst of volcanic proportions, stony silence or, at the most extreme, threats of dismissal that meant he would return her to her family. Whoever had kidnapped him, thought Priscilla, would soon realise what a handful he could be.

Turning her attention back to what Charlie might wear, Priscilla selected some casual clothes that Elvis often wore around the house, light slacks with flared bottoms and a dark red velvet shirt with oversized collar. Charlie, who wasn't so slim himself, fitted reasonably well into them, though the slacks were a bit loose around the waist, even with one of Elvis' outsize buckled belts. Priscilla added a gold chain that she draped around his neck and a matching bracelet. Finally she slipped three jewelled rings on his fingers.

Charlie looked at himself in the mirror and realised that if he sneered, twisting his lip in the way that Elvis had made his own, he could pass off for his boss, at least from a distance. He went downstairs and into the living room, where Vernon, Lamar Fike and Linda Thompson greeted him with smirks. He turned very red.

'Hey, I think I look pretty good!' he announced.

Lisa Marie sauntered in dragging a teddy bear upside down by its legs, then stopped to scrutinise Charlie.

'Are you tryin' to look like my daddy?' she asked, matter-of-factly.

Priscilla, who had followed Charlie downstairs, felt a

twinge of remorse. 'Yes, well, Charlie's going to make an extra special effort to play with you this time, he's gonna take you to the movies and pretend to be your daddy, but you must promise you'll go along with the game.'

'Okayye,' sighed Lisa wearily. 'But I want daddy to come back. I'd rather go the movies with my real daddy.'

Up in the hills of Kentucky, Del and Roy had woken early to resume their search for Elvis, drifting a considerable distance from the cabin as they rummaged around in the undergrowth. After four hours of skirting Lake Cumberland they had caught neither hide nor hair of him. Back at the cabin Sandra, recovering from her ordeal, waited for them. She'd woken up with sore head but had no other ill effects aside from a tiny graze above her left eye.

'Let's get back and eat,' said Del, gazing out into the distance at the grey line of mountains against the horizon. 'I'm hungry.'

'OK. We'll try again later, in the opposite direction,' said Roy, who was carrying a rifle and seemed prepared to use it should they find their prey. 'I wanna get that fat bastard. He hurt Sandra, and I aim to make him pay for that.'

'Me too. We'll stay out here till dark if we have to, and keep trying, and search tomorrow if we don't find him.'

'But what if we don't find him tomorrow?' asked Roy. 'If he gets back to Memphis, we're history. By the time we get up in the morning and begin another search he could be on his way back here with cops, if he isn't already.'

Del turned in the direction of the cabin. 'He doesn't know where he is. For all Elvis knows he could be anywhere in Tennessee or Georgia or anywhere where there's mountains like this. It's a big country. In any case he ain't fit enough to reach a main road, even if he knew which way to walk.'

'He'll know where he is if he reaches the highway,' said Roy. 'After lunch we'll search in the other direction.' The attachment to Elvis that Roy discovered when they were alone in the cabin was rapidly declining while his frustration at being unable to find him only worsened his mood.

'I think Elvis might find it hard to get anywhere even if he does reach the road,' said Del. 'He has no money. Imagine trying to explain who he is to someone who picks him up. And he ain't exactly one for hitching is he?'

Roy could see the funny side. 'Imagine some dude stopping and finding Elvis... I'd like to film that, sure sounds like some Candid Camera thing to me.' He looked up at the clouds drifting across the sky. 'I'd say the weather's turning, so let's eat and get out looking again as soon as we can.' Taking up a stick he had found earlier, he began thrashing at the undergrowth.

'Careful,' warned Del, as they neared cabin, 'you don't wanna alert him if he is in there.'

'Don't I?' said Roy, to which Del only shrugged. Even Sandra probably wouldn't care much about Elvis's well-being right now, Del thought.

After a quick lunch they went out again, this time driving Del's truck along the track that led from the cabin to the road, stopping after about half a mile to head back into the undergrowth. It was then that they noticed traces of a recently flattened trail. Ray cocked his rifle.

Elvis heard them coming. He'd spent his first night out in the open since he was on army manoeuvres back in

1958, and he was feeling about as bad as he'd ever felt. Hopelessly lost and unable to cover himself, with only the white t-shirt to keep out the cold, he'd shivered as darkness fell; a combination of the chilly night and his own deteriorating health had brought him about as low as he thought possible. As the hours passed and he stared up at thousands of stars, he realised the utter stupidity in thinking he might somehow escape out here in the open country. Forced to decide whether to give himself up or hide, he opted to spend the night in the open and give himself up the following day by trying to retrace his steps back to the cabin. He knew that even if he stayed hidden his captors would keep on coming and find him eventually. So he called out, and Del and Roy were on to him in a flash. He looked a sorry sight, even more unkempt than when they last seen him. Roy pointed his gun at Elvis.

'Don't shoot,' said Elvis. 'I'm sorry for what I did. It was… it was wrong of me.'

'Give me one good reason why I shouldn't kill you,' said Roy.

'Because I'm worth more to you alive than dead,' replied Elvis.

Del walked up to Elvis and punched him in the face. 'That's for what you did to my wife,' he said, walking back to where Roy was standing, still pointing the rifle at Elvis' head. 'I'll get some rope,' he said, making his way back to the truck.

'Kneel down Elvis,' Roy ordered.

Elvis got down on his knees. 'Now stay right there you sonofabitch.'

When Del returned they tied his arms behind his back and frogmarched him to the truck, then they tied his legs together and bundled him into the back before setting off for the cabin.

Inside, Sandra was sprinkling some cracked black pepper into another rabbit stew and tasting a little from the edge of a ladle. It was piping hot so she had to blow on it first and as she did so she heard the sound of the truck pulling up outside. Abandoning the ladle, which slid into the bubbling casserole, she dashed outside.

Del and Roy alighted from the truck and released the backboard. Then they pushed Elvis hard so that he fell out. Elvis landed on the ground and cried out, obviously hurt.

'Just look at what we found out there,' cried Del, his face aglow.

Roy overzealously kicked Elvis in the stomach and Elvis groaned. Sandra went over to him and kicked him too, not quite as hard. Elvis looked up and

flinched when he saw Sandra looming over him. He felt deeply ashamed at having hit her. Sandra stared down with a mixture of distrust and disdain at the puffy-eyed man who had struck her head with the guitar. A bluish bruise had appeared beneath his left eye where Del had punched him earlier. He appeared to be suffering from some form of exhaustion, and was visibly shaking.

'You hurt me,' she said. 'How could you?'

'I'm sorry. I had to get away. I shouldn't have hit you.'

Sandra ignored him and turned to Del and Roy. 'Come on inside, supper's ready,' she said.

'Pills,' whispered Elvis hoarsely, his throat all dried up from lack of moisture. 'Pills.'

'Oh, no you don't!' said Del. 'You actually think those things have been doin' you any good? What you need, Elvis, is a lesson in manners. Get up.'

When Elvis had struggled to his feet Del and Roy marched him towards the nearest tree, fastened the ropes around him and left him. 'You can wait here while we eat,' said Del. 'If there's anything left over, we'll feed you the scraps.'

They disappeared into the cabin, leaving Elvis tied up outside. After eating they went back outside and hauled Elvis into the cabin, gave him a broom and ordered him to sweep the floor. 'We'll be waiting outside. Do it properly.'

Elvis had no choice but to sweep out the cabin. A wave of shame passed over him as he did so, and when he'd finished he went into the bedroom and sat on the side of the bed. He felt like crying again but would never do so in front of a woman, so he called out. 'I've done the sweeping.'

Del came into the cabin and brought a glass of water into the bedroom.'Starving you is good punishment for hitting my wife, I reckon,' said Del.

Elvis sipped the water and hung his head low. 'I said I'm real sorry about that.'

'What's that you say?' asked Roy, who had joined him to heap on the humiliation. 'It ain't us you should be apologising to.'

Elvis coughed as the dust dislodged in his throat. 'Tell Sandra, I'm sorry,' he croaked.

'Tell her yourself,' said Del, as she walked into the room. 'On your knees.'

Elvis got down off the bed and knelt down. 'I'm so sorry for what I did,' he said. 'My mamma would scold me real bad if she knew I ever hit a woman, and I didn't ever want to do anything to make her mad at me.'

'So you should be,' replied Sandra. Then she fetched

a plate with the remains of the rabbit stew and handed it to him. Elvis ate greedily while the others watched and when he put the plate down he looked up and said simply, 'Thank you. I have been taught a lesson.'

Roy handed Elvis two pills, one red and one yellow, and another glass of water. Then he tied his feet securely to the bed with ropes, closed and bolted the bedroom door, and joined Del and Sandra outside. They needed to discuss what to do next.

Exhausted after his sleepless night in the open, Elvis was sound asleep when they went back inside. 'He's lucky we don't lock him in the john,' said Del as he checked the ropes. 'Any more crap from him and we will.'

They heard nothing from Elvis throughout the night and in the morning fed him fatty bacon and scrambled eggs, washed down with coffee, and gave him one of his red pills. He seemed to have recovered from his night sleeping rough and even offered to chop wood for the fire. 'And let you have our axe,' laughed Roy.

'I said I wouldn't try anything again and I meant it,' said Elvis. 'You can train the gun on me if you want.'

While Roy held the gun, Del loosened the ropes around Elvis, then marched him outside, handed him the axe and watched while he chopped logs. He tired after about ten minutes and sat on a tree stump to catch his breath. Del decided to take over, chopping twice as many logs in half the time that Elvis took. Sandra, watching from the porch of the cabin, took note. Then they marched their captive back into the cabin, secured him to the bed and bolted the bedroom door again.

They had decided that Roy would drive all the way to Memphis and mingle with the fans at Graceland, checking on the comings and goings there. He would leave immediately. Outside the cabin, against the backdrop of the sky and mountains, Roy swung open the heavy truck door and took out a .38 Special revolver that had been left on the seat.

'I'd say there's a storm brewing,' he said as he felt a few spots of rain on his hand. He tossed his backpack into the truck as Del slid the spare gun into his belt.

'You have ammo?' asked Roy.

'Plenty,' confirmed Del.

'You might not need it. Don't leave Sandra alone with him again. I'll snoop around Graceland to see if anything's happening there, and buy a newspaper. I'll be back sometime tomorrow Del.'

'Good. Well, safe trip then,' said Del, putting his arm against the door ready to slam it shut, then watching as his friend manoeuvred the truck down the dirt road that led from the cabin to the main road.

After the witness to the kidnapping left his office, Lieutenant Shriver drove slowly along Shelby Drive East, his head poking lazily out of the car window in the hope that he might catch a glimpse of something left behind from the kidnapping.

It was a gloriously bright sunny day in Memphis, and Shriver decided, at last, to pull over just a short distance from the freeway ramp to make the most of the good visibility. He stepped out onto the tarmac and wandered along the grass verge, his eyes locked firmly to the ground so that nothing would escape his attention. When he reached the freeway ramp he found the spot where one of the kidnappers would have waited with Elvis while the other went to fetch their truck, but he found nothing beyond flattened grass, a tell tale sign that someone had lain there within the last few days.

It occurred to him that if the man who'd witnessed the kidnap with his married girlfriend had only raised the alarm sooner the white truck might have been waylaid on the freeway. Then again, how would anyone know which direction they had taken after leaving Memphis? After another cursory glance among the weeds that grew beneath the ramp he got back into his car and made his way to Elvis Presley Boulevard. He was cruising past Graceland at the same moment that Charlie West, dressed as Elvis, stepped out onto the porch, secretly hoping that no one would notice him.

Charlie had come to the conclusion he'd been made him wear the outfit for no other reason than to make a spectacle of him. It might have looked alright on Elvis, but Elvis was Elvis and he could wear what he liked and still look good. Charlie wriggled uncomfortably and tugged at the high collar before realising that Lisa Marie had slipped by him.

'God damn, where has that kid got to now?' he complained aloud.

'Here daddy,' replied Lisa Marie, appearing in the doorway.Charlie put his head in his hands and groaned.

'Are you sure this is working?' asked Priscilla as she watched from the window with Linda. Charlie and her daughter were being ushered into a car by Lamar Fike who would act as their chauffeur.

'Relax,' said Linda. 'It'll stop the speculation about where Elvis is and whether he's recovering his health.'

'So, what movie are we gonna see, Char – I mean, daddy,' asked Lisa Marie as they secured their safety belts.

'Gee, well what's on?' asked Charlie, feeling worn out already.

'Well, daddy likes Monty Python, but I'd prefer Escape To Witch Mountain.'

On the other side of the street in the Elvis bar, Frankie Wilson sipped meditatively on an ice-cold beer. As the warm air from the room condensed on the frosted beer bottle, it reminded him of an Andy Warhol painting. He would make his beer last a while, maybe talk to some more fans, see if he could find out anything new.

It wasn't long, however, before Frankie noticed a buzz of excitement rippling around the bar area. He swivelled on his high stool to peer across the street. Sure enough, quite a gathering had appeared at the gates over the last quarter of an hour or so, suggesting that something must be happening in the Graceland grounds. Abandoning his drink, Frankie left the bar to investigate, pushing his way through the crowd to get near the gates where he found the girls from Nashville that he had met in the bar.

'Hey, Freddie! You were right, Elvis is much better!'

'Yeah, he must be, he's in that car with Lisa Marie.'

Frankie was puzzled. He stared up the drive towards the house and, sure enough, a car was moving ever so slowly towards them and Elvis – or someone impersonating Elvis – was waving at them from the opened rear window.

'I guess he's still unsteady on his feet,' said one of the girls as they exchanged sweets. 'That's why he got straight into the car at the top of the hill. Want some marshmallow, Freddie?'

'No, thanks,' replied Frankie, trying hard to make out the figure in the dark red shirt as the car sped through the Graceland gates. He knew it couldn't be Elvis, but he decided to head straight back to his office and call Al Shriver anyway, just to be sure.

Back at the cabin, Del was chopping wood in a clearing close by. Sandra and Elvis were alone together inside, but now Elvis was tied with both legs to the bed and Del had thrust the .38 into his wife's hands on the way out the door.

Sandra fingered the gun carefully as she sat at the wooden table, a safe distance from Elvis. It wasn't loaded, but the bullets were in her pocket. She ran her hand over the smooth surface of the barrel.

'You wouldn't really use that thing on me, would you?' asked Elvis, whose fascination with guns was well known.

'That depends,' she said, 'depends on whether you'd try to hurt me again.'

Elvis frowned. 'I didn't mean to hurt you, I said so before...' He trailed off.

'Well, you didn't hypnotise me then smash the guitar over my head by accident now, did you?'

'How d'you mean, hypnotise you?' asked Elvis, shuffling himself to a sitting position.

'You know, whatever it is you do when you sing, when you make music.'

'Why, I just sing, Sandra...'

'Well, it sounds like more than that to me. But I know Del and Roy don't get it. Men don't get it like women do.'

'I'm not sure I get it.'

'You must see it in all their faces,' said Sandra. 'You gotta hear it when all those girls scream at you, even if you don't know what it is, you must see the reflection of it come back at you?'

Elvis thought for a moment. 'Yeah, I suppose I do,' he replied, nodding in agreement. 'I never meant to hypnotise you or them but that's what happens. Back at the beginning it was crazy, all that screaming. It was impulsive somehow, like they couldn't help themselves. Once one started they all joined in. Now I think it's like... planned. Like it's expected of women to scream so they do. Don't matter how old they are either. It's the same for my friend Tom Jones. They throw their underwear at him.'

Sandra laughed. 'I would never do that,' she said.

'Oh, they bring it specially…. in their purses. It's not like they're wearing it and take it off. It's like some strange ritual… to let him know he can have them if he wants, even when their husbands are watching. He wipes his face with it and throws it back. They go wild.'

Sandra put the gun down and twisted a lock of hair around her finger, losing herself in silence for a while. 'I've been thinking,' she said at last. 'Well, there is one more song I'd like you to perform for me.'

'What's that?' asked Elvis.

''One Night',' she replied. 'It's sort of sentimental to me. You sang it on that Singer Special TV show. I thought it the best song you did. I just wanna see if the fire's gone out. Now I'm here with you like this, I see the man, not the myth. And in some ways that's a good thing, because there can't be many girls that can say that now, are there? But in some ways it's bad, because the myth was better. And then there are other times when I'm not altogether sure where the man ends and the myth begins.'

Elvis wasn't sure he understood. What he did know

was that he had behaved badly to this woman and that bothered him, but in a strange kind of way he also felt free from having to act like the mythical Elvis in front of her. Opening up to her meant he no longer had to act the part.

Sandra untied the ropes that secured Elvis' legs together and handed him the guitar. She sat at the opposite end of the bed, still holding the gun.

'Should you be sitting there?' Elvis asked. 'I mean, how can you trust me after what happened yesterday?'

'I can't, but perhaps that's part of the thrill,' she said. 'I don't think you'd do it again. In any case my husband is outside and I have this gun. Besides, you looked kinda vulnerable all roped to the bed like that.'

Elvis was vulnerable, but he felt safe next to Sandra. He was coming to the realisation that she was different from all the sweet-talking, money-grabbing fakes and phoneys that were always swarming round him, and he was able to connect with this woman as one human being to another. When she said she saw the man and the myth as merging entities, he understood exactly what she meant as he often wondered to himself who Elvis really was. The more he thought about it all, the more he regretted hurting her in his foolish attempt to escape.

Sandra touched the guitar. 'Please, just sing 'One Night',' she begged.

'That song,' began Elvis, 'I recorded two versions, one that was released and another that wasn't.'

'What was the difference?' she asked.

'Well, my record company was worried about the lyrics. They thought it was too, er, suggestive. The original version said 'One night of sin is what I'm paying for', and my version said 'One night with you is what I'm praying for'.'

'I see what you mean,' she said. 'Sing the original version.'

Elvis cradled the guitar, slid his fingers down its neck so its strings began to resonate from the womanly curves of its body. He found the right chord and began to strum.

'One night of sin, is what I'm paying for...'

Sandra closed her eyes and felt herself drawn back again into that dizzy world of lights and colour with her one true god, unable to tell the difference between fact and fantasy – or desire and disappointment – that she couldn't separate out. She felt a thrill inside as Elvis sang his famously erotic ballad, the same feeling of arousal she'd felt last night as Del's fingers probed between her legs, the same feeling of yearning she'd had all those years ago when she first laid eyes on the youthful, handsome Elvis, and as she looked up at the sad, unkempt and unshaven face of the singer to whom she was once so devoted, she felt that same warm glow of arousal and turned her face away so that he was unable to see the look in her eyes as they moistened and filled with tender tears.

'The things we two could plan, would make my dreams come true.'

Del re-entered the cabin just as Elvis finished singing and one glance at Sandra told him something had changed. He also noticed that he was no longer roped up.

'I was singing for Miss Sandra,' said Elvis, almost apologetically. He placed the guitar on the bed beside him. 'She asked me to.'

'Yes, I did, and thank you Elvis.' Sandra dried her eyes on her sleeve and looked at her husband. 'I need some air,' she said.

Del closed and locked the bedroom door with Elvis inside and followed Sandra. As they were leaving the cabin she picked up a rug that was on a chair by the door. 'He sang to me and it was lovely,' said Sandra as they held hands and walked away from the cabin. 'But I don't love him. I don't think I ever did, not really. He's not as good as you. And you're better at chopping wood.'

Del laughed. 'I know I am. I might not be able to sing but I love...'

Sandra placed a finger on his lips. 'I know you do. You don't need to say it. You proved it with this stunt. I don't know how it'll play out but I love you for doing it, for doing it for me. Now... it's time for, you know.' Sandra smiled suggestively at her man and took his hand. 'Come on, it's ages since we did it in the open air.'

In the trees they found a clearing where Sandra spread the rug out on soft earth covered by bracken. Words were no longer necessary. They kissed and undressed each other hurriedly and when they were both completely naked they made love on the ground surrounded by trees and woodland, and when Sandra felt her climax approaching she gripped Del tight, clawing at his back and crying out as he emptied himself into her. They didn't speak for a long time afterwards but held on to one another tightly, enjoying the sensation of being naked in the open air. It was Sandra who eventually broke the silence.

'What do we do now?'

'We let him go.'

'We can ransom him, surely. We can profit from this.'

'I thought you wouldn't want to do that.'

'I've changed my mind. He doesn't mean anything to me now. He's just a commodity. I'm sure Roy will agree with me when he gets back.'

'Of course he will. That was his intention all along.'

They dressed and walked back to the cabin hand in hand. As Del unfastened the lock on the door Sandra whispered in his ear. 'There's no way Elvis could make me feel like you do. That song he sang, you know, about making dreams come true, it's you and not Elvis that does that for me.'

Chapter Nine

(October 11 – 13)

Roy reached Memphis late in the evening and went straight home and to bed. The next morning he shopped for food at a Walmart store, picking up the copy of the Memphis Press Scimitar that carried Frankie Wilson's story about Elvis recovering at home and the quotes about his next Las Vegas season from Colonel Parker. Back in his truck he scanned the paper until he came across the page, read it twice and stashed it behind the seat. From it he deduced that the story was a cover-up and that its author, this Frankie Wilson guy, had either been duped or, more worryingly, been told about Elvis' disappearance. Then he took a drive down Elvis Presley Boulevard and parked in the lot by the restaurants opposite Graceland.

Standing by the wrought-iron gates of Elvis' mansion was the usual crowd of fans, so Roy crossed the street to join them. It didn't take him long to discover that in the past 24 hours Elvis had been seen in the grounds, playing with his daughter Lisa Marie close to the house, driving around in a golf buggy and occasionally waving in the direction of the gates. He'd also been driven out in a car with Lisa Marie and arrived back a few hours later.

'Are you sure it was Elvis?' he asked one fan.

'Sure looked like him to me,' she replied. 'It seems like he's getting better after his illness. We all sent him our best wishes. Uncle Vester said he'd pass them on. Last night he took Lisa Marie out somewhere, or so I heard. Some fans saw him in the back of the car as it came through the gates, even though the windows were tinted.'

Roy was still standing amid the throng of fans when a police car pulled up outside the gates and a member of Elvis' staff came down the drive to open them and let it through.

'Do the police often visit Elvis?' he asked the fan.

'Not usually,' she replied, 'but they have recently. Funny that, especially as he's well again.'

'Yes,' muttered Roy. 'Funny that.'

Al Shriver alighted from the police car that had arrived at Graceland and hurried inside. He'd already called Priscilla to alert her of his impending arrival and requested she hold off from telling Colonel Parker.

'Why?' she asked.

'I'll explain when I get there.'

Priscilla ushered Shriver into the living room and closed the door. Shriver felt more confident talking to Elvis' ex-wife alone without Parker to browbeat him and ask awkward questions. Priscilla felt the same. She looked at Shriver expectantly.

'We've had a breakthrough, of sorts,' said the policeman. 'A witness. A man who saw what happened. He didn't report it immediately because he's a married man who was with another man's wife at the time and they don't want anything said. But he gave us a pretty good description of the actual kidnap and although it's not going to lead us to the kidnappers it fills in a few gaps in the story. They were wearing crash helmets of course so couldn't be recognised. However, we can be absolutely certain now that Elvis was taken alive, bundled into a truck and driven away by two men. Where they went and where he is now is anybody's guess, but it sort of confirms what I've been thinking all along, that it was two guys who knew what they were doing.'

Priscilla stared hard at the policeman, absorbing what she'd been told. 'Thank you, Lieutenant,' she replied. 'It's a relief to know that Elvis is probably alive. I appreciate you telling me this before you tell Colonel Parker. I know he'd still like to inform the media about what's happened, no doubt because he thinks it'll boost sales of Elvis' records, which it probably will, but I want to prevent this at all costs. I think Elvis will remain unharmed so long as we keep silent.'

'I understand ma'am,' said Shiver. 'Parker gave me a deadline to find Elvis before he'd tell the media but I agree with you though I'm being pressured by my own superiors as well as Parker to get results. Although my Captain wants to keep it under wraps for the time being I fear he might come round to believing that an announcement to the media will bring about those results. But like you I think that might jeopardise Elvis' safety.'

Priscilla hesitated, as if in deep thought. 'I'm glad of this opportunity to speak to you alone,' she said finally. 'I've been thinking. I have an idea to make absolutely sure the kidnapping remains a secret. This may sound like a fantasy to you but hear me out please. This whole kidnap is like a fantasy, a bad dream fantasy, anyway. Living with Elvis for as long as I did was a fantasy for that matter.'

'Go on,' said Shiver.

'Are you aware that Elvis was on friendly terms with ex-President Nixon?' she asked.

'No, I was not.'

'Elvis visited him at the White House in 1970 when he was President, more or less uninvited but Nixon saw him and they talked for some time. He gave Elvis some narcotics agent badge or something, crazy I know, but

that's what it was like with Elvis. I happen to know that
Nixon called Elvis at the hospital here in Memphis, called
to wish him a speedy recovery. The nurses told me.'

Shriver held on to Priscilla's words, fascinated,
wondering where this was leading.

'I think we should tell Nixon what has happened
and ask him to tell everyone, Parker, your superiors,
that under no circumstances must the news of Elvis'
kidnapping be revealed to the press. He might even be
able to get President Ford to tell them too.'

'You think Nixon would do that?'

'Oh, I think he would. He's star struck around Elvis.
He's a groupie. He'd be flattered if we took him into our
confidence, and he'd be keen to help. He doesn't have
much to do nowadays, so he'd probably welcome a bit
of intrigue like this. He might be a former President but
I would imagine he still carries some weight. I'm sure
Parker would do as he says. And if he could get to Ford…'

'Do you know how to reach Nixon?' asked Shiver.

'No, but I can find out.'

Roy wasn't the only visitor to Graceland that morning
that knew that the 'Elvis' seen by fans wasn't who they
thought it was. Summoned to Graceland by Priscilla,
Frankie Wilson almost bumped into him amid the throng
of fans outside the gate, the two men stepping aside to
let each other pass. Roy was out of earshot when a fan
who recognised Wilson commented to him how delighted
everyone was that Elvis was up and about again.

'It's so great to see Elvis getting better,' she said,
echoing the sentiments that Roy had heard not 15 minutes
before.

'Sure is,' said Wilson. 'Won't be long before he's up on

stage again,' he added before speaking quietly to the staff man at the gate who swung it open to let Wilson through.

Wilson made his way up the drive to the front door of Graceland. It was opened by Charlie West. He was ushered into the presence of Priscilla and Shriver in the living room.

'Mr Wilson, thank you for coming so promptly,' she said, offering a limp handshake. 'Thank you also for writing the story in today's paper. It will quieten down any rumours about Elvis' whereabouts.'

'The Colonel asked me to write that,' said Wilson.

'I know and for once I agree with him. But there is something else you can help us with.'

'What's that?' asked the reporter.

'Lieutenant Shriver here has been telling me about a witness to the kidnap that seems to confirm all our theories. The most important thing is that Elvis was evidently taken alive. However, we are still no closer to knowing where he is.'

Wilson nodded, producing a notebook into which he scribbled a few words. 'Is that all?' he asked.

'No, the Lieutenant and myself wish to ensure that certain others who know about what's happened do not carry out their plans to inform the media. I think you know who we are talking about.'

'Yes.'

'And we think you may be able to help us.'

'How?'

'As you know Elvis is on friendly terms with ex-President Nixon. We would like to ask for his help in this. If he were to tell Colonel Parker and the Lieutenant's superiors to keep a lid on it, or instruct the FBI to do so, they would be obliged to do as he says, especially if, just maybe, he could get President Ford to back him up.'

'No doubt, you're right,' said Wilson. 'But how can I help?'

'You're a reporter. You have contacts. I want to speak with Nixon. Surely you can set that up. Think about it... when you write your story you can say that it went all the way to the White House.'

'May I use your phone?'

'Of course,' said Priscilla, handing him the gold plated handset that Elvis used to make his calls.

Within ten minutes Wilson had secured a number for Nixon's office in California.

Priscilla Presley was quite correct in her estimation of Richard Nixon, the now disgraced former Present of the USA. He was a show business groupie and he didn't have much to do with his time. Like Elvis alone in the hunting lodge in the hills of Kentucky, he spent a great deal of it brooding on his lot. Former friends and allies tended to stay away, so any call was welcome. He was therefore delighted when Ron Zeigler, his former press secretary and one of few who had stood by him after Watergate, came into the room to tell him that Priscilla Presley, the ex-wife of the famous singer, wished to speak with him.

'Put her through,' he said eagerly, surprised yet intrigued that the former Mrs Presley should seek his counsel. When the phone rang he snatched it up. 'Good morning Mrs Presley,' he said. 'Richard Nixon here. How may I be of assistance?'

'It's about Elvis,' she said.

'I thought as much. Is his health deteriorating? I'm sorry if that's the case. Your husband made a big impression on me when he visited me in the White House some years ago.'

'No, no... it's not that. He's recovered from his illness.'

'I'm glad.'

'It's worse than that. He's been kidnapped.'

Those elected to the presidency of the United States of America are not often lost for words but Priscilla's words had rendered even Richard Nixon momentarily speechless.

'Mr Nixon?' inquired Priscilla. 'Are you still there?'

'Yes, yes, I'm sorry,' he replied. 'What you said came as, well, a shock. Please go on.'

For the next 10 minutes Priscilla told Nixon everything she knew about Elvis' disappearance. Nixon interrupted her from time to time with a question, almost all of which she was able to answer. He seemed particularly concerned about the confidentially of the case, agreeing with Priscilla's view that the media be kept in the dark, and assured her that he would do anything he could to ensure this was maintained. When Priscilla explained that Elvis' manager, the formidable Colonel Parker, was keen to release details to the press, Nixon agreed this was the wrong approach.

'I will do what I can to help Mrs Presley,' he gallantly promised as the conversation drew to a close. 'I still have some authority in Washington and elsewhere. You can reply on me... Richard Nixon won't let you down.'

'Thank you, sir,' said Priscilla, hoping that her helpless-little-girl-who didn't-know-where-to-turn act would appeal to whatever sense of chivalry might linger in the psyche of the disgraced former Commander-in-Chief.

Nixon replaced the phone and after consulting a file in a cabinet by his desk asked Zeigler to call an old friend at the department of the Pentagon where records of illegal aliens were kept. 'Marty, how are you?' he said when he was connected. 'You remember when I told you about how Elvis Presley visited me in the Oval office? Yeah, well I recall a conversation with you afterwards when you told me something very interesting about Presley's manager, that Colonel Parker guy. Tell me again, what was it that the FBI had on him?'

Lamar Fike, in the continued absence of Joe Esposito the senior member of the Memphis Mafia on regular duty at Graceland, had left instructions with Charlie West that if Lieutenant Shriver were to visit the house and speak with Priscilla when he or the Colonel weren't present he was to tell them immediately. In the event neither Fike nor West were at Graceland that morning, Fike having decided to spend a rare moment at home with his family, and West having opted to attend to the servicing of one of Elvis' cars. Colonel Parker, meanwhile, was on a flight to New York to pick up the money that Rocco Laginestra has squirreled away for him.

Parker didn't linger long in New York after collecting the cash that Laginestra handed over, though he did assure RCA's president that he was pressuring the Memphis Police to release details of the kidnap to the media. A certain Captain Jim Magill might favour this move eventually but was restrained only by the reluctance of Lieutenant Shriver and Priscilla Presley, and his own unwillingness to detonate the media storm that he knew would follow. 'I think he'll come round to our way of thinking soon, if only to get results,' said Parker. 'He seems like the kind of guy who doesn't like doing nothing.'

Laginestra nodded, aware that his position was on the line after helping himself to $1.5 million of RCA's money.

'Remember I've pressed up millions of albums and handed over one and a half million dollars to you,' he told Parker. 'I must have something to show for it.'

'You can have the money back if we don't need it,' he assured Laginestra, who knew full well that the chances of Colonel Parker ever handing back any money to RCA, whether it was one dollar or a million, was about as likely as Richard Nixon reoccupying the White House.

Parker was back in Memphis by the mid-afternoon. His first port of call was to a bank where he rented a safety deposit box in which he placed the money he'd extracted from RCA, then he stopped by his hotel to see if there were any messages. To his astonishment there was a message to call former President Richard Nixon, with a California Area Code.

In his room Parker dialled the number and asked for Nixon. Zeigler answered and put him through.

'This is Colonel Tom Parker, the personal manager of Elvis Presley,' he said. 'Is that Mr Nixon, the former President?'

'Yes it is,' said Nixon. 'Mr Parker, I'll come straight to the point. I have been made aware of the circumstances surrounding the disappearance of your client Elvis Presley.'

Parker spluttered. Who had told him?

'I have told no one else about this,' continued Nixon, 'nor will I. The only other person I may speak to on the matter, apart from my secretary, is President Ford, should that become necessary.'

'Mr Nixon...' interrupted the Colonel, who disliked intensely being called Mr Parker. He was about to ask how Nixon knew of the kidnap but Nixon cut him off.

'Please hear me out. I understand from Priscilla Presley,

Elvis' former wife, that you are in favour of announcing this kidnapping to the media. I am calling to advise you, to instruct you in fact, in the strongest possible terms not to do so, at least until Elvis is freed.'

So Priscilla had a hand in this, thought Parker. 'Surely that's up to me,' he said.

'Indeed, it is. But if this were to happen it would put Elvis' life in great danger, and we don't want that do we? Past experience of high profile kidnapping cases points to the fact that keeping the circumstances secret almost always results in a successful outcome. By that I mean the victim is generally released unharmed, even if the ransom has had to be paid.'

'I understand,' said Parker. 'Of course we don't want anything to happen to Elvis, but at the moment the investigation is limited because of the secrecy. Strip that away and we can have a full-scale manhunt.'

'Which is precisely what we want to avoid. As I understand it the police have no idea where Elvis is being held, nor have they identified the kidnappers. If this story suddenly hits the newspapers, the TV, it'll be the biggest story ever. Every newspaper in the world will put it on their front page and every TV station will broadcast it. Elvis' face will be everywhere. We both know that. They might panic, kill Elvis and hide the body where it might never be found. And then disappear.'

'We have to take that risk,' said the Colonel.

'No we don't. And this would not look good for the authorities, which they want to avoid.'

'I can't help that.'

'No, but there is one other thing I need to mention,' continued Nixon. 'It concerns your status here in America.'

'I don't understand,' said Parker.

'I think you do,' replied Nixon. He paused for a moment, consulting notes he had written earlier that morning. 'The FBI and the Internal Revenue Service have known for some time that your name is not Colonel Thomas Andrew Parker, born in Huntington, West Virginia in 1909, but Andreas Cornelis van Kujik and that you are a Dutch citizen, born that year in Breda in Holland, and an illegal alien. Not only that but the Dutch authorities would like to talk to you about an unsolved murder. The FBI and IRS have turned a blind eye to this because you pay your taxes and stay out of trouble. However, although I am now only an ex-President I have many contacts in Washington and elsewhere and it is in my power to make things difficult for you in this regard. President Ford still takes my calls and sometimes even asks for advice. He owes me a favour or two, as do a number of friends of mine in the FBI.'

Parker remained silent.

'Deportation orders are easily obtained,' continued Nixon. 'I nearly managed to get that John Lennon deported and would have succeeded were it not for Watergate and Lennon's influential friends. Also, the pretext to deport him, a minor drugs infraction in London in 1968, may have been a miscarriage of justice. Furthermore, he entered the country legally. You didn't. It's much easier to deport illegal aliens who jumped ship.'

Parker was unused to being browbeaten, on the losing side of an argument, and only rarely conceded, but this was different. He was cornered.

'OK, Mr Nixon. You win. I shall give instructions that no one must know,' he said, finally. 'Now, but perhaps not forever.'

'What happens when Elvis is released, if Elvis is released, is a different matter,' said Nixon. 'It may well be that the FBI might prefer the story never to be released. We shall see and it will be up to them. But until then, if word gets out, you could face deportation, Mr van Kujik.'

Livid that he had been outmanoeuvred, Colonel Parker replaced the phone and called Graceland to inform Priscilla that he was on his way over. His taxi dropped him outside the door 20 minutes later.

Gathering together Priscilla, Linda Thompson, Vernon Presley, Lamar Fike and Charlie West, he made a formal announcement that under no circumstances was anyone to ever breathe a word about the kidnap to a soul, not now or for evermore.

'That's for the better,' said Vernon.

Priscilla, who had informed Linda of the morning's meeting with Shriver and her call to Nixon, looked smug. Linda smiled. Fike and West looked embarrassed. None of them had any idea of the hold that Nixon, and by extension the US Government, had over Parker. All of them believed he was an American citizen. Parker, knowing that Priscilla was behind the call from Nixon, probably with the assistance of Lieutenant Shriver, was still fuming.

Unwilling to confront Priscilla directly on the matter lest it disrupt the uneasy truce between them, Elvis' manager left abruptly, slamming the door behind him. He was wondering how he would tell Rocco Laginestra that the extra Elvis records he'd pressed up might just as well be dumped in a landfill, or placed in a warehouse until the day Elvis died which, if his failing health was anything to go by, might happen any day now anyway. Then there was the matter of the $1.5 million. He was also wondering how

Frankie Wilson would react if it was necessary to tell him that the exclusive story he'd been promised in return for his co-operation was to be embargoed indefinitely. A call from Nixon or Ford would probably silence him as well, he thought.

Roy returned to the cabin in the early evening and reported on what he had seen in Memphis, the scene outside Graceland, the talk with the fans who claimed to have seen Elvis and the story in the Memphis newspaper that he'd brought back to the cabin to show to Sandra and Del. They talked outside the cabin so that Elvis couldn't hear them and agreed between themselves that ransoming their captive was the next move. After discussing how to deliver a ransom note they went back inside and informed Elvis of their decision.

'You were right about being worth more to us alive than dead,' Del told him. 'We think maybe one million dollars is the price on your head. It seems that the story of your being kidnapped is being kept secret, and that someone is even impersonating you at Graceland. The Memphis newspaper continues to publish stories to the effect that you are recovering from your illness, which implies a cover up is taking place, with your manager's co-operation. It's lucky for you that this is the case, otherwise we'd have to dispose of you some other way.'

Elvis shuddered but did not speak.

'We have decided to deliver a ransom note to Graceland telling them we want $1 million in cash and that the arrangements for dropping it off will be confirmed in a phone call by you to your home 24 hours after the note has been delivered. We assume you know the phone number of Graceland, a private line?'

Elvis nodded.

'We think that you and only you will be able to convey the seriousness of the situation. Besides, talking to whoever picks up the phone will prove you're alive and we mean business. They'll know your voice. You'd better hope they take us seriously and don't try anything stupid. One of us will pick up the money and we'll release you within 24 hours. If anything happens to whichever one of us goes to get the money, then you'll suffer.'

'How will they know the ransom note is genuine?' asked Elvis.

'You're going to help,' replied Roy. 'We're going to take a Polaroid picture of you holding a copy of yesterday's Memphis newspaper, cut off a lock of your hair and steam the label off one of your prescription pill bottles. We'll put the photo and the rest in the envelope. Then a day later you'll phone Graceland from a pay phone on the highway and give them instructions.'

That night they lined up Elvis against the wall of the cabin and photographed him with the paper before using it to concoct a ransom note, cutting out the letters from headlines and pasting them on to a piece of notepaper. 'WE HAVE ELVIS,' it said. 'WE WILL RELEASE HIM ON PAYMENT OF $1 MILLION IN USED $50 AND $100 BILLS. ELVIS WILL CALL YOU AT GRACELAND AT EXACTLY 10 AM ON OCTOBER 13. BE READY TO RECEIVE THE CALL AND FURTHER INSTRUCTIONS. IF YOU DO NOT DO AS WE SAY YOU WILL NOT SEE ELVIS AGAIN.'

'We'll post it in Louisville,' said Roy after he'd snipped off a few locks from Elvis' head to put in the envelope along with the note, photo and pill bottle label. It was addressed, in anonymous block capital letters, to Vernon Presley at Graceland, and Elvis sullenly supplied the correct Zip Code. 'If we post it from there it won't give them any clue where we are. We could be in Kentucky, Indiana, Ohio, anywhere.'

After eating they locked Elvis in the bedroom and settled down for the night, Roy again sleeping in the hammock out on the porch while Del and Sandra occupied the sleeping bags. Next morning Roy set off to Louisville, the envelope on the seat beside him.

After he'd spoken to Colonel Parker Richard Nixon had put in a call to the White House and spoken briefly with President Gerald Ford. The following morning Captain Jim Magill of the Memphis Police Department received a call from Ford instructing him in no uncertain terms that the investigation into the disappearance of Elvis Presley was to remain strictly confidential. The Police Captain sent for Al Shriver.

'Lieutenant,' he began when Shriver arrived in his office, 'I'm not quite sure how it came to their notice but I have had orders from the President in the White House that under no circumstances must the Elvis case go any further than us. Colonel Parker has been informed. He didn't take it kindly. What progress have you made since we last spoke?'

'We have a witness,' replied Shiver, who knew precisely how the case had come to the attention of the White House but thought it best not to explain. He went on to inform his chief about the man who saw the kidnap, along with his companion. They agreed that this man's testimony pointed to Elvis having been taken alive.

'What about Frankie Wilson?' asked Shriver.

'String him along. It may well be that at the end of the line we will have to pretend it never happened. The others who know will be happy to maintain their silence, Elvis too if he's released alive. Wilson may be more difficult to rein in, so we need to come up with a plan for him. Think about that Lieutenant…'

'Yes, sir,' said Shriver.

'There is one more thing,' said Magill, as Shriver was about to leave the room. 'Because of the interest that the President has taken in this case it is probably best that I make no inquiries as to how he came to know about Elvis' disappearance. From what you've told me I suspect that Priscilla Presley had a hand in it, but I couldn't help but notice that you didn't seem surprised when I told you about the call from President Ford just now. Do you have anything to say?'

'No, sir,' said Shriver.

'If this situation ends in a tragedy,' continued Magill, 'I will expect your resignation. You'd better be right Lieutenant, or a million Elvis fans will be after your lynching, and I might not have the manpower to prevent it.'

With Roy making a long round trip to Louisville, Del and Sandra found themselves spending another 24 hours in Elvis' company. The frosty atmosphere created by his attack on Sandra had thawed, and the decision to ransom him had somehow eased the tension between abductors and abducted. Sandra proposed that the three of them take a hike towards Lake Cumberland and Elvis, not normally one for walking, surprised himself by agreeing to the proposal.

'The exercise will do you good,' said Del, who still carried his revolver in case their captive tried another escape. He knew now that this was very unlikely, that

Elvis had realised the futility of trying to run away.

'Where are we?' asked Elvis as they began their hike.

'Well, I don't suppose it'll do any harm to tell you now. Tell him Sandra.'

'We're in Kentucky,' she said. 'Over that ridge is Lake Cumberland, a man-made lake but still as lovely a sight as anyone could ever hope to see, even you, and I guess you've seen more than most. In the other direction is the Daniel Boone National Park.'

'I don't get to see much when I'm tour,' replied Elvis. 'Just hotel rooms and airports and dressing rooms. And faces staring at me from the crowd. I look out of the limousine windows and it all looks the same, the same streets, the same stores, the same gas stations, the same motels, the same fast food places. I don't get to see much country, Colorado a few times maybe, and Hawaii, but not country like this. I can't remember ever being this far away from people.'

Elvis stopped in his tracks and looked around him at the tall trees. The ridge they were climbing was the one that he had decided against climbing in his thoughtless attempt to get away from the cabin after hitting Sandra with the guitar. He walked slower than his companions and every so often stopped to gather his breath, but it seemed to them that the more Elvis walked, the more determined he was to carry on. And he seemed almost eager to chat.

'Have you ever been abroad, out of the US?' he asked.

'No,' replied Sandra. 'That's something my husband and I wanna do. Maybe one day.'

'The only time I ever left the United States was when I was in the army, when they posted me to Germany at the end of 1958,' said Elvis. 'But I was surrounded by other GIs, so I could have been anywhere really, not much different from boot camp in Texas. I was in Frankfurt, and I stayed in a house with my pappy and some of the guys. That was way back in 1959, the whole year, maybe longer. Then I came home and was discharged. I went to Paris once. They knew who I was, but not like it is here. On the way home the plane touched down in Scotland, and some fans were there to greet me. I'd like to have gone to London.'

'Why didn't you?' asked Sandra.

'Not enough time.'

'But you could go now. You can go anywhere you want.'

'Well most of the time I can but not right now.'

'She don't mean that,' said Del. 'She means you have the money to go anywhere in the world, so what's stopping you?'

Elvis paused again, not because he was tiring but because he wasn't sure how to answer the question. It was one that had occurred to him many times over the years, at least since he resumed live performances in 1969. Every time he'd broached the subject of performing concerts in Europe or anywhere outside of the US, Colonel Parker had found some excuse not to go: poor security, venues not big enough, not enough money on the table, conflicting schedules, the same reasons over and over again. Yet other big acts regularly played in Europe, in London, in Paris, in Rome. These big English rock bands like the Rolling Stones, the Who and Led Zeppelin, and stars like Elton John, were selling more records than him and attracting huge audiences on the road, and they played in Europe. The same with Americans groups he knew about like the Beach Boys and Crosby, Stills, Nash & Young, and singers like Bob Dylan. Frank Sinatra regularly performed in

London, before and after his many 'retirements'. So why can't I, Elvis wondered time and time again. It never occurred to him in his wildest dreams that the reason was because his manager didn't hold an American passport and was unable to apply for one because he was an illegal immigrant.

'Well, what's stopping you?' repeated Del.

Elvis came to his senses. 'Well, I don't really know,' he said. 'My manager doesn't seem like he wants me to go to Europe. I sometimes wonder why myself. I think I owe it to my fans there. I guess they come to me, so it doesn't matter that much.'

'Who makes the decisions, you or him?' asked Del.

Once again Elvis slipped into silence. He didn't want to admit to Del and Sandra that he wasn't in command of his own affairs, yet at the same time realised they'd inadvertently hit on a sore point with him. 'I do,' he replied, 'but he wants to do what's best for me.'

'Does 'what's best' always have to mean 'what makes the most money'?' asked Del, fascinated by the way the conversation was going. Sandra, too, was beginning to feel that they were touching on Elvis' vulnerabilities; also, that they were allowing him to get things off his mind, things he wanted to say but had no one to say them to in the life he led.

Elvis shrugged. 'That's the way he looks at it,' he replied. 'Ah, don't really know what else to say.' As ever when he was cornered, Elvis sulked and said nothing. Here on this mountain, without those who invariably deferred to him no matter what, he felt insecure and greatly ashamed that he wasn't able to answer in ways that didn't expose his weaknesses.

Del laughed. 'Seems to me you need to stand up for

yourself more Elvis.'

'I think maybe I should change my ways,' he said finally. 'You two… you're making me see things more clearly. I do need to stand up to Parker, I know I do, but he's guided me for so long. I don't have anyone else, never have had, apart from my mother.'

'Did your mother know Parker?' asked Sandra.

'Yes, and she was suspicious of him. I think maybe if she'd lived things would have turned out differently. My pappa worships him, never wants me to cross him.'

Elvis lapsed into silence. He was tiring now, treading heavily, but very much wanted to look out over this lake that he'd been told about. No one spoke for the next few minutes and as they approached the top of the ridge the gradient became steeper. Gradually Elvis fell back as if the effort was too much for him. Del was some way ahead, maybe 15 yards in front, with Sandra between them. Del was the first to reach the top and gaze out over the water. Sandra was only a few paces behind but Elvis was struggling to keep up. He sat down with about 20 yards of the ridge still to climb. 'I don't think I can make it,' he said.

Sandra went back to where he was sat. 'Sure you can. Be a man. Be like Del. You're Elvis. THE Elvis. If you can't climb this hill you ain't the man I thought you were.'

Elvis struggled to his feet. He felt humiliated. Sandra held out her hand and he grasped it. 'Come on Elvis,' she said. 'You can make it. Do it for me.'

Del watched from the top of the ridge as Sandra cajoled Elvis into finishing the climb. Eventually, after what seemed to Del and Sandra like a gargantuan effort, Elvis reached the top, sat down on a rock and stared out over the lake, taking in the magnificent, unspoilt scenery of rural Kentucky.

'I told you it was worth the effort,' said Sandra, watching Elvis as he scanned the landscape. He seemed electrified, taken aback by the endless beauty that was spread out before him. In all his travels across America he'd never been confronted by such a sight, the splendour of nature at its most impressive.

'The Lord God made this,' he said eventually, raising his hand to his eyes to shield them from the glare of the sunlight. 'I've always believed in God. He gave me my talent and He gave us this.'

Del and Sandra, neither of whom held any deep religious beliefs, listened while the most famous singer in America, a man once despised by the religious establishment for espousing the devil's music, talked abut his faith. 'I've read the Bible many times. I've tried to make sense of how we came here, how I came to be here. I felt I was sent for a purpose. That's why I made those spiritual records, you know,' he said. 'I sing hymns in my concerts.'

'I know,' said Sandra. 'I have those records, How Great Thou Art and He Touched Me. You sing hymns beautifully.'

'They are my favourite recordings, truly the only records that mean anything to me now. If there is a heaven and if entry is barred to me, well I can look at those records and know that my sins will be forgiven in the Lord's good time.'

Up here on this mountain, surrounded by the most beautiful scenery nature could devise, Del and Sandra felt they were closing in on the inner core of Elvis Presley. It was as if Elvis was making a last confession and they were the priests he'd chosen to hear it.

Elvis said nothing for a moment or two, then began to hum the melody of his favourite hymn. After a few attempts he found the right key and started to sing, quietly at first. 'Well, I'm tired and so weary, but I must go alone. 'Till the Lord comes and calls, calls me away, oh yeah.' Growing in confidence as he reached the final two lines of the verse, Elvis seemed inspired by the melody and his own extraordinary voice. 'Well the morning's so bright, and the lamp is alight, and the night, night is as black as the sea, oh yea.'

Elvis stood up and gazed at the sky, singing with all his power, with all his sincerity, every emotion now untapped. He looked out over the panorama spread before him and it seemed to Del and Sandra as if he had entered into a trancelike state, unaware of anything but his own presence. The voice that she and so many others adored boomed out over the lake towards the horizon, as if Elvis wanted the entire population of America to hear him sing this treasured hymn. 'There will be peace in the valley for me, some day. There will be peace in the valley for me, oh Lord I pray. There'll be no sadness, no sorrow, no trouble, trouble I see. There will be peace in the valley for me, for me.'

Finally, turning to Del and Sandra, he lowered his voice and repeated the final lines of the chorus and, at the end, added: 'For Jessie and me'.

'Jessie was my twin, you know,' Elvis told them, sitting down again, his eyes moist. 'He died before he was born. I survived, he didn't. Why did I live and he die? I've always wondered about that. And what would have happened to me, happened to us, if he'd lived? Would he have been able to sing like me? Better than me? Did my life become what it did because he died? Did I take on his life as well as my own? Am I living two lives at once? My mamma used to tell me that when one twin died, the one that lived had the strength of both. I would give everything I have to talk to him, for Jessie to tell me what he thinks of the life I've had.

'I've done some bad things and I've done some good things. These two sides of me... is one Elvis and the other Jessie? Is Jessie good and Elvis bad? Or is it the other way round. All my life I've wondered about that.

'Oh, he used to speak to me in dreams when I was young. Lying in bed at night he'd tell me these things but I can't remember them now. Then I'd wake up and he'd be gone. I think about how we were in my mother's womb together, breathing, alive together there, close together, as close as anyone can be to another, and I made it and he didn't. Maybe I took on whatever he had and it is his voice I sing with. Sometimes I'm singing in some big stadium somewhere and I look out over the audience and wonder if he can hear me, if he can see me? Is he judging me? Is he out there somewhere? Is he beside me on this stage? In the spotlight next to me? Invisible. Has he entered my body as I sing 'Peace In the Valley'?'

Elvis shook his head slowly, deep inside himself. 'I've cried so many tears for Jessie, and for my mamma. It's always been hard being Elvis Presley you know, real hard.'

They made their way back to the cabin in virtual silence, Sandra leading the way, followed by Elvis with Del keeping up the rear. Elvis found the going easier downhill. Once inside Elvis went to rest on the bed while Del chopped wood for the fire and Sandra chose something to cook from the provisions that remained. She served up fried chicken, potatoes and onions and Elvis ate greedily, saying little until his plate was empty. Then he spoke.

'I've told you everything about me but I don't know

anything about you,' he said. 'I know you're married and I know your names and I'm guessing you live in Memphis but I don't know for sure or where you come from or what sort of lives you've had, you or your friend that keeps leaving to drive off somewhere.'

'We can't tell you,' said Del, 'otherwise when we release you, you could set the police on to us.'

'Why would I do that?'

'To get your revenge. To see justice done.'

'From what you tell me, my disappearance has been kept secret. Is that right?'

'As of yesterday, yes,' said Del. 'There's been no mention of it on the radio. Nothing in any newspapers. Those who do know probably think it's safer to keep it quiet.'

'In case you kill me?' asked Elvis.

'We wouldn't do that, not now,' said Sandra.

'Good.' Elvis smiled. 'I don't want to die yet. I might not live as long as most folk but I'm not ready to go just yet. In fact, these last few days... well, I've started to feel better than I did a week or so ago.'

'I know,' said Del. 'I can tell. But we still ain't telling you who we are. The least you know the better.'

'What if I was to give you my word that when you let me go and I get back to Graceland, I don't say a word of what's happened to anyone?'

'It's too late. My buddy will have sent the ransom note,' said Del.

'OK, but what if I refuse to identify you? What if I insist that this secret is maintained even after I'm freed and the ransom paid? You say someone is impersonating me at Graceland. Well, that's good. What if I get back and with my help it's agreed no one ever talks about this ever again? No one need ever know.'

'Why should we trust you to do that?'

'Because I have nothing to gain by the story becoming public. Oh, maybe the police might recover some of the ransom money if you haven't spent it. But why would anyone who knows about this want the world to know that Elvis had been kidnapped and held to ransom?'

'Maybe,' said Del. 'But I still ain't telling you more than we need to.'

'Well, I do give you my word,' said Elvis. 'I promise on my Bible and the memory of Jesse and my dear mother that I won't try to identify you to the police or anyone else. And what's more I'll say nothing about this to anyone, ever. Now I'm sleepy, that walk tired me out.'

Elvis went into the bedroom, took off his overall and lay down on the bed. He was asleep in seconds. He didn't even ask for a yellow pill.

When Roy arrived in Louisville in the early evening he located a main Post Office and put the envelope in a mailbox. Then he got back into his truck and drove directly back towards Kentucky, stopping to eat along the way and arriving at the cabin in the late evening. Del and Sandra filled him in on the day's events, including the walk with Elvis to the top of the ridge and the conversations they had with him.

'Seems to me like you've tamed him,' said Roy.

'He's a different person than the one we kidnapped five days ago,' agreed Del. 'I'm getting round to thinking that this experience has maybe even done him some good.'

'All that stuff about his twin,' said Sandra. 'That was weird. Makes you think, though. There's something about Elvis that certainly is mighty strange. He just ain't like other men. Or women. It's no wonder he thinks he's Jesus Christ or something.'

'Well, he's worth a million dollars to us if we pull this off,' said Roy. 'That certainly makes him different from other men to me.'

'We've got one more day with him tomorrow, then he has to make the phone call. He won't mess us around. I actually think he's beginning to like us, well me and Sandra anyway. Not sure abut you Roy.'

Before they slept they checked on Elvis in the locked bedroom. He was sleeping soundly. The following day, after breakfast, all four of them, Elvis, Roy, Del and Sandra, squeezed into the truck and drove into the Daniel Boone National Park, stopping at a gas station on the outskirts of Montecello to buy food for a picnic lunch. Elvis was in a buoyant mood and had to be persuaded to stay in the truck with Roy while Del and Sandra went inside to pick up the provisions, and when they returned he pleaded with them to be able to step outside.

'I just want to be able to be normal in the midst of ordinary people,' he said. 'That's something I never had, not since I was famous anyway. Let me use the bathroom. I won't try anything.'

Del and Roy looked at one another. 'Should we let him?' asked Del.

'Yes,' said Sandra. 'I trust him.'

'OK, but you gotta wear this hat,' said Roy, handing Elvis a floppy hat in green camouflage material that he wore while out shooting. Elvis reluctantly placed it on his head.

Public appearances by Elvis Presley were almost always pre-planned, tightly choreographed and reported in the press, no matter how brief. On such occasions Elvis made sure he looked the part, dressing up in his capes, buckles and belts, the way he and his fans thought he ought to look. He usually wore outsize sunglasses. Elvis would no sooner slip out of the house in everyday clothes to pick up a pint of milk than the Queen of England would be seen in her nightdress.

During pre-production meetings in Los Angeles for the Singer special in May of 1968 its producer Steve Binder had suggested he and Elvis step out of his office on Sunset Boulevard and mingle with passers-by. Elvis was appalled by the suggestion, fearing that he would be mobbed on the street and some sort of disturbance ensue. He was therefore deeply humbled when no one recognised him. 'We were just four guys standing in front of this building,' Bones Howe, Binder's audio engineer, said afterwards.

It was quite another thing, however, for Elvis to use the bathroom in a roadside gas station without a security detail checking out the building first, making sure no one else was inside and waiting outside while he relieved himself. However, Elvis had been a captive now for five nights and, although he'd been given a change of clothing, the overalls and t-shirt he loathed so much, he hadn't had a shave in all that time, nor been able to wash properly and re-dye his hair as was his custom. As a result Elvis' natural brown colour was starting to show at the roots and, as each day passed, his stubble had continued to grow but it wasn't black like the dyed hair on his head, more salt and peppery. The camouflage hat only added to the obvious reality that he no longer resembled anything like the Elvis Presley that the world would recognise.

'OK,' said Roy. 'But I'm coming with you.'

Elvis stepped down from the truck and walked across the forecourt to the bathroom. The only other customer, a young man dressed in a check shirt and similar overalls to those Elvis wore, was filling up a station wagon, and as they approached the bathroom a middle-aged woman pulled up in a sedan, got out and walked towards the shop. Neither gave Elvis and Roy a second glance.

Inside the bathroom was another man, splashing water on his face at the basin. He turned and stepped aside as Elvis passed close by him, glancing at Elvis but showing no signs of recognition. After relieving themselves Elvis and Roy walked back to the truck, passing close to the woman from the sedan who was lingering by a newspaper stand close to the entrance to the shop. She ignored them.

Back in the truck Elvis appeared overjoyed. 'You have no idea what that felt like for me,' he said. 'That's the first time in 20 years I've been able to walk around outside in public and not be recognised. Now I know what it's like not to be Elvis Presley.'

Emboldened by the success of their experiment at the gas station, the quartet drove on into the National Park, eventually stopping at a picnic area and eating lunch. Although the area was far from crowded, a handful of other groups of picnickers settled nearby, among them a family of four, father, mother and two boys below the age of 10. After their meal the boys began to throw a football to one another and when one boy failed to catch the ball it rolled to where Elvis, Roy, Del and Sandra were sat. Elvis glanced at the others. Roy nodded. Elvis picked up the ball, stood up and threw it back to the boy.

'Thanks mister,' he shouted from about 10 yards away. The father of the boys waved in acknowledgement and Elvis waved back. He smiled and sat down. Elvis was beginning to enjoy normality.

In the afternoon the four of them continued their drive

through the National Park, stopping now and then and getting out of the truck to admire the scenery. At one particular spot they mingled with a coach party. Elvis again went unrecognised. Driving back to the cabin in the early evening they passed a roadside diner and Elvis suggested they stop to eat. 'I can't remember what it was like to go into a restaurant and be served, just like a normal person, no one making a fuss,' he said.

There were three other vehicles parked outside, and it was safe to assume one of them belonged to the staff. Roy parked the truck and sent Sandra inside to check on how crowded it was.

'There's only two tables occupied,' she reported back. 'A young couple on one and an old guy on the other.'

'OK,' said Del. 'I'm sick of eating in the cabin anyway.'

'Me, too,' said Elvis. 'But that's not to say I don't like your cooking Miss Sandra,' he added hurriedly.

Sandra smiled at Elvis, and Elvis grinned back. It seemed like any natural exchange between old friends.

'You sit facing the wall Elvis,' said Roy. 'If anything happens we're out of here quick.'

The four of them ate burgers and fries washed down with coke. No one paid them the slightest notice. Elvis said little throughout the meal, relishing his anonymity. It never even occurred to him to go up to the counter and identify himself, not that the waitress would have recognised him anyway. As they walked back to the truck he asked, 'Do y'all trust me now?'

'I guess so,' said Roy. 'But I still had this with me, just in case.' He opened his jacket to reveal the .38 stuffed into his belt.

Elvis winced. 'You didn't need that,' he said. 'I gave you my word.'

Sandra thought she detected a touch of hurt in his voice. 'I believe you,' she said.

Back at the cabin Elvis joined Roy, Del and Sandra on the porch before they turned in for the night. Roy and Del were drinking beer, Elvis and Sandra coke. 'Did you guys serve in the army?' Elvis asked them.

Roy and Del nodded.

'Vietnam?'

'Yea,' said Roy. 'But we don't talk about it.'

'They don't like to,' said Sandra. 'Even I can't get them to tell me anything about what they did there.'

'Why not?' asked Elvis.

'The way the Americans treated the Vietcong,' said Del. 'It wasn't good.'

They lapsed into silence. Then Roy spoke. 'I'll tell y'all one story. We took a prisoner once, me and Del. A stray Vietcong man we found in the jungle. We ought to have killed him but we didn't. We couldn't. Not in cold blood. He wasn't a soldier, just a simple man, a farmer maybe. So we tied him up and took him with us, back to where we thought our camp was located. But we got lost in the jungle, didn't know where we were, lost our sense of direction. It was night, there were no lights, nothing, just a torch that I had.'

Elvis nodded. 'So what happened?'

'The Vietcong guy sensed that we were lost and he showed us the way,' said Del, picking up the story. 'He couldn't speak no English and we couldn't understand him but he led us out of the jungle even though he was our prisoner. And when we got near the camp he pleaded with us to let him go because he knew that if we took him into the camp he'd be shot.'

'Did you let him go?' asked Elvis.

'Yea,' said Del. 'He'd saved us. We thought maybe he had a wife and kids. He could have led us back to where his people were, and we'd have been captured or killed.'

'He ran off back into the jungle as fast his legs could carry him,' said Roy. 'The thing is… we trusted him and he trusted us. We repaid his trust.'

'Just like today,' said Elvis. 'You trusted me, and I repaid it. I can't lead a normal life, and never will, even after you let me go. But you showed me what it was like. Millions of men dream of being Elvis Presley, and I dream of being one of those millions. Today a little piece that dream came true for me. Because of the same trust you shared with that Vietcong guy in the jungle.'

Addressed to 'Vernon Presley, Graceland, 3764 Elvis Presley Boulevard, TN 38116', the envelope with the ransom note was sorted in Louisville and the following day delivered to Memphis where it was placed in a sack with all the other mail addressed to Graceland. It wasn't until the following day that the batch of mail containing the ransom demand was delivered.

Most of the mail that arrived at Graceland was addressed to Elvis and it was usually the job of Vester Presley to sort this out from mail sent to the other occupants of the house. Nevertheless, everyone at Graceland received plenty of mail so it was late in the day when Vernon was handed his share in a bundle passed on to him by his elder brother. Vernon was in no mood to attend to his mail and it wasn't until Priscilla reminded him that a message from Elvis' kidnappers might arrive any time, addressed to anyone at Graceland, that he began to scan the envelopes up in his bedroom. The envelope with the ransom demand was about half way down the pile and when he opened it and the photograph and lock of hair fell out into his hand he knew immediately what it was without even having to read to the note.

Vernon had already suffered one heart attack earlier that year and felt decidedly uneasy as he walked down to the stairs, calling to anyone within earshot. Linda Thompson heard him first and rushed to see what was troubling the old man. 'Here,' he said. 'It's a ransom note for my boy. Take it, show the Colonel.'

As it happened, the Colonel wasn't in residence but Priscilla was, at that moment playing with Lisa Marie in the Trophy Room. Linda rushed down and showed it to her, together with the lock of hair, the label from the pill bottle and the photograph that fell from the envelope. 'It's genuine,' she said, gazing at the Polaroid photo. 'Call Shriver.'

Priscilla and Linda studied the photo together.

'He looks strange,' said Linda.

'I know. He won't have wanted to put those clothes on. I don't like seeing him like that.'

'Well, at least we know he's OK.'

'Can I see?' asked Lisa Marie.

'No darling,' said Priscilla.

The little girl made a face. 'Is that a letter from daddy?' she asked.

'Yes,' replied her mother. 'You can see it later maybe. We have to show it to the policeman first.'

Lisa Marie made another face and went back to playing with her dolls house.

Lieutenant Shriver wasted no time in getting to Graceland and examining the note and photograph himself. Since it had been handled by Vernon, Linda and now Priscilla there was little point dusting it for fingerprints.

'Well, I guessed we would hear from them sooner or later,' he said, re-examining the letter. 'Are you sure this is a lock of Elvis' hair?'

'As sure as I can be,' replied Priscilla. 'It's dyed back, just like Elvis did. Of course, it'll have grown out a little now after the time he's been away. And this looks like the label from one of Elvis' Tuinal bottles. Anyway, the photo confirms it's genuine. That's a paper from two days ago, the one with the story by Frankie Wilson. The kidnappers made sure of that.'

'Yes,' said Shriver. 'There's no doubts now. Looks to me from the type style that they've cut up that same copy of the *Memphis Press-Scimitar*. It's often the case that ransom notes are delivered like this but this is the first one I've ever seen. We'd better get Colonel Parker here, and my Police Chief. Things are moving at last.'

It was late in the afternoon when Colonel Parker, Police Captain Jim Magill, Lieutenant Al Shriver, Lamar Fike and Priscilla Presley gathered in the Trophy Room at Graceland and pored over the random note together. It was the first time Magill has visited Graceland and he was impressed. Linda Thompson was looking after Lisa Marie in the Music Room, Charlie West was standing outside the door and Vernon Presley was upstairs in his bedroom praying to God that his son would be released unharmed. Those present had decided not to bring Frankie Wilson into their confidence for the time being.

'It seems we're nearing the end,' said Magill. 'Elvis must be unharmed. I have it from the highest authority, President Ford, that if anything happens to him we will be held responsible. The American public won't stand for it. We must do as the kidnappers demand. Do you have access to $1 million in cash?'

The question was addressed to Colonel Parker. 'Yes I do,' he replied, coughing slightly, secure in the knowledge that he had $500,000 more than that in a Memphis bank deposit box.

Priscilla, who with the possible exception of Lamar Fike knew Parker better than anyone else in that room, thought for moment that the Colonel wasn't so much coughing as suppressing a chuckle. He was quick to compose himself. 'But surely we can set up an undercover operation and follow whoever collects the money?' he asked.

'We could but we'd be taking a big risk,' said Magill. Shriver nodded, deferring to his chief now that the endgame was at hand. 'Elvis won't be released until maybe 24 hours after the money has been collected. If whoever collects the money suspects it's a trap, Elvis might never be released. He or she will be looking out for anything suspicious. Oh, you'd get your money back Colonel but you might not get your client back.'

Priscilla leapt in. 'One million dollars is nothing to you,' she told Parker. 'You lose that on the tables in Vegas all the time, or so I've heard. What's worth more to you, Elvis alive or another million?'

'Er, Elvis, of course,' said Parker, but the moment's hesitation confirmed Priscilla's long-held suspicion that Parker was motivated solely by the golden eggs that Elvis could lay. 'We will pay the ransom. I'll get the cash tomorrow. Let's just hope we can catch the kidnappers after Elvis is released.'

Magill said nothing. He had already decided in his

own mind that aside from Frankie Wilson, the abductors and their victim, no one in the world outside of this room would ever know that Elvis Presley had been kidnapped. And if that meant letting the kidnappers get away with their crime, so be it. 'If they stick to what they say in the note, Elvis will call tomorrow at 10 in the morning,' he said. 'I suggest we all gather here tomorrow at that time. Good night to you all.'

Frankie Wilson, unaware of the events happening in Graceland, slipped a sheet of paper into his typewriter and began to type. 'ELVIS KIDNAP SENSATION,' he typed in capital letters, adding: 'World Exclusive by Frankie Wilson in Memphis.'

'Elvis Presley, the King of Rock'n'Roll, was released today after a week's captivity as a ransom victim. In a top-secret operation headed by Captain Jim Magill and Lieutenant Al Shriver of the Memphis Police Department that went all the way up to the White House, a $1 million ransom was paid and the singer was freed and returned unharmed to Graceland. 'It's great to be back,' Elvis told me as he relaxed in the Trophy Room of his luxury mansion. 'It's been one hell of a week.'

Charlie looked at what he had written and smiled to himself. It was conjecture, of course, as he had no idea about the size of the ransom demand, not yet, but it was the biggest story of his lifetime and it belonged to him and him alone. He continued to write, and as he did so it occurred to him that he would need to interview Elvis about his ordeal as soon as he returned to Graceland. 'Some scoop,' he whispered to himself. 'Some fucking scoop.'

Chapter Ten

(October 14-15)

They awoke early and had finished breakfast by 7.30. Sandra opted to stay behind while Del and Roy drove Elvis over the rough terrain to the main road, then headed east for an hour in the direction of Somerset before switching west towards Russell Springs and Columbia. Having spent their time south of Lake Cumberland they had decided that Elvis would make the call to Graceland from north of the lake so that, in the unlikely event that the police tried to trace the call and from it their whereabouts, they would be some distance from the cabin with a 100-mile long lake in between.

Del stopped the truck at a gas station about three miles beyond Russell Springs and waited until 10 am precisely. In the meantime they again went through what Elvis had been instructed to say. It was to be brief and depended to an extent on who was listening at the other end.

In the Trophy Room at Graceland Vernon Presley, Captain Jim Magill, Lieutenant Al Shriver, Colonel Tom Parker and Priscilla waited for the phone to ring. Lamar Fike stood outside the door to make sure no one walked in to interrupt and Linda Thompson was playing with Lisa Marie in the garden at the rear of the house while Charlie West, again dressed up as Elvis, looked on. It had been decided that Vernon would answer the call, but the phone had been rigged up so that Magill could listen on one extension and Parker on another. Vernon would pass his phone to Shriver and, if Elvis asked, Priscilla.

Vernon was staring at the Polaroid photo in his hand

when the phone rang. He picked it up immediately.

'Is that you son?' he said. 'Are you OK?'

'I'm fine pappy. Is there a policeman with you?'

'Yes.'

'Put him on. I don't have long.'

Vernon passed the phone to Shriver.

'Lieutenant Al Shriver of the Memphis Police Department here. Is that Elvis Presley?'

'Yes Lieutenant. Have you been assigned to deal with this er… my case?'

'Yes sir, Elvis. I was the first officer that Lamar Fike called, the day after you went missing.'

'Good. Listen carefully. A ransom of $1 million dollars in cash, used bills, fifties and hundreds, must be left in a brief case by the roadside at the Kentucky-Tennessee state line on Route 200 between Powersburg and Forbus. There's a sign indicating where the state line runs and it must be left at the foot of the sign between six and seven pm today. If you are driving from Memphis it will take between six and seven hours to get there. Leave the case and leave the area immediately, driving south. If whoever picks up the brief case does not return with it to where I am being held before midnight, then I will be killed. If the individual is followed, then he will know about it, and this will also mean I will be killed. The men who kidnapped me mean business and will be ruthless. Do you understand?'

'Yes Elvis, I do,' said Shriver, who had made a note of where to make the drop.

'Who else is there with you?'

'Colonel Parker, Captain Magill, my boss, and Priscilla.'

'Let me speak to Colonel Parker.'

Shriver nodded to Parker who was listening on the extension.

'Elvis, is that you?' he asked,

'Yes, Colonel. It's up to you to make sure this ransom is paid and I'm freed. This is far and away the most important thing you've ever had to do for me in our long association. If you want to see me again, make sure the instructions are carried out. If something goes wrong, my kidnappers will almost certainly kill me. I know we've had our differences in the past but this time I'm forgetting all about that. Don't let me down. My life is in your hands.'

'I'll do what I can son.'

'I'm counting on you Tom,' said Elvis, using Parker's assumed Christian name for the first time ever. 'Now put Priscilla on the line.'

Parker handed the phone over.

'Nungen,' said Elvis, using the pet nickname he'd coined when they met in Germany. 'Nungen, how's Lisa?'

'She's fine,' said Priscilla. 'She misses her pa awfully.'

'Is she there?'

'She's outside playing, with Linda.'

'If you want Lisa Marie to see her pappy again, you make sure this is done as the kidnappers say. I've given instructions to that policeman, and Colonel Parker will see they're carried out. You make sure they are.'

'I will, Elvis, I will. I promise.'

'Put me back on to my pappa.'

Priscilla handed the phone back to Vernon.

'I'll be home soon pappa,' he said. 'Pray for me. I gotta go now.'

Then the phone went dead.

'Good job Elvis,' said Roy, patting him on the back after he replaced the payphone. 'Now we need to get out of here quick in case those police try to trace the call, not that it'll do them much good.'

'Would you have used that gun on me if I hadn't stuck to the script,'

asked Elvis as they accelerated down the highway.

'I guess we'll never know,' said Roy. 'You think they'll try anything stupid?'

'No,' replied Elvis. 'Priscilla will see to that.'

'What was that you called her?'

'Nungen,' said Elvis. 'It's a make-up word we had. It means 'young one' to us.'

'How old was Priscilla when you first met her?'

'Fourteen,' said Elvis hesitantly.

'That's a bit young isn't it?' asked Roy. 'You could be put in jail for that in most states.'

'I know. It killed Jerry Lee's career,' said Elvis. 'He was married to his cousin, thirteen I think she was. He's crazy, some day he might kill me. Always was jealous of my success.'

'You were lucky no one asked too many questions about Priscilla,' said Del. 'Same thing coulda happened to you.'

'Her parents threatened me. We had to get married.'

'Did you make her pregnant?' asked Del.

'Oh, no. We never touched one another before our wedding night. Well, what I mean is we didn't do it until our wedding night.'

'I don't believe that,' said Roy.

'No one does,' said Elvis. 'But it's true. Oh, we maybe fooled around a bit, you know, got to second or third base as they say. She wanted to but I held back. We didn't go all the way together.'

'So how come you had to marry her.'

'The morals clause in my contract. My image. I became an all-American boy after I came out of the army. Her parents threatened to go to the newspapers, expose me, all about the Mann Act, you know, taking minors across state lines for immoral purposes. They got Chuck Berry for that. Priscilla's folks said that if I didn't marry her, they'd ruin me.'

'Did Priscilla know this?' asked Roy.

'I don't think so. I never told her. I think she always expected that I'd marry her one day and I did. I did the honourable thing.'

'Were there any other girls you wanted to marry?' asked Roy.

Elvis laughed. 'Too many, far too many. There was Dixie back at the beginning, and June, then Anita. Natalie Wood, the actress. She was beautiful but too clever for me. Elisabeth in Germany before Priscilla. She was my secretary. Some of the girls that were in my movies... Nancy Sinatra, some others. Ann-Margret was fantastic. I really loved her. So many, too many. I don't know if any of them would have married me. Priscilla was the one who held out for me, always there. When I sing 'You Were Always On My Mind', it's her I'm singing it to now.'

'Why didn't you marry any of them until Priscilla?' asked Del.

'My manager didn't want me to get married, or even to be seen with girls,' replied Elvis. 'Not before I went into the army anyway. He blew his top over June, my second real girlfriend. I loved her, and my mom liked her too. But the Colonel said no. He thought it would be bad for business. He thought it might get bad publicity. He wanted me to appear single and, er, available, I guess.'

'It seems to me that this Colonel guy, your manager, fucked up your life,' said Del. 'What you were saying about him to me and Sandra yesterday... he's bad news.'

Elvis thought for minute for a minute before replying. 'Colonel Parker made me and he ruined me,' Elvis finally said. 'I maybe wouldn't have made it without him but at the same time when I did make it he didn't know what to do with me. He's an ol' showbiz guy, a carney man. He worked fun fairs before he went into music. He had an elephant show once. Maybe he still thinks like that, that I'm his elephant show now. He don't know nothing about music, or blues, or rock'n'roll. I don't think he even likes it. I ain't ever been to his house in Palm Springs but I'd bet a dollar to a dime you won't find a single Elvis Presley record in his collection, even if he has a record collection. Oh, he's good for business, good for makin' money for me an' him and all that. But it don't go no further with Colonel Parker.'

Elvis hesitated, then continued: 'I've often thought about leaving him if I could, getting a new manager, but I can't. There's too much of me tied up with too much of him. But he doesn't tell me what he doesn't want me to know, an' I think there's a lot of that. 'Taking Care of Business' is what he calls it, and I even had this jewellery made up with 'TCB' on it that I give to folks that help me.'

Elvis laughed. 'I'd give one to you guys if I had one on me. You sure know how to take care of business.'

'What does Priscilla think of Colonel Parker?' asked Del.

'Oh, Priscilla an' him don't get along,' Elvis replied. 'She was always on at me about the Colonel's ways. She's sharp, she knows what's going on, or wants to get to the bottom of what's goin' on. But he won't let her near him, hates even talkin' to her. I can't imagine how they're dealin' with this kidnappin', the two of them. Holy shit!'

Elvis banged his first on the dashboard. 'Talk about suspicious minds,' he laughed. 'It's ma pappy I worry about more. He's under the Colonel's spell. Priscilla sees through him. Losing her was…'

Elvis didn't finish the sentence. They drove on in silence for a minute or two, with Elvis humming to himself. Then he began to sing: 'Maybe I didn't treat you….'

Del and Roy were spellbound as Elvis sang for them. Both recognised 'You Were Always On Mind', the country song recorded by Brenda Lee that Elvis had recorded shortly after his separation from Priscilla. At the close of the first verse Elvis paused and Del slowed the truck down to a crawl. 'Don't stop,' he said. Elvis smiled and began the second verse, giving it all he had 'Maybe I didn't hold you…' Then he sang the third, bringing the song to a climax with the repeated final line, 'You were always on my mind… you were always on my mind.'

'That was…' Del was lost for words.

'Woah Elvis. Now I get why you're the man you are,' Roy, equally impressed.

'It might have been written for me, for me to sing to Priscilla, that

song,' said Elvis. 'I know Sandra was fan of mine, but were you?'

Roy laughed. 'Not really, but I am now. Me and Del like country music, Merle Haggard, Johnny Cash, that kind of thing.'

'I've recorded lots of country songs,' said Elvis. 'Some of the first songs I did back at Sun were country songs.' He began to sing a verse of 'I Don't Care If The Sun Don't Shine', then stopped. 'Some fans think that the best songs I ever recorded were the early ones, the rock'n'roll and country songs I did for Sam Phillips at Sun Records, but I don't. I prefer the ballads that came later. 'Can't Help Falling In Love' was my favourite for a long time, from the Blue Hawaii film. That film was so successful but it wrecked my

chances of ever being taken seriously as an actor. From
then on all I had to do was smile, kiss some girl and win
a fight or two. All the roles were the same. And I know I
was a laughing stock in Hollywood, but you couldn't argue
with the money those films made. Colonel Parker might
not know shit from a shovel but he sure knew how to make
money for me an' him.'

Elvis paused. 'I ain't told many people all this,' he added.
'And I know this won't go no place further. Will it?'

'There's no reason for us to tell anyone, expect maybe
Sandra,' said Del.

'She knows already, or at least I think she does,' said
Elvis. 'She's smart. She sees right through me. I need a
woman like that.'

'You can't have her,' laughed Del. 'She's mine.'

'I know. She'll be a great mother some day. Do you have
kids?'

'No, not yet. Maybe someday.'

'I have a daughter, Lisa Marie. I wonder whether they've
told her about her pappy being missing.'

'How come you only had one child Elvis?' asked Roy.

Elvis hesitated. 'Well,' he began. 'It just didn't happen a
second time.'

'Did Priscilla not want another.'

'I didn't,' said Elvis. 'I was alone, no brothers or sisters,
and I figured my child should be too.'

'Didn't you try again?'

Elvis remained silent. He knew perfectly well that the
reason why Priscilla hadn't fallen pregnant a second time
was because he'd rarely lain with her after the birth of Lisa
Marie, and that this was the reason why she had left him for
Mike Stone. He'd opened himself up to these men but this
was an area of his life that was strictly off limits. He decided

to change the subject.

'I can't talk about that,' he said finally. 'So which of you is going to collect this ransom money?'

'You are Elvis,' said Roy. 'And you'll have a gun trained on you the whole time.'

When Vernon Presley replaced the telephone at Graceland, all that remained was for those present to consult a map and decide which of them would deliver the ransom money. After a brief discussion it was agreed that Frankie Wilson was the right choice, along with Shriver, and the police Lieutenant called the reporter to request his immediate presence at Graceland. In the meantime Parker went to the bank to collect $1 million in cash, leaving the rest in the vault.

Both returned to Graceland within an hour. Wilson was delighted to be asked to be in on the delivery, knowing it would add a bit of spice to his eventual story. They calculated it would take between five and seven hours to drive from Memphis to the state line where the money was to be dropped, the fastest route along Route 40 north eastwards to Nashville, then east to Cookeville before turning north to Forbus. They were on the road by 11.30, a briefcase containing the cash on the seat between them.

'I've already began to write my story,' Wilson told Shriver as they headed east out of Memphis along Route 40. 'It'll be a sensation.'

'Sure will,' said Shriver, who wasn't yet ready to tell Wilson that there would be no story. 'You'll have to hold off until we tell you of course,' he added.

'Yes, I want to interview Elvis after he's released. If Elvis will talk about what's been happening to him, it might even make a book.'

Shriver hadn't yet decided on precisely how and when he was going to tell Wilson what he wouldn't want to hear, but the thought of Elvis being interviewed by Wilson gave him an idea. Elvis would tell him. That way Wilson would be forced to bury it. He wouldn't want to cross Elvis. He made a mental note to ask Colonel Parker to arrange an interview between Wilson and Elvis, with Elvis primed beforehand to insist the kidnapping never become public knowledge.

'Oh, I think we'll be able to arrange that,' said Shriver. 'In fact I'll make absolutely certain that you get to interview Elvis. Have you met him before?'

'Many times,' replied Wilson. 'He doesn't give interviews really, doesn't talk about his life or what's on his mind. He isn't specific. He doesn't want to reveal things, like what the real Elvis is thinking. He just says what people want to hear. But that's fine with me.'

The two men lapsed into silence as the drove along, Wilson at the wheel. They maintained a steady 55 mph, staying on the freeway as they passed through Nashville, then heading east towards Lebanon and Cookeville.

It took Del, Roy and Elvis slightly over an hour to get back to the cabin where Sandra was waiting. They ushered Elvis into the bedroom and locked the door. 'You don't need to lock me in any more,' he said.

'One last time. We need to talk amongst ourselves,' said Roy.

'How did it go?' asked Sandra when the three of them were sat out on the porch.

'Fine,' said Del. 'Elvis played his part superbly.'

'Who's going to collect the money,' she asked,

'Roy and Elvis,' replied Del. 'Elvis will pick it up from

the roadside and Roy will watch him from a way off, like maybe 50 yards or so. When Elvis returns to the truck, they'll come back here, pick us up and we'll head down to Nashville. We'll let Elvis go there, and he can make his own way back to Memphis. Ain't no one gonna recognise him now that's for sure. And what's more, he won't want to be recognised either. We'll give him enough money for a Greyhound bus ticket and to get some food along the way.'

'A Greyhound bus?' laughed Sandra. 'That'll be a first for sure. We'll clean up the cabin while you're gone.'

'We'll burn everything, bury our traces,' added Del.

Then they went back into the cabin to tell Elvis that all being well he'd be a free man by midnight.

Wilson and Shriver made the drop at shortly after five and, as instructed, left the area immediately after placing the briefcase at the base of the state line sign. The road was deserted in both directions. 'If they want us to drive south then they must be approaching from the north,' said Wilson. 'I'd sure like to see them. Elvis might even be with them.'

'Don't even think about it,' said Shriver as they got back into the car. 'Not if you want that exclusive interview with him. Don't get me wrong but I have a lot of respect for these kidnappers. They've covered all the bases. I really do think they might kill Elvis if we try to double-cross them somehow. We have to play their game.'

'I know,' said Wilson, 'Still…'

'There is no still Frankie.'

No one saw Shriver and Wilson make the drop. Back in the car Shriver made a U-turn and headed south back to Forbus as instructed, retracing his route to Memphis via Nashville and Jackson. The two men barely spoke, listening instead to country music stations. In his mind Wilson was composing his story: '$1 million in cash was the price on Elvis' head, left by the Tennessee-Kentucky state line by myself and Lieutenant Shriver…'

Roy and Elvis left the cabin in Del's truck at five and drove to Monticello and on to Powersburg. They reached the state line shortly after six. Roy braked 50 yards away and instructed Elvis to get out and walk to the sign. 'I'll be covering you,' he said. 'Just pick up the case, real slow like, no runnin' or anythin', and walk back here. If a car passes look like you're about to take a leak.'

'In these overalls?' said Elvis as he stepped from the truck.

Watching Elvis walk away, Roy took the .38 handgun from his pocket and trained it on his back. He was certain Elvis wouldn't try anything. No traffic passed in either direction as Elvis walked along the side of the road, stooped when he reached the sign and picked up a case. Then he walked back to the truck and climbed in. Roy leaned over, opened the case and looked inside. 'Looks like a million to me,' he said. Elvis reached inside and grabbed a bundle of notes wrapped together with an elastic band. 'Hey, hands off. That's ours,' said Roy.

'I guess it is,' said Elvis. 'Still, I always did like the feel of money.'

Elvis grinned as Roy put the truck back into gear, made a U-turn and headed north again. As was the case with Wilson and Shriver, not a soul had seen them.

Back in the cabin Del and Sandra busied themselves clearing away, packing up whatever clothes they had brought with them and leaving the cabin as it was when

Del and Roy arrived with Elvis eight night ago. They built a fire outside and burned any spare provisions and shopping bags, together with the bed sheets and sleeping bags. It was their intention to leave as little trace of their occupation as possible.

When the fire was roaring Sandra went back into the cabin bedroom, telling Del she was double-checking to make sure that they hadn't forgotten anything. She was carrying the case she'd brought with her and once inside she nudged the door so that it remained only slightly ajar. Satisfied that Del couldn't see what she was doing, she took a brush from her case and combed her hair, quickly put on new make-up and rummaged in the case until she found the white negligee she'd packed as an afterthought. It was a bit crumpled but that didn't matter. She undressed completely and put it on, along with the matching panties, wishing there was a large mirror in the room so she could see herself. No matter, she was pretty sure the nightdress would have the desired effect on her husband. Opening the door slightly she called for him. 'Del, come in here. I want to show you something.'

When Del walked into the room and saw Sandra he stopped in his tracks, mesmerised. Sandra crossed over to him and put a finger to his lips. 'Don't talk,' she said. 'Just listen. I bought this nightdress specially to take to Las Vegas and packed it, but after Elvis cancelled his show I didn't want to wear it. So I put it away. It reminded me of that terrible morning when I was watching the news on TV, when we found out Elvis wasn't going to do his show, and you threw the ashtray and smashed the TV set. I don't know why but when you said we were coming up here I packed it again. I didn't think I'd get a chance to wear it for you with everyone else around but this seems like the right moment.

Do you like it?'

She did a twirl so that the hem of nightdress rose slightly, revealing the matching see-through underwear. 'I asked whether you like it. Well?'

'Oh my, oh Sandra honey.' Del was already unbuttoning his shirt. 'What do you think?'

'Hurry,' said Sandra, '… on the bed where Elvis slept.'

In the post-coital calm that followed Sandra was idly wondering whether she might finally fall pregnant when her eyes fell upon the guitar that Del had bought for Elvis to play. She untangled herself from Del's embrace, rose from the bed and walked to the corner of the room where it was resting against the wall. Del watched as she picked it up by the neck and carried it back to where he was lying. 'Guess we won't be needing this any more,' she said.

Then, dressed only in her sheer negligee, Sandra walked outside and tossed it on the fire. Del joined her, holding her hand as they watched the flames devour the last trace of Elvis' presence.

Roy and Elvis arrived back at the cabin before eight and the four of them took the money from the case and laid it out on the table. It was in bundles of $10,000, of which there were 100, $1 million dollars exactly, in used notes, fifties and hundreds as they'd requested.

Even Elvis had never seen so much cash in one place, though he'd spent many more times that during the past decade. 'What are you going to do now?' he asked as Del and Sandra replaced the money inside the case.

'We're going to let you go free Elvis,' said Roy. 'We'll drop you in Nashville, at the Greyhound Bus Station. We'll give you $20. You can buy a bus ticket and get on the Greyhound to Memphis. Don't suppose you've ever travelled on a

Greyhound before. Ain't no one going to recognise you now. And I don't suppose you'd want any one to recognise you dressed like that anyway.'

'No, I don't suppose I would,' said Elvis. 'I guess I'm gonna' spend a bit more time like a normal person again, only this time I'll be on my own.'

'You happy with that?' asked Sandra.

'Guess I ain't got no choice,' replied Elvis. 'Ah can handle it.'

An hour later the four of them were squeezed into the front seat of the truck and Del was driving south towards Nashville, taking the same route that Wilson and Shriver had driven down not two hours earlier. They didn't talk much. It was night time and there wasn't much traffic on the road. They reached Nashville around midnight and found the Greyhound Bus Station in the Pie Town area of the city. It was pretty much deserted but there was a waiting room where Elvis could stay until the first bus for Memphis left the following morning.

Del found two $10 bills in his pocket and gave them to Elvis. 'Here,' he said. 'That's for your ticket, food, whatever.' He also gave Elvis an old coat, a shabby green anorak with a fur-lined hood that had been left in the cabin, and the fishing hat he'd worn on their drive into Daniel Boone National Park. Elvis stuffed it into the pocket of the anorak. It was too small for his vast bulk but he put it on all the same and pulled the hood over his head.

Del, Sandra and Roy climbed down from the truck to say farewell and Elvis hugged the three of them individually. 'I won't forget you guys,' he said. 'I won't identify you to the police. I won't even speak to anyone about what's passed between us. I will do all I can to make sure no one ever gets to know about how I was kidnapped.'

'We appreciate that,' said Del. 'Thanks man.'

'No, it's me that needs to thank you,' said Elvis. 'You've made me realise a few things about myself that I needed to know. You've taught me things. Hell, I don't even feel as sick as I did last week before you snatched me. I feel like… like I can stand up for myself now.'

Elvis hesitated, as if searching for the right words, then looked into the faces of his kidnappers and mumbled something about walking down a lonely street. 'I was your prisoner,' he finally said, 'but somehow, for these last few days, I didn't feel quite so lonely as I've felt for most of my life.'

Sandra stepped forward and planted a kiss on Elvis' cheek. 'I've always wanted to do that,' she said. 'For years I was in love with you, and I still love you, but as a brother now, or maybe an eccentric old uncle. Mind how you go Elvis.'

Elvis kissed Sandra on the forehead. 'Thanks Miss Sandra. You forgiven me for belting you with that guitar?'

'Maybe.'

'Ah won't forget you. Really, ah won't. Ah… ah hope you have kids some day, you and your husband. You'll make a fine mother to them.'

Roy was last to say goodbye. 'It's been a pleasure knowing you Mr Guitar Man,' he said, shaking Elvis by the hand. Then he grinned. 'Don't let the bastards grind you down, man.'

All three of them stared into the face of the captive they were freeing. And all three would later swear amongst themselves that Elvis had a tear in his eye as he turned to walk towards the waiting room of the bus station.

Watching the truck carrying Del, Sandra and Roy

move off from the kerb and disappear into the night, Elvis realised for the first time that he really was alone now, alone and unrecognisable. And exposed. The fantasy that he'd dreamed so many times was now a reality, and despite what he told his kidnappers he wasn't sure if he could handle it. He couldn't remember ever having done anything as simple as walk into a shop and buy something to wear or eat, or buy a ticket to go some place, or even have a casual conversation with a stranger who didn't know who he was. As a result Elvis was profoundly unsure of himself. He was like a child, a child whose parents had abandoned him, but he was a child aged 40.

Elvis looked around and saw two or three other strangers in the night, none of whom paid any attention to him. He saw a sign for a men's restroom, so he crossed the area where busses parked and went inside. There was a row of urinals, three stalls with WCs and a pair of washbasins. Above both were mirrors.

Elvis hadn't seen himself for over a week, not since the day he was captured. He was desperate to look at himself again but just as he approached the mirror he heard a WC being flushed and a stall door opened. Out stepped a burly young coloured man in jeans and a dark coat who walked past Elvis and towards the basins, turned on the tap and rinsed his hands. He paid no heed as Elvis stood beside him and did the same, rinsing his hands beneath the tap. Then he glanced up and saw himself in the mirror. The shock made him gasp audibly, and the coloured man turned to look at him.

'Whoa, man,' he said. 'You okay, buddy.'

Elvis squinted at the man. 'Ahm fine,' he murmured. 'Just... just a bit tired.'

'Ain't we all bro,' said the man.

Elvis turned away, terrified that he might be recognised but the black man showed no sign of knowing whom Elvis might be.

'Y'all take it easy now,' he said, stepping back from the basin, turning around and walking out. 'Mind how you go.'

Alone again, Elvis stared back at his reflection in the mirror. Only in his 1968 film *Charro*, one of the last movies he had made and the only one in which he hadn't sang, had he worn a beard. But that beard was neatly trimmed, cosmeticised, and matched his hair. What he saw in the mirror was rough, week-old stubble, the look of a man who had simply not bothered to shave, was perhaps too lazy to shave or couldn't even afford a razor, and it disgusted him. His face was dirty and his hair was unkempt, the roots just beginning to show a shade lighter than the uncombed mop on top. It was unwashed and dirty too, and matted. He wished he had a brush or a comb. The overalls he wore were shapeless and there were traces of dirt around the kneecaps, the white t-shirt was grimy and the anorak soiled, old and worn. Elvis knew he looked like a bum and might be treated as such by anyone who saw him. The black guy showed no prejudice but others, especially well-to-do white folk, might not be so forgiving. Still, well-to-do white folk weren't likely to be hanging around Greyhound Bus stations after midnight.

After rinsing his face Elvis left the restroom and found a seat in the waiting area outside, slumping down on a bench and pulling the hood down so that only his mouth, nose and eyes were visible. Unable to understand a timetable pinned to the wall, he'd decided to wait until the morning when the busses would start running. Then he'd buy a ticket for Memphis. He thought about making a call to Graceland from a payphone but he had no change and, in any case, hadn't used a payphone for over twenty years. All he could do was pretend to sleep. It occurred to him that he'd forgotten all about the red and yellow pills that he'd had on him and taken in the cabin. After his kidnappers had taken the bottles from him to scrape off the labels, he hadn't even asked for them back. He felt drowsy and closed his eyes.

Lieutenant Shriver and Frankie Wilson arrived back in Memphis shortly after midnight and headed straight for Graceland where they reported to those that gathered in the living room, Parker, Priscilla, Linda and Vernon, that they had left the ransom money at the agreed site without seeing anyone. They saw no one retrieve it and didn't wait for this to happen. Everyone now assumed that Elvis had been held captive nearby, but it could have been anywhere in north Tennessee or southern Kentucky, a vast area.

Priscilla seemed relieved, as did Linda. Vernon Presley nodded and Colonel Parker, who had waited up for their arrival, grunted. 'Ain't no more we can do then?' he said. 'I guess we'd just better wait 'till we hear from Elvis, then collect him from someplace.'

'If they simply drop him somewhere between here and Kentucky, he'll be lost,' said Linda. 'Elvis hasn't mixed with the public for decades. He'll be helpless. He doesn't carry money. He might be recognised. If he is there'll be a scene.'

'I think you underestimate Elvis,' said Priscilla. 'I think he'll find his way back to us somehow. He's done a lot of acting in his lifetime and that might come in useful now.'

'I think you're right,' said Shriver, replacing the phone after having reported back to Captain Magill. 'He won't want to be recognised. It'll be a test but a test he'll pass.'

'Well, he isn't going to show up until tomorrow at the earliest,' said Parker. 'I'm going back to my hotel. Where's

Lamar? He can drive me.'

Frankie Wilson followed Parker into the hallway of Graceland. 'Colonel,' he said. 'When Elvis does return, I'd like to sit down and talk to him. Could you arrange that?'

'OK,' said Parker. 'It'll be a pleasure Mr Wilson. Maybe we can give you a ride into Memphis.'

After dropping Elvis in Nashville, Delmore, Sandra and Roy headed straight for Memphis and their separate homes. In the morning they planned to pack their bags for a holiday together, their first stop New Orleans, after which they would split up, Roy to head down to the sun, first to Acapulco in Mexico and then on to Rio in Brazil. Del and Sandra would fly to California, visiting San Francisco, Los Angeles and one other destination before they came home. Although confident that Elvis wouldn't reach Memphis until much later in the day and that the kidnapping would not be investigated, they had all decided to steer clear of the city for the remainder of the year.

It was four in the morning when they reached the outskirts of Memphis and pulled into a truck stop. Taking care that no one was watching, they shared out the money between them, Del and Sandra taking $600,000 and Roy the remaining $400,000. They dropped Roy off at his apartment and agreed to meet him at Memphis Airport in the early evening after they'd all had time to catch up on some sleep. There was a flight to New Orleans at 8 pm.

At around the time that his kidnappers were counting out the bundles of $100 and $50 bills, Elvis was awakened by someone kicking him in the shin. He wasn't sure where he was for a moment and when he looked up he saw a skinny young white guy with long uncombed hair holding a knife. He was trembling slightly, either from nerves or drugs. 'I want your money,' he said. 'Whatcha got? I got a knife.'

Realising for the second time in eight days that his life was being threatened, Elvis decided it was finally time to act tough. More importantly, he wasn't afraid. 'I ain't got no money,' he drawled.

'Then what you waitin' on a bus for?'

'I ain't. I'm just resting. I ain't got nowhere to sleep.'

Film critics who'd been unkind about Elvis' acting talent in the past might have revised their opinion had they seen this little performance, but the exchange gave Elvis time to consider his next move. He knew that if he stood up he would tower over this little guy and that's what he did, rising slowly from the bench until he was looking down on him. Elvis was a good foot taller and more than twice as heavy.

'You fuckin' motherfuckin' lil' shit,' said Elvis, screwing up his face. 'You wouldn't use that. I could smash you to pulp in seconds.'

The mugger, who hadn't realised the size of his victim, looked terrified. 'Don't I know you someplace,' he said. 'Your voice sounds familiar.'

'Get the fuck outa here before I kick your fuckin' ass,' drawled Elvis.

The man backed off, then ran away.

Elvis sat back down on the bench. No one appeared to have seen the encounter. Another man was sleeping about twenty yards away, on another bench, and the restroom lights were still on. He didn't have a watch so he didn't know what time it was, but it seemed to him that the sky was getting lighter. Soon he'd have to buy a ticket, which meant he'd have to speak. He knew his voice might give him away, as it could have done with the junkie who'd tried to mug him if Elvis hadn't scared him off. He felt pleased with himself for that, as if he'd gained in self-respect what he might have lost a week before. He also felt hungry. There was a vending machine that dispensed soft drinks and candies but he had no coins and didn't want to risk asking someone for change from one of his $10 bills. He would have to wait.

The ticket office opened at 6 am. Elvis, dozing lightly, was awakened by the sound of a Greyhound pulling into the bus terminus. He came to his senses quickly, knowing that it was likely he'd have to act his way out of any situation by behaving as if he wasn't Elvis. Instead of swaggering, he decided to affect a limp, and he decided to try and alter his voice, speaking without a southern twang, if he could. He'd heard plenty of Yankees talking and figured he could sound like them if he dropped the drawl.

Elvis got to his feet, shambled towards the ticket office and went inside. The clerk barely gave him a second glance as Elvis approached the counter.

'Where you headed?' he asked.

'Memphis,' said Elvis. He'd decided to say as little as possible.

'That'll be four dollars and 50 cents.'

Elvis handed over one of his $10 bills. He was given a ticket and change, a $5 bill and two quarters. Unused to dealing with cash, he was momentarily confused. 'Ah,' Elvis began, then corrected himself. 'I… I need more change.'

The clerk looked up at the customer, squinted, and took the $5 bill. In return he gave Elvis three dollar bills and a handful of quarters and dimes. 'That do you?'

'Thanks,' murmured Elvis, then he asked, 'When's the bus leave?'

'There's a bus to Memphis at seven, get you there by noon, maybe a bit sooner.'

'Where do I board?'

'Over there, station five.'

'Thanks,' said Elvis, turning away.

The clerk watched him leave the office with a pensive look on his face. Then shook his head. 'No way. Can't be,' he muttered to himself.

Elvis crossed over the parking area to another vending machine and after studying it for a moment inserted some coins, pressed some buttons and was rewarded with a vacuum-packed ham sandwich, two packets of potato chips, a bar of chocolate and a coke. Sitting down to eat, he was feeling quite pleased with himself but he knew his trial was far from over.

The Memphis coach arrived on station five at a quarter to seven, by which time half a dozen passengers beside himself were waiting to board. Elvis took his time and boarded last, that way ensuring that no one would sit next to him. He showed his ticket to the driver, keeping most of his face covered by the hood, then clambered aboard. He headed towards the rear, found a seat and sat down next to the window. The seat was far too small for someone of his bulk and he realised too late that he ought to have picked a seat on the very back row where there appeared to be more room, but he didn't want to draw attention to himself by moving so he stayed where he was, squeezed into a seat designed for someone not much bigger than half his size. Six more passengers boarded in the next ten minutes, none of whom sat next to him, and the bus began its five-hour journey promptly at seven, pulling out of Nashville and heading west on Route 40. Elvis reckoned that to pretend to be asleep was the best way to avoid anyone making small talk. He closed his eyes as the State of Tennessee slipped by, opening them only when the bus slowed down.

Until the bus reached Jackson, about two thirds of the way, it was an uneventful trip, as Elvis had hoped. The bus had stopped three or four times to allow passengers to alight and others to board but once it reached Jackson, the biggest city en route, there was a longer delay and most passengers got off to find something to eat or use the bathroom. Elvis, hungry as ever, decided to join them, once again seeking out a vending machine so as to avoid having to speak to anyone. This time he bought two chicken sandwiches and another coke, but when he re-boarded the bus the seat in which he'd been sitting was taken, and nowhere could he see two empty seats together. The back row was full. Many more passengers had boarded the bus at Jackson and he had no choice but to sit in an aisle seat next to another passenger.

As he made his way up the aisle Elvis was trying to decide which of the other passengers was the least likely to recognise him. He opted for an elderly coloured lady who offered him a kindly smile as he squeezed into the seat.

'Them seats sure ain't designed for a big man like you,' she said as Elvis sat down.

'No, ma'am,' muttered Elvis.

'You goin' to Memphis?'

'Yes, ma'am,' Elvis replied. 'An' ah'm mighty tired. If you'all excuse me, I'm goin' to try to get some rest.'

Too late Elvis realised he'd slipped back into his southern drawl. The old lady eyed him closely. She was wearing a threadbare green coat over a jersey with frayed strands of wool at the cuffs.

'This is the darndest thing,' she said. 'But you remind me somehow of Elvis Presley, the singer. Mind you, ain't no way Elvis be dressed like you is on a Greyhound bus at this time of day.'

'Shure wouldn't,' said Elvis, his heart pounding. Then he pulled the hood down over his face as far as it would reach, closed his eyes and began to pray.

The Greyhound bus carrying Elvis pulled into the Memphis terminal at just before twelve noon. It was a sunny fall day with barely a trace of cloud. The coloured lady in the seat next to Elvis paid no more attention to him until the bus slowed to a halt and when it did she nudged him in the ribs. 'We's in Memphis now big guy,' she said.

Elvis opened his eyes and looked around. Other passengers were rising from their seats and pulling down luggage from the racks above. Elvis had no luggage but the old lady did.

'Would you mind awfully reaching up and getting that case f'me?' she asked.

As Elvis did so he noticed that her suitcase was held together with a length of thick twine. He saw a label with a name and address: 'Mrs M. Jefferson, 2097 Elmbrook Drive, Southaven, Mississippi 38671.' He knew that Southaven was on the south side of the city, an area occupied by poor African Americans. Elvis handed the bag to the lady and committed the name and address to memory.

'Thank you,' she said as Elvis handed her the shabby case. 'You is a kindly soul.'

'Ma pleasure ma'am.'

Elvis followed the lady off the bus and found himself amidst a crowd of travellers. He looked downwards, trying to hide his face. The lady turned to him. 'May the good Lord bless you,' she said.

'An' you too ma'am,' replied Elvis. 'Ah gotta be on ma

way now.'

Elvis rarely walked anywhere, especially in Memphis
where he was the city's most celebrated citizen, but it
was out of the question for him to hail a taxi, let alone to
Graceland. Although he travelled everywhere by limousine,
he was sufficiently familiar with the layout of the city to
know that if he left the bus station on East Brooks Road he
could walk for half a mile to Elvis Presley Boulevard and
then turn left and walk down towards Graceland about a
mile away. But it was daylight, there would be fans outside
the gates and he would be seen if he tried to enter the gates
where his uncle Vester as likely to be on duty. He needed to
wait somewhere until it got dark.

Forest Hill Cemetery, where his mother was buried, was
another four miles down the Boulevard past Graceland. He
would walk there and wait. He remembered the fishing hat
in his pocket, put it on and began to trudge away from the
bus terminus, along Brooks Road, affecting a slight limp.
No one paid him much attention and he was careful to
avoid eye contact with anyone walking towards him. He
figured that any fellow pedestrians would assume he was a
homeless drifter, a down and out.

Elvis turned into the road that had been named after
him and continued walking. Within fifteen minutes he was
approaching Graceland, so he crossed over to the opposite
side of the road and, head down, limped a bit faster, past
the restaurant that sold Elvisburgers and a souvenir shop.
He was unable to resist a glance and, sure enough, there
was a gaggle of fans outside the gate with his wrought-iron
likeness on the front, and a man on duty that he assumed
was his uncle. He slowed and looked beyond the gate,
up the drive to his home, and as he did so collided with a
woman who was walking in the opposite direction.

'Whoa there, watch where you're going mister,' she said.

'Ah, ahm real sorry, ma'am. Please excuse me.'

The woman paused, squinted up into the sun and examined Elvis, but she showed no sign of recognition. 'Wait Lucy,' she said, addressing another woman two paces ahead of her that Elvis had failed to see.

She and her friend had been about to cross the road to the Elvis gates but she stopped, put her hand inside her purse and fished out two one dollar bills and some change. 'Here,' she said, handing the money to Elvis. 'You look like you could use a decent meal. We're Christians and we believe in helping those less fortunate than ourselves.'

Elvis was too stunned to respond. He accepted the money and stuffed it into his coat pocket. 'Thank you ma'am,' he murmured. 'You're kindly folk. You'll find a place in heaven.'

And then Elvis turned away and hurried off in the direction of Forest Hill Cemetery where two small white angels and the figure of Jesus in front of a cross marked his mother's last resting place.

Gladys Love Smith was four years older than Vernon Presley, and when they eloped to marry in June of 1933 Vernon had lied about his age. Born 20 months later, Elvis inherited many qualities from his mother, not least the impulsive nature that saw Cadillacs bought for total strangers and his sudden, irrational outbursts of temper. That she adored her only son, the surviving twin, and he adored her was never in doubt. No loss was more keenly felt than when she died following a heart attack at the Baptist Memorial Hospital on August 14, 1958, her husband at her side. Elvis arrived minutes later, summoned from Graceland by Vernon, and they knelt down by her deathbed and wept together. It was the worst day of his life.

Since that day Elvis had often wondered whether his sudden success and the riches it brought had accelerated the liver problems from which his mother suffered. As a result he sometimes blamed himself for her death.

It took Elvis almost two hours to walk to the cemetery and when he arrived he made his way straight to Gladys' grave and knelt down to pray. 'Mamma forgive me,' he said beneath his breath. 'I have done some bad things. I have done things that I would never have done if you had lived as pappa has lived. I have been mean sometimes, and I have acted crazy. I have been greedy and I have cheated on women. I… I struck a woman just recently and I was so sorry I did that. I knew afterwards that you would have scolded me. I have been bad but I have been good too. I have given away things to people. I have been generous to some. I have lived an extraordinary life that I can't begin to describe, and my only wish has always been that you'd been here beside me to enjoy it with me. If you had then maybe we'd have been able to carry each other through, just like Jessie might have done too. I have always wanted to make you proud of me. I love you Satnin'. I never stopped loving you and never will. You is the only woman I have ever truly loved. God bless you.'

Elvis crossed himself, rose from his kneeling position and walked towards a bench opposite. He was still sitting there, still staring at his mother's headstone, when a young couple approached the grave site and paused to gaze at it also, then walked towards the bench where Elvis was sat, and they too sat down, just a few feet away from him.

'They say he really loved his mamma,' said the girl.

'I read somewhere that she wouldn't let him out of her sight, not till the day he went to school,' said the boy. 'She loved him too.'

'Such a shame,' said the girl, 'losing his mamma like that. It must have broke his poor heart. All that fame and riches he had, but it couldn't bring his momma back.'

'He's sick, you know,' said the boy. 'Fat too. He looks like a broken man. There's something awfully sad about him these days. I don't think he'll live long. Such a life, such a sad thing.'

'But that voice...'

Elvis shuffled along to the end of the bench. They were talking as if he wasn't there, not just as if he wasn't able to hear them but as if no one was actually there. It seemed to Elvis that here in this cemetery, sat opposite his mother's grave he'd become invisible at last, that he was finally passing through the world unseen by anyone. Now even this recurring fantasy had come true; Elvis really was invisible, not just a normal person, the normality he'd often craved and now tasted, but completely hidden from sight by the clothes he wore, the clothes of a bum, a drifter on the lowest rung. His transformation was complete. The young couple didn't even notice when he stood up and limped away.

Elvis spent another hour strolling around the cemetery, pausing to look at other graves and read the inscriptions, and as the sun dipped below the tree tops he walked slowly back down Elvis Presley Boulevard, arriving at Graceland in the twilight. A handful of fans were clustered around the front gates but no one was on guard duty. It was out of the question for him to clamber over the front gates dressed as he was but he knew the estate's outer perimeter well, and figured that if he could make his way to the grassland and wooded area at the back of the house he could climb a wall there. If he was caught, then so be it. With a bit of luck it would be Lamar or another of his guys that saw him.

Elvis made his way around the back, shinned the wall and dropped down on the other side. No one saw him until he came within about 50 feet of the house when a man carrying a powerful torch came running towards him, shouting. It was Charlie West, dressed in Elvis' clothes.

'Whoa there, stop. This is private land.'

Elvis said nothing. The man came closer, shining the torch in his direction.

'You get outta here. Y'hear me.'

Elvis waited until the man was real close, then took off his hat and the anorak, and stood there in his white t-shirt and dirty blue overalls.

'What you doin' wearing ma things Charlie?' he asked. 'Take 'em off and give 'em to me. Ah ain't walking into Graceland dressed like this.'

EPILOGUE

The day after he arrived back at Graceland Elvis Presley gave instructions to everyone that knew about his disappearance never to mention it again, never to say a word about it to anyone ever, and they obeyed him, as they always had and always would. After a while it was forgotten.

Frankie Wilson, summoned to Graceland by the Colonel, took it hard but he was unable to refuse when Elvis personally requested that he decline from writing his story. 'A'll always remember this, this promise you made to me today Frankie,' said Elvis, hugging him as he left the house. Frankie wrote his story anyway and filed it away, never showing it to anyone.

Colonel Parker didn't take it quite so hard, saying it was for the best, and since everyone expected him to be fuming over the outcome they couldn't understand the reason why, nor would they. His relaxed attitude certainly puzzled Priscilla but she was delighted that Elvis had been returned unharmed, as was Linda Thompson. Both women sensed a slight change in his nature in the days after his return, a tempering of his moods, an out-of-character element of humility entering into his dealings with the others in his household. Vernon Presley noticed it too, but it wasn't to last, and within a few weeks Elvis was the same as ever, capricious and calculating, stubborn and easily irritated.

Realising it was the only tangible memento of the kidnapping, Priscilla kept the Polaroid photo of Elvis in a drawer with other souvenirs from their time together, some pictures from Germany and elsewhere, a lock of his hair and the ring that Elvis had placed on her finger on the day of their marriage.

Lamar Fike vowed that never again would Elvis go out riding his motorbike with less than three members of the Memphis Mafia to accompany him. Vernon forgave Lamar for his lapse of judgement that day and thereafter each Sabbath knelt to thank God for returning his son unharmed.

Lieutenant Al Shriver and Captain Jim Magill were relieved at the satisfactory conclusion of the case and agreed to halt further investigations into its circumstances. When weeks passed and nothing more was heard of Elvis' disappearance Richard Nixon placed a call to President Ford, ostensibly to exchange Christmas greetings. 'Oh, and that Elvis business… a conspiracy of silence,' he said.

'It's for the best,' replied Ford.

'Yes,' said Tricky Dickie, musing on how his life might have turned out had his attempt to hush up Watergate been as successful.

A week after Elvis returned to Graceland a Mrs Monica Jefferson who lived in Southaven on the south side of Memphis woke up to a knock on the door from a deliveryman carrying what looked like a brand new and very expensive suitcase. When she opened it she found a pristine and costly green winter coat, along with two warm woollen jerseys and an envelope containing $1,000 in cash. There was also a card inside on which was written, 'Sincerely, Elvis'.

'Well, this is the darndest thing,' she told her son when he arrived home that night. 'Maybe it was…'

On November 27 Elvis Presley flew to Las Vegas in the Convair 880 jet that he had bought for $250,000, refurbished at a cost of $450,000 and christened the Lisa Marie. He spent the next four days preparing for a two-week season at the Hilton Hotel that opened on December 2 and continued until December 15, for which 32,000 fans contributed to a box-office take of $800,000. The season had been scheduled to make up for the cancelled shows in August and Elvis, feeling much fitter than he did then, put on a good show most nights. Early December was traditionally a slow period in Vegas but 1975 would be remembered as an exception to the rule. As ever, Elvis defied expectations by selling out every night.

Among those in the front row on opening night were Frankie Wilson and his wife Grace. Still seething inwardly over what he saw as a broken promise, obliging him to sit on the story of the century, he'd accepted complimentary tickets for Vegas as well as their plane fare and hotel bills paid for by Elvis. Some compensation, thought Frankie, as he and Grace waited in their seats to see him perform one more time.

Also in the audience on that opening night was Colonel Tom Parker, as ever dealing with arrangements, peddling tawdry souvenirs and losing Elvis' money on the gaming tables. He had done his best to avoid Rocco Laginestra, the President of RCA Records, but Rocco also flew in for the opening and when he saw the Colonel at the roulette wheel he steered Elvis' manager into a quiet corner.

'Colonel, what the fuck am I to do with three million Elvis albums no one wants?' he asked.

'Just sit on them. Remember what I said, Elvis won't live forever.'

'I won't say anything about this kidnap business but tell

me one thing, was it true? Did it really happen or was it just another of your scams?'

The Colonel smiled. 'You can think what you like Rocco. I'm not in a position to answer that. I have too much to lose.'

'And RCA has lost one and a half million dollars. Where is it?'

'I'm afraid we spent it, the ransom, expenses. You can charge it back… treat it as an advance.'

'A million and fucking half? An advance against what.'

'Future sales, Rocco. Future sales. They'll come one day.'

The Colonel went back to the tables a happy man. Neither Rocco nor anyone else would ever know about the other half million dollars sitting in a bank vault in Memphis; or that the kidnapping of Elvis had enabled the wily ol' Colonel to come out of the whole deal with half as much as the kidnappers themselves.

Priscilla Presley was also among the first night crowd, overjoyed that Elvis was back on stage, his health evidently much improved. She was sitting next to Linda Thompson, two of the three most important girls in Elvis' life maintaining the conspiratorial silence about recent events.

'Was daddy just hiding somewhere?' asked the third, Lisa-Marie, when she was told that Elvis had returned to Graceland.

'Yes, darling,' Priscilla answered. 'Just hiding. He wanted to be alone for a few days.'

Frankie Wilson, Colonel Parker, Rocco Laginestra, Priscilla Presley and Linda Thompson did not recognise the smartly dressed couple occupying another table in the front row, close to the centre of the stage. They had lately enjoyed a vacation in New Orleans before flying west to California, visiting first San Francisco and then Los Angeles before heading to Las Vegas for Elvis' opening night performance. The pretty lady's blonde hair was in ringlets and she was in the early stages of pregnancy, towards the end of her first trimester, the swelling of her baby just beginning to show beneath the clingy, ankle-length white gown that she wore. A tiny scar above her left eye was all that marred her comeliness. On the fourth finger of her left hand was a sparkling diamond ring that her husband had placed there that very evening, immediately before they left their luxury suite to take their seats in the auditorium. He was a rugged, handsome man dressed in a tuxedo, his straight back suggesting he'd been in the military at one time.

Elvis recognised them, of course. When the curtains parted and the band struck up, he walked on from the side in his glittering white jumpsuit and gazed out over the cheering audience, stopping in his tracks when he noticed the elegant couple in the front row. He silenced the band with a wave of his hand, took the microphone from its stand and waited for the applause to die down.

'Well, ah'am mighty glad to be back here on stage and ah'am real sorry for cancelling those shows back in August,' he began. 'I've been, er, convalescing, getting ma'self back to fighting fit.' He made a sudden karate chop and the women in the audience screamed. Elvis grinned. 'Ah had a bit of help along the way,' he continued. 'Doctors, nurses, that kinda thing. Ah'd like to dedicate this first song to a couple here tonight, they know who they are, two friends of mine and a buddy of theirs that maybe ain't here. They kinda helped me get better too. They had tickets for those cancelled shows so it's... it's....'

Elvis hesitated, and some in the audience that night would later swear that the King of Rock'n'Roll's unease was due to a lump in his throat. He coughed, turned away to compose himself then turned to face his audience again. An expectant hush had descended over the auditorium. 'It's truly an honour for me to be able to welcome them back,' he said, 'and to sing for them tonight. Ah can't say no more than that.'

Elvis stepped back from the mike and Charlie Hodge handed him a Gibson acoustic guitar. Charlie helped him with the strap and Elvis found the right chord. Off mike, looking straight at the mother-to-be with the twinkling ring on her finger, he murmured, 'This one's for you, Miss Sandra,' and began the song.

'One night with you…'

During the remainder of his life Elvis Presley never did visit Europe to perform, though he raised the issue many times with his manager. After his stay in the cabin in the Kentucky hills he went back to his old ways, a combination of gluttony and pill popping, never again mentioning the missing week of his life to anyone after the day he arrived back at Graceland.

Elvis continued to tour and perform in Las Vegas for the best part of two more years, his shows often lacklustre though his fans never seemed to mind. The hymn 'Peace In The Valley' remained a feature of his concerts, towards the end the only song that he performed with sincerity and solemnity. He dated more girls but the loneliness that afflicted him never went away. When he died, at Graceland on August 16, 1977, the headline over Frankie Wilson's account in the *Memphis Press-Scimitar* read: 'A Lonely Life Ends on Elvis Presley Boulevard'.

Unusually, RCA had ample stocks of his albums already pressed up to cater for the enormous demand that autumn. Elvis was laid to rest next to his mother Gladys and twin Jessie Garon at Forest Hill where he'd knelt down and prayed that day in October 1975. Their graves were eventually moved to Graceland where they became a Mecca for his fans everywhere. The grave of Vernon Presley was placed beside them after his death in 1979.

Colonel Tom Parker's stewardship of the Elvis Presley Estate was terminated in 1981, after which it became one of the most profitable legacies in the history of show business, this due in large part to the efforts of Priscilla Presley. Among her accomplishments in this regard was to turn Graceland into a hugely popular tourist attraction, the second most visited private home in America after the White House.

Not until after his death in Las Vegas in 1997 at the age of 87 was Colonel Parker's true identity revealed, although he had occasionally dropped hints about his Dutch ancestry to puzzled members of his staff. Representing Elvis Presley Enterprises at his memorial service was his nemesis Priscilla, who by this time had carved out a successful career for herself as an actress, notably in the Naked Gun series of comedy films, and adopted a no-nonsense attitude to the running of her late husband's estate that plentifully enriched their daughter Lisa-Marie.

Time, it is said, can repair all ills and in this respect Priscilla Presley, as she would always be known, demonstrated a keen sense of humour with regard to the Colonel's capricious ways. In her eulogy at his memorial service she stated: 'Elvis and the Colonel made history together, and the world is richer, better and far more interesting because of their collaboration. And now I need to locate my wallet, because I noticed there was no ticket booth on the way in here, but I'm sure that the Colonel must have arranged for some toll on the way out.'

In May of 1976, almost nine months to the day since she wore the sheer white nightdress on their last afternoon in the cabin by the shores of Lake Cumberland, Sandra Pandel gave birth to a son that she and her husband Delmore named Jessie Garon. Delmore died in 2012, outliving his wild pal Royston Kruger by almost three years. Sandra, heartbroken at losing the loving husband who would do anything to make her happy, died in 2014.

Frankie Wilson's story about Elvis' kidnapping was filed away amongst his papers where it remained unpublished and unseen by anyone for almost four decades. Keeping the promise he made to Elvis, he told no one, not even Grace, about the events of October 1975. He died in 1993 and in his will left his literary archives to the Memphis City Library.

Frankie's story was finally discovered by Jessie Garon Pandel. In 2015, aged 39 and curious to find out why he shared his name with the brother of Elvis Presley, the twin who had died in childbirth, he was poring through documents at the library when he came across the Wilson Archive. Inside he discovered a lengthy narrative that corresponded almost exactly with a bizarre story about the kidnapping of Elvis that his mother had told him on her deathbed.

After reading Frankie Wilson's account he finally understood.

AUTHOR'S NOTE & ACKNOWLEDGEMENTS

I never saw Elvis perform but his music has thrilled me since I first heard it. Beginning with 'Heartbreak Hotel', it's to blame for my life-long love of rock'n'roll music. Elvis' life, the triumphs and the disasters, the magic and the missteps, has always fascinated me. As a boy of 12 I cut out photographs of Elvis from magazines and stuck them on my bedroom wall. I bought or was given 10 of the first twelve LP records he released (stopping after *Blue Hawaii*), four EPs, and about a dozen singles. In 1973, as *Melody Maker's* US editor temporarily stationed in Los Angeles, I read *Elvis: A Biography* by Jerry Hopkins, the first serious account of his life, which prompted me to write to Colonel Tom Parker requesting an interview with Elvis. I never received a reply.

In 1977, a month before Elvis died there, I had my photo taken outside the gates of Graceland in Memphis. I actually had a ticket to see him at Nassau Coliseum on Long Island on the tour that was due to have taken place that Fall. I was living in New York when I heard he had died and I called a friend in Memphis to request he send me three copies of that day's Memphis Press Scimitar, the edition with the headline 'A Lonely Life Ends on Elvis Presley Boulevard'. I happened to be walking down 57th Street with them when I encountered Ray Davies of The Kinks with whom I was acquainted in those days, so I gave him one. I still have the other two.

In 1980, as the employee of RCA Records charged with handling PR for his estate, I stood on stage at an Elvis Fan Club convention in Leicester, accepted an award on the company's behalf and made a short speech. The newsreader Reginald Bosanquet, unsober, was the guest speaker. I've since read about 20 further books on Elvis, written a brief one myself (to accompany a cassette of his hits), and edited and/or been responsible for the publication of six more.

I began this book was several years ago but sidelined it until last year when, semi-retired, I finally had time to focus properly and complete it. I am grateful to Anne Meehan, Lisa Pettibone, Sarah Morrison, Paul Moorcraft, Sarah Hopkins, Paul Charles, Helen Donlon, Amy Frey Floch, Lucy Beevor and a few others who read it in draft stage for help and encouragement along the way. It would have been nice to acknowledge the co-operation of Elvis Presley Enterprises, the corporation that administers the estate, but they denied me permission to quote certain lyrics they control.

A large number of Elvis biographies and reference works were consulted, and among the most useful were the two-volume definitive biographical books *Last Train To Memphis* (1994) and *Careless Love* (1999), by Peter Guralnick, both published by Little Brown; *Elvis Inc* (Prima, 1996) by Sean O'Neal; *The Elvis Encyclopedia* (General Publishing Group, 1994) by David E. Stanley; *All Shook Up: Elvis Day By Day 1954-1977* (Pierian Press, 1985) by Lee Cotton; *The Colonel: The Extraordinary Story of Col Tom Parker and Elvis Presley* (Aurum, 2004) by Alana Nash; and *Elvis And Me* by Priscilla Beaulieu Presley (with Sandra Harmon) (Putnam, 1985). Various maps and guidebooks to Tennessee and Kentucky were also consulted.

For anyone unfamiliar with the music of Elvis, the video/DVD documentary *Elvis 56: In The Beginning*, narrated by Levon Helm, is a must, as are the three multi-CD box sets of Elvis recordings, *The King Of Rock'n'Roll: The Complete 50s Masters, From Nashville To Memphis: Essential 60s Masters and Walk A Mile In My Shoes: Essential 70s Masters.* I'm also partial to the songs 'Elvis Presley Blues' by Gillian Welch, covered with distinction by Tom Jones, 'From Galway To Graceland' by Richard Thompson, 'Johnny Bye Bye' by Bruce Springsteen and 'The Smile Of Elvis' by Jim Lea.

Chris Charlesworth, June 2017

ROCK ATLAS
UK AND IRELAND SECOND EDITION

*800 great music locations and the
fascinating stories behind them*

Rock Atlas is more than just a guide to over 800 music locations. You can visit many of the places or simply enjoy reading this extraordinary fact-packed book's fascinating stories. Some are iconic, others are just plain weird or unusual, such as Bob Dylan turning up unannounced on a public tour of John Lennon's childhood home or the musical park bench commemorating Ian Dury's life that plays recordings of his hits and his appearance on Desert Island Discs.

Providing insights into many performers' lives, Rock Atlas includes artists as diverse as The Beatles, Sex Pistols, Lady Gaga and Lonnie Donegan. Presented in an easy-to-read, region-by-region format, every entry provides detailed instructions on how to find each location together with extensive lists of the pop and rock stars born in each county.

Illustrated with hundreds of rare, unseen and iconic colour and black and white photographs, Rock Atlas is a must for anyone with an emotional tie to contemporary music and the important places associated with it.

Discover music history and
facts 365 days a year

www.thisdayinmusic.com

Sign up now
for the
**Red Planet
Newsletter**
and receive
news about
our new
books and
special
offers
(its free, it'll
save you money,
and we promise
not to mail you
too often or sell
your details):

sign up right now at
www.redplanetzone.com

650
GREAT MUSIC LOCATIONS

ROCK ATLAS USA

David Roberts

The musical landscape of America

Album cover & music video locations

Venues, festivals, studios, & homes

Statues, graves, museums, memorials, & plaques

Exclusive interviews and more than 500 fascinating photographs

Crosby, Stills & Nash Cover shoot by Henry Diltz, West Hollywood, 1969

PLUS! THE BRILL BUILDING • DEAD MAN'S CURVE • THE JOSHUA TREE • PAISLEY PARK • AND MORE

Rock Atlas USA
The musical landscape of America

www.redplanetzone.com

Printed in Great Britain
by Amazon